The Slave Trade Debate

The Slave Trade Debate
contemporary writings for and against

Bodleian Library
UNIVERSITY OF OXFORD

First published in 2007 by the Bodleian Library
Broad Street
Oxford OX1 3BG

www.bodleianbookshop.co.uk

ISBN: 1 85124 316 X
ISBN 13: 978 1 85124 316 7

The Publisher gratefully acknowledges the contribution of Melanie Bigold in transcribing the journal of Rev. James Ramsay

Designed by Dot Little
Printed and bound by Biddles Limited, Kings Lynn, Norfolk
British Library Catalogue in Publishing Data
A CIP record of this publication is available from the British Library

Contents

Introduction

2007 marks the two-hundreth anniversary of the abolition of the slave trade, with the bill passing Parliament on 25 March and the ensuing Act of Parliament coming into force on 1 May. The passing of the Act was the culmination of a long campaign by the Society for Effecting the Abolition of the Slave Trade and other abolitionist bodies, and had been fiercely resisted by those who had a vested interest in the trade, primarily the West Indian merchants and planters.

Token commemorating the abolition of the slave trade, Sierra Leone, 1807, Franklin Smith Collection

Despite some earlier efforts, systematic campaigning against the slave trade is generally regarded as having begun in the 1780s. The Quakers were the first to highlight the issue, and it was they who organized the first petition to Parliament on the subject in 1783. The Quakers set up a committee to obtain and publish information 'as may tend to the abolition of the slave trade', and this work was carried on by the more broadly based Society for Effecting the Abolition of the Slave Trade, which was established in 1787. With Thomas Clarkson travelling the country to gather information and to sir up the local committees of the Society, this was able to attract the support of a considerably wider segment of the population, and in 1788 over one hundred petitions were presented to Parliament. A further wave of petitions followed in 1792, when no fewer than 519 were presented, the largest number ever presented during a single session of Parliament. On this occasion every single English county was represented amongst the petitions, with some also from Scotland and Wales, and it has been estimated that around 400,000 people, roughly 13 per cent of the adult male population of the time, had put their names to them.

With such a weight of popular opinion behind it, it may seem surprising that abolition did not happen for a further fifteen years, being finally achieved in 1807. The reason lies almost entirely with the war against revolutionary France which broke out in 1793. In reaction to events across the English Channel, the government became increasingly suspicious of the radicalism represented by mass petitioning, a feeling strengthened by the news of the slave revolts in the French West Indian islands. At the same time, those in favour of the trade successfully presented themselves as the patriotic party and were able to argue both that the trade itself was an important nursery for British seamen and that its abolition would lead to the loss of the British West Indies to the French or the Americans.

In the long run, however, the course of the war may have helped the abolitionist cause. After Napoleon had had himself crowned Emperor, he reinstituted slavery on the French West Indian islands, and France under the Empire, although still Britain's foe, was clearly no longer tainted by the Jacobinism of the earlier revolutionary regimes. Moreover, by 1805 many of the French and Dutch possessions in the West Indies had fallen

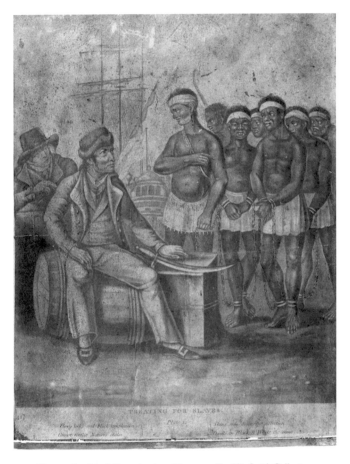

'**Treating for slaves**', Engraving, late 18th century. Franklin Smith Collection.
A contemporary illustration of a slave market in the West Indies, published by
an anti-slave trade body. The inscription reads:

Fleecy looks and black complexion
Cannot forfeit Nature's claim.
Skins may differ, but affection
Dwells in Black and White the same.

into British hands, thus removing the fear of competition which had dominated much of the thinking of the West Indian merchants and planters. In 1805 a Bill abolishing the slave trade to the newly conquered islands passed Parliament, and from this it was an easy step to move to outright abolition of the trade.[1]

The success of the abolitionists' campaign was for many years largely attributed to its moral force. This was seen as awakening the conscience of a nation which was becoming increasingly influenced by humanitarian concerns, with the result that these were perceived as having a higher value than the selfish, purely economic, considerations of the West Indian merchants and planters. William Lecky, for example, wrote that 'The unweary, unostentatious, and inglorious crusade of England against Slavery may be regarded as among the three or four perfectly virtuous pages comprised in the history of nations'; this was echoed by Sir Reginald Coupland, who wrote in his standard history *The British Anti-Slavery Movement*:

> It would be hard to overstate what the movement has owed to the character of its leaders ... but they could not have done what they did if a great body of opinion among the British people had not been resolutely and persistently bent on the destruction of an evil which Britain had one done so much to create and sustain. There are dark and dubious passages enough in British history, but that one at least is clean.[2]

This view was later challenged by Eric Williams in his influential book *Capitalism and Slavery*, in which he argued that abolition only occurred after the West Indies had entered a period of economic decline. The sugar plantation industry, he maintained, was becoming increasingly inefficient and the West Indian interest was losing much of the influence it had formerly wielded in England; thus the slave trade could safely be abolished because it was no longer viable. Whilst not denying the importance of the abolitionists, he also felt that their role had been 'grossly exaggerated'.[3]

More recent research has suggested that Williams overstated his case. Many of the economic points he made seem more relevant to the period before the abolition of slavery itself in 1833 than to this earlier period, and the slave trade itself was continuing to generate handsome profits right up to the time of its abolition. Thus the emphasis has returned to the 'moral' aspects of the campaign for abolition, with many writers stressing the growth of humanitarianism during the eighteenth century. The religious aspect of the debate has also been returned to centre stage.

It has also come to be increasingly recognized that the anti-slave-trade campaign was in many ways the prototype for all the mass political and humanitarian campaigns which have followed it, up to and including the Anti-Apartheid Movement and the campaign to Make Poverty History in our own day. The leaders of the campaign saw their role as mobilizing public opinion to such an extent that Parliament would be forced to act. This would be achieved through public meetings, the publication and distribution of books, pamphlets and circular letters, the drawing up of petitions and using the burgeoning newspaper press to highlight the issue. The sheer number of petitions presented to Parliament in 1788 and 1792 shows how successful these tactics had been in raising awareness of the issue.

The anti-slave-trade campaign was also one of the first to adopt an easily recognizable emblem or logo. Josiah Wedgwood's design, depicting a kneeling slave, with the famous motto

'Am I not a man and a brother?', was reproduced on pottery and medallions, which were widely distributed and became the most familiar image of the campaign. Later, recognizing the important role played by women in the campaign, cameo brooches with the inscription 'Am I not a woman and a sister?' were also produced.[4]

Almost equally recognizable was the depiction of the Liverpool slave-trade vessel *Brookes*, which Clarkson realized early on was a powerful piece of propaganda for the abolitionist cause. First published in 1789, this was widely reproduced in pamphlets and broadsides of the time and has appeared in many books about the slave trade since. In this volume it appears in the pamphlet produced by the anti-slave trade society in Glasgow. The image of the slaves tightly packed into the lower decks of the ship was, and remains, a powerfully emotive one. It showed them as dehumanized objects, passively submitting to their fate and being packed on to the ships like herrings in a barrel. The message was clear: as the slaves were unable to rescue themselves, it was up to the British public to demonstrate their humanitarian instincts and right this terrible wrong.

It was the abolitionists who set the tone of the debate, but the defenders of the trade responded in kind, and throughout the 1780s and 1790s each side issued a flood of pamphlets in an attempt to influence not just the lawmakers in Parliament, but public opinion more generally.

The Bodleian Library of Commonwealth and African Studies at Rhodes House possesses a substantial number of these pamphlets, and this book brings together a representative selection from each side of the argument. The debate touched on many issues, including humanitarianism and the Rights of

Man, the economic well-being of Britain's colonial territories in the aftermath of the loss of the American colonies, the state of the British mercantile marine and the Royal Navy (seen as crucial at a time of war with France), the condition of the poor in England, and, not least, the economic and moral condition of the African slaves themselves, not only in the West Indies, but also in Africa. Both sides drew freely on scriptural sources to support their case, thus providing a fascinating sidelight on the theological debates of the time.

Central to the arguments of the abolitionists was the humanitarian issue. To them the slave trade was unchristian and inhuman, and the avarice which underpinned it had created 'an oppression which, in the injustice of its origin, and the inhumanity of its progress, has not ... been exceeded, or even equalled, in the most barbarous ages', as the 1784 Quaker pamphlet included in this volume put it. 'Justice and humanity' demanded that an end be put to this 'inhuman business', and it is surely significant that in the title of this pamphlet the Africans are called 'our fellow creatures'. The abolitionists went on to argue that it was the greed and avarice of the traders which caused many of the wars in Africa and which led to families becoming enslaved and separated before being forced to undertake a voyage from which they could have no hope of returning.

The abolitionists also made much of the conditions on board the slave ships during the Middle Passage, the second leg of the round trip voyage, from Africa to the Americas, drawing attention to the violence on board, as manifested for example through frequent instances of floggings and rape, and to the inhuman conditions caused by what was called 'tight packing' below decks. The diagram of the *Brookes* referred to above was powerful evidence of the latter, and it was this aspect of the campaign which seems to have had the greatest impact. The abolitionists' first significant success in Parliament was the passing of Sir William Dolben's Act in 1788, which limited the number of slaves which could carried in proportion to each ship's tonnage. This Act also offered a bounty of £50 to the captain of any ship on which the mortality rate amongst the slaves was less than 3 per cent; this was increased to £100 if the mortality rate was below 2 per cent.

Paradoxically, this Act, seen as the first great victory of the abolitionists, had the effect of increasing the profits of both the slave traders and the West Indian planters, whilst also enabling them to pose as agents of humanity. Perhaps unwittingly, the Duke of Clarence (later king William IV) revealed this in his speech to the House of Lords in 1799 (included in this volume), when he said:

> it is wise and praiseworthy of this Great Commercial Nation, to prevent diseased and infected Negroes from being imported into the British West India Plantations. Let foreign nations … make no regulations for their own vessels, and let them import into their own islands, disease and discontent amongst the slaves brought from the coast of Africa; but we, thank God, are actuated by other considerations than mere gain. We are actuated by principles of humanity.

Hugh Crow, the captain of the last slave trade ship to sail from Liverpool was, as befitted a blunt seafaring man, more direct in his judgement on the Act, writing in his *Memoirs*:

> could any one in his senses suppose, that after paying £25 for a negro, their owners would not take especial care of them, and give them those

comforts which would conduce to their health? Many a laugh I and others have had at Mr. Wilberforce and his party, when we received our hundred pounds bounty.[5]

In order to substantiate their case, the abolitionists realized early on that it was not enough to appeal to people's emotions; it was also important to establish the facts. This led Thomas Clarkson, on his tour through England in 1788, to question some of those with direct experience of the trade, including slave captains, mates and crewmen. The results appeared in his *Substance of the Evidence of Sundry Persons on the Slave Trade*, which, it has been claimed 'can rightfully be considered as the first detailed account of the slave trade in the English language'.[6] In the book as originally published, the names of Clarkson's informants were left blank, perhaps to protect them from any form of harassment on the part of their employers, but the Rhodes House Library copy has the majority of their names written in by hand, possibly by one of Clarkson's assistants who knew their identities. Two sections of this book, giving the evidence of a Mr Ellison and a Mr Parker, who between them had made thirteen voyages on slave trade ships to Africa, are reproduced in this volume.

The abolitionists realized that raising the question of the legitimacy of the slave trade meant that the whole question of slavery in the colonial territories in the West Indies had to be tackled as well, for clearly the former existed only in order to feed the latter. Many of their publications, therefore, dwelt as much on the horrors of life on the plantations as on the conditions endured on the Middle Passage. They set out to document the brutality of the masters and overseers, the long working hours and inadequate periods of rest, and the poor diet and living conditions inflicted on the slaves. The model questions and answers provided by James Ramsay, which are included in this volume, were intended to substantiate through hard factual evidence what was essentially an emotional appeal. They gained added weight by coming from someone who had first-hand knowledge of the conditions in the West Indies (as most of the abolitionists had not).

Ramsay was an important figure in the abolitionist campaign, but, perhaps because he died eighteen years before the successful conclusion of the campaign, he has not received the attention of some of the other leaders such as Wilberforce or Clarkson.[7] Nevertheless, his entry in the *Oxford Dictionary of National Biography* concludes that 'the abolition of the British slave trade in 1807 probably owed more to [his] personal integrity, ethical arguments and constructive proposals than to any other influence'.

He was born in 1733, at Fraserburgh, Aberdeenshire, and, after training as a surgeon, joined the Royal Navy, serving aboard HMS *Arundel* on the West Indies station. On 27 November 1759 the *Arundel* intercepted a British slave-trade ship, the *Swift*, and Ramsay was so horrified by what he saw of the condition of the slaves that he later resigned from the Navy and sought ordination to enable him to work amongst the slaves. From 1762 to 1777 he served as a clergyman on St Kitts, arousing the antagonism of many of the planters and government officials for his attempts to improve the welfare of the slaves. Later he rejoined the Navy and served as a chaplain, again on the West Indian station. He returned to England in 1781 and became vicar of Teston, near Maidstone in Kent. There he wrote *An essay on*

Ramsay's church at Teston, Kent.

the treatment and conversion of African slaves in the British sugar colonies, which exposed the appalling conditions under which the slaves in the West Indies lived and worked. This was published in 1784 by James Phillips (1745–99), who subsequently became the leading publisher of abolitionist literature. This book generated an enormous amount of interest and in many ways set the tone for the debates which were to follow. It also led to Ramsay being vilified by the planter community and their associates in England. Undeterred, he went on to publish *An inquiry into the effects of putting a stop to the African slave trade* (London, 1784), included in this volume, in which he proposed that emancipated slaves should be settled on the African coast, where they could trade their produce for British manufactured goods. Thus an illegitimate trade in human beings could be replaced by a legitimate one in goods, to the benefit of all parties.

In addition to publishing his own works Ramsay also worked behind the scenes, preparing briefs for Wilberforce and other politicians, and providing the evidence and arguments which they could use in their speeches, both in Parliament and at public meetings around the country. His unpublished journal, now held by the Bodleian Library of Commonwealth and African Studies,[8] contains a series of questions and answers, which he himself used when giving evidence to the Parliamentary commission of enquiry in 1788, and which provides a fascinating insight into how the abolitionists prepared for their campaigns. The journal also contains the draft texts of several of his publications, including his pamphlet on a proposed bill to abolish the slave trade, which sets out the abolitionists' case in a clear and succinct manner (included in this volume), and copies of some of his letters to Wilberforce and other abolitionists.

Ramsay died in 1789 and was buried at Teston. It seems appropriate that his gravestone in the churchyard is close to that of Nestor, his African servant of twenty years and himself a former slave. Sadly, Nestor's gravestone is now so badly worn as to be virtually unreadable, but both men are also commemorated by a plaque in the church which reproduces the inscriptions on the gravestones. Ramsay's reads as follows:

> While firm integrity, unaffected zeal for the public good, steady
> contempt of self-interest, tender attention to each social duty,
> benevolence to the whole human race, and humble piety to God are held
> in estimation, the memory of the Rev. JAMES RAMSAY (whose earthly
> reliques are here deposited) will claim respect, mingled with sorrow that
> his labours were no longer spared to the poor, the friendless and the
> oppressed, for each of whom, of whatever clime or colour, his Christian
> love and generous exertions not disappointment could exhaust, calumny
> slacken, or persecution abate.
> He died on the 20th July 1789 aged 56

That for Nestor reads:

> Buried here Dec 1787 aged 36
> NESTOR
> A Black. 22 years a servant of James Ramsay. By robbers torn from his
> country and enslaved, he attached himself to his master. Hating idle
> visiting he was employed constantly in his work. Being himself careful,
> he suffered not other servants to waste his property. His neat dress, his
> chaste sober life, his inoffensive manners, subdued the prejudice his
> colour raised, and made friends of his acquaintance. He fixed his faith in
> Christ and looked up to Heaven for happiness.
> Reader, use thy advantage as this honest Negro did his misfortunes, for
> a spur to diligence in duty, and when thy Redeemer comes to Judgement
> Thou shalt hear pronounced "Well done, thou good and faithful servant.
> Enter into the joy of the Lord'.

It would be hard to imagine two finer or more appropriate
epitaphs.

The defenders of the slave trade, although clearly motivated
by self-interest as much as anything, were forced to address the
humanitarian issue in their replies to the abolitionists. Their
argument relied very heavily on the assertion that the conditions
under which the slaves lived in the West Indies were actually

One penny coin. Barbados, 1788. Franklin Smith Collection.
The reverse depicts an African slave with a headdress of sugar cane, and the motto 'I serve'.

preferable to those under which they had lived in Africa. It was argued that most of the slaves were criminals or prisoners of war, whose fate at the hands of the African rulers was likely to be death or human sacrifice. Thus transporting them to the West Indies saved their lives, and in return they owed the Europeans a debt of service, that is, labouring on the plantations. Henry Wilckens, a Liverpool salt merchant, expressed this argument very directly when he wrote:

> The advantage which the Negroes, the objects of the slave trade, thus derive appears to me sufficient to justify the continuation of it; and that the Europeans, by preserving the lives of the slaves, are very much entitled to their services.

Mathusian sentiments also played a part in this argument. It was stated that there was a surplus population in Africa, and that therefore the removal of much of this 'surplus' not only prevented the slaves from dying from starvation, but also allowed the living standards for those who remained in Africa to rise. As Wilckens put it:

> If this trade were … abolished it would place Africa and the negro states in a more wretched situation than they are at present.[9]

This line of argument was also emphasized by the Duke of Clarence in his speech to the House of Lords in 1799, when he said:

> For the sake of humanity, therefore, my Lords – and I repeat it – for the sake of humanity – this Trade ought to continue; for how many thousands, how many millions of lives have been saved in the Kingdom of Dahomey! And how much bloodshed has been spared amongst the wretched and miserable victims in that quarter of the globe, thus rescued from the knife.

A second line of defence was that the living conditions of the slaves were better than those of many of the poor at home. Slave-trade captain Hugh Crow wrote in his *Memoirs* that:

> I would rather be a black slave in the West Indies, than a white one at home; for there is no comparison between the comforts of one and those of the other.[10]

Fishermen, miners, factory workers, those in jail or the workhouse were amongst those Crow categorized as 'some of the greatest slaves in existence', and he also drew attention to the system under which many of the poor were shipped from the British Isles to America as indentured labour, a condition little better than slavery itself. In his *Memoirs* there is a striking passage in which he describes the sale of some Irish labourers in Charleston as indentured labour, with the clear implication that this was little different from a slave market.

That this element of the defence in favour of the slave trade had an impact on public opinion is clearly shown by the pamphlet in this collection by 'A Plain Man'. The anonymous author, who signed one of the petitions against the slave trade at Derby, later came to regret that he had done so. Influenced by a 'Chaplain to a Regiment in Jamaica', he was led to believe that the slaves had 'each a little snug house and garden and plenty of pigs and poultry' and that it was 'a common thing to see at their feasts, fine fowls, very good beef, English bottled porter, and wine'. Misled in this way it is easy to see why he should have wished that the English 'labouring poor were half as well off as the Negroes', and that 'we should in the first instance restore freedom to, and relieve the wants of our own poor'. There must have been many others who found such propaganda equally convincing.

Although the anti-abolitionists made great play with these supposedly humanitarian arguments, there can be little doubt that the cornerstone of their case was the economic one. They began with the premise that the mortality rates on the West Indian islands were very high, and thus, as 'Mercator', in the pamphlet included in this volume, expressed it, 'a constant supply of negroes from Africa is requisite to continue the cultivation of the islands'. From this it was an easy step to argue that unless the slave trade was continued the lot of the existing slaves on the

Clay pipe bowl. Late 18th century, depicting an African head. Franklin Smith Collection. Clay pipes such as this, with outsized bowls, were probably not designed for smoking, but as objects of display, to indicate that the owner was also a slave-owner.

plantations would become worse, as they would 'no longer be joined by new recruits to share and lighten their burdens'. And, if the labour supply dried up, the planters would emigrate and Britain would lose its colonies in the West Indies, which might then fall into the hands of France or the recently independent United States. Thus, it was argued:

23

> The West India planters and merchants have only been the humble
> instruments ... for extending the commerce and thereby adding to the
> wealth and strength of the British Empire.

'Mercator' is generally reckoned to have been a pseudonym for
Sir John Gladstone (1764–1851), the father of W.E. Gladstone,
the prime minister. Originally from Scotland, Gladstone was a
leading Liverpool merchant who in 1803 began trading in sugar
and cotton from the West Indies. In that year he purchased
the Belmont estate in Demerara and this was followed by the
purchase of other estates in later years. He subsequently also
became chairman of the Liverpool West Indian Association,
and was a staunch defender of the rights of the West Indian
planters. He was never involved directly in the slave trade itself,
but he was a considerable slave owner, and as late as 1830 he was
still arguing against the total abolition of slavery in the West
Indian colonies.[11]

Although the aim of the majority of the abolitionists was
the eradication of slavery itself, as well as of the slave trade, they
accepted that the sugar trade was of immense value to Britain
and that the West Indian islands should remain under British
rather than French or American sovereignty. They tended to
argue that common economic interests, together with, as James
Ramsay put it, 'long habits of acquaintance [and] the sameness
of laws and customs', would continue to bind the planters to
Britain, and that British naval power should be sufficient to
protect them from France or America. As to the labour question,
Ramsay argued that had the slaves been treated with greater
humanity, or even liberated, they 'would long ago have been so
greatly multiplied as to have afforded sufficient numbers to have

Tobacco jar. Early 19th century. Franklin Smith Collection. Shaped to depict an African head, this jar, like the clay pipe, would have indicated that its owner was a slave owner.

peopled the islands', and that it would be 'most profitable in the end if we begin even this late to treat them generally like human creatures'. Thus the humanitarian argument was neatly used to turn the planters' economic arguments on their head.

The defenders of the slave trade also argued that if the British gave up this very lucrative trade, other nations would not be slow to take their place, and they might not treat their 'human cargo' so well. 'Mercator' argued that:

> The result ... of the abolition of the slave trade by Great Britain alone, will be the aggrandisement of foreign merchants and foreign colonies at the expense of our own, and that the slave trade, instead of being carried on in British ships, subject to the humane regulations adopted by parliament for the accommodation of slaves on their passage, will be carried on in American and other foreign ships not subject to these restrictions, and thus the cause of humanity will be injured instead of being benefited.

This was, of course, quite a clever argument because it fused humanitarianism with nationalism. At a time of war with France this was a compelling argument for many people. As 'An Individual of Little Note' wrote in the pamphlet included in this collection:

> We should never lose Sight of that great Truth which the French most certainly ever have in View, that they can only rise by our Fall, and that our Ruin must be the Foundation on which alone they can establish their Greatness.

Just as the abolitionists tackled the question of slavery itself, as well as the narrower issue of the transatlantic slave trade, so the anti-abolitionists tended to fuse their defence of the slave trade with a defence of slavery in general. This was quite a clever tactic, because there is much evidence to show that, not just in Britain but throughout Europe, slavery was viewed as part of the natural order. David Hume, for example, wrote in his *Essay on national character*:

> I am apt to suspect the negroes, and in general, all the other species of men (for there are four or five different kinds) to be naturally inferior to the whites.

If a leading member of the Scottish Enlightenment could hold this view, then it should not be surprising that most of the defenders of the slave trade followed the same line. Henry Wilckens, the Liverpool salt merchant, put it thus:

> The assertion that slavery is not the same thing even in idea to an African as to a European is highly probable:– Many of the Negroes are born in a state of slavery; it is even interwoven in the government, customs and manners of the African Negro; he feels not the indignity, he scarcely wishes for a change in his situation; or if he would change, it he knows not how to devise advantage from it.[12]

Moreover, by careful selection of quotations from the Bible, principally the Old Testament, slavery could be portrayed as part of the divine order too. This line of argument is represented in the present collection by the Rev. Raymund Harris's *Scriptural researches on the licitness of the slave trade* (Liverpool, 1788) in which he attempted to show that 'the Slave Trade is perfectly consonant to the principles of the law of nations, the Mosaic Dispensation and the Christian Law, as delineated to us in the Sacred Writings of the Word of God'. Indeed, he went further and quoted Leviticus 25:44–6 to argue that:

> the Slave Trade has not only the sanction of Divine Authority in its support, but was positively encouraged (I had almost said *commanded*) by that Authority, under the Dispensation of the Mosaic law.

The passage in Leviticus to which Harris refers concerns the enslavement of the heathen, and he was quick to add that God 'does not say … *of them MAY ye buy bond-men and bond-maids*, but *of them SHALL ye buy bond-men and bond-maids*'. He was thus able to draw the apparently logical conclusion that 'the word of God

Plate. Early 19th century. Retailed by Goode & Co. Franklin Smith Collection. Depicts an African head, surmounted by a crown. Thomas Goode established his first shop in London in 1827 and this plate probably dates from shortly after that date.

encourages the persecution of the slave trade'.

This interpretation of the Bible met with such approbation amongst members of the Corporation of Liverpool that they presented Harris with £100 as a mark of their appreciation.

Harris himself is a rather shadowy figure. A Spaniard whose real name was Hormasa, he was a Jesuit priest who had been expelled from his homeland with his Order and came to Liverpool, aged thirty-one, in 1773. There he worked together with Father Joseph Gittins as joint priest of a secret Catholic church concealed within a warehouse building in Edmund Street. It was not a happy partnership, as Gittins and Hormasa quarrelled over the administration of the church's finances, a quarrel which became more bitter as it divided the congregation. After five years of wrangling, during which even the arbitrators appointed by the Bishop took sides and failed to agree, the Bishop finally lost patience and, in 1783, handed the church over to the Benedictines and forbade both Gittins and Hormasa from exercising their ministry within ten miles of Liverpool. Hormasa was then appointed chaplain at Lydiate Hall (just outside the ten-mile exclusion zone), but he only went there to say Mass on Sundays, continuing to live in Liverpool and carrying on the dispute, now principally with the Benedictines. Eventually the Bishop ordered him to take charge of a parish in Yorkshire, but he refused to go, preferring to remain as a layman in Liverpool. It was after this enforced retirement that he devoted himself to the defence of the slave trade. He died, aged only forty-seven, in 1789.[13]

The abolitionists were swift to respond to Harris's pamphlet, with Ramsay, himself an Anglican clergyman, writing *Examination of the Rev. Mr. Harris's Scriptural researches on the licitness of the slave trade* (London, 1788), also included in the present collection. Ramsay ridiculed Harris's logic by showing that if everything in the Old Testament was accepted as the divine will, then crimes such as incest should be regarded as lawful, and he went on to argue that the New Testament amended and improved the human understanding of God's will. In his view, 'the law of Moses was enacted in aid of natural religion, till the perfect religion of Christ should be given to the world'. Moreover, even in the Old Testament 'nothing ... countenances a trade in slaves', and Hebrew laws guarded against their ill-treatment.

This point was reinforced by the Rev. William Agutter (1758–1835), who, in a sermon preached at Oxford on 3 February 1788 (also included in the present volume), argued that:

> Slavery, or servitude, was indeed connived at by the Jewish Laws; but it was constrained by wise and merciful regulations; and we know that God winked at the times of that ignorance when men could not receive a purer law, or be influenced by better motives than those temporary rewards and punishments which were the sanctions of that disposition.

Significantly, Agutter chose to preach on the text 'God hath made of one blood all the nations of men, to dwell on the face of the Earth' (Acts 12:26).

At the time of this sermon Agutter held a demyship (scholarship) at Magdalen College, Oxford. He was well known as a preacher and many of his sermons were later published. Politically, he was a conservative, but he also held strong humanitarian views and was a consistent and long-standing supporter of the abolitionists.

Finally, the defenders of the slave trade sometimes claimed

that it was an important nursery for British sailors and that the Navy would suffer if it were to be abolished. The abolitionists had little difficulty in demolishing these claims. As Ramsay wrote in his *Inquiry into the effects of putting a stop to the African slave trade*, 'That the African trade is destructive to our seamen is known to every person who has an acquaintance with it'. Thomas Clarkson estimated crew mortality at about 20 per cent, and this has been broadly confirmed by modern research.[14] It is a telling fact that mortality rates amongst the crews of slave-trade ships were consistently higher than those amongst the slaves themselves.

The abolition of the transatlantic slave trade was in many ways only the beginning rather than the end. The abolitionists had never made any secret of the fact that their ultimate aim was the abolition of the institution of slavery itself in any British territory, but it was to take another quarter of a century's campaigning before this was achieved in 1833. Nor of course was this the end of the story. Abolition was not achieved in the United States until 1865 or in Brazil until 1888. The Royal Navy devoted considerable resources throughout the nineteenth century to patrolling the Indian Ocean in an attempt to suppress the slave trade between East Africa and the Arabian peninsula. Today Anti-Slavery International, the lineal descendant of the Society for Effecting the Abolition of the Slave Trade, remains the world's oldest human rights organization, and is still actively campaigning against all forms of slavery worldwide. In 2003, after Anti-Slavery International conducted the first national survey of slavery in Niger, the government of that country introduced a new law against slavery. Within the first six months of this measure coming into force over two hundred slaves were freed. The humanitarian concerns first raised by the abolitionists in the second half of the eighteenth century remain equally important today, in the first decade of the twenty-first.

John Pinfold
Bodleian Library of Commonwealth and African Studies at Rhodes House
2007

Notes

1   J. Oldfield, *Popular politics and British anti-slavery: the mobilisation of public opinion against the slave trade, 1787-1807* (Manchester, 1995) is the best general introduction to the campaign.

2   R. Coupland, *The British Anti-Slavery Movement*, 2nd edn. (London, 1964), pp.250–1.

3   E. Williams, *Capitalism and slavery* (Chapel Hill, NC, 1944), p.178.

4   It has been estimated that about 10 per cent of the subscribers to the Abolition Society in 1787–8 were women.

5   H. Crow, *Memoirs* (London, 1830), p.42. For further reading please note the following new edition of the memoirs: *The Memoirs of Captain Hugh Crow: The Life and Times of a Slave Trade Captain* (Oxford, 2007).

6   J.Oldfield (ed.), *The British transatlantic slave trade*, vol. 3, *The abolitionist struggle: opponents of the slave trade* (London, 2003), p.xxiv.

7   F.O. Shyllon, *James Ramsay: the unknown abolitionist* (Edinburgh, 1977) is the only book-length biography of him.

8   Mss. Brit. Emp. s.2.

9   H. Wilckens, *Letters concerning the slave trade and with respect to its intended abolition* (Liverpool, 1793), pp.4, 19–20.

10 Crow 1830, p.176.

11 See, for example, his *A Statement of facts connected with the present state of slavery in the British sugar and coffee colonies* (London, 1830).

12 Wilckens 1793, p.29.

13 R.J. Stonor, *Liverpool's hidden story* (Billinge, 1957), pp.33–5.

14 P.D. Curtin, *The Atlantic slave trade: a census* (Madison, WI, 1969), pp.282–6.

Dish. 19th century. Franklin Smith Collection.
Depicts a scene from Harriet Becher Stowe's anti-slavery novel *Uncle Tom's Cabin*, first published in 1852. Items like this would have been distributed as part of the anti-slavery campaign in the United States before emancipation

THE
CASE
OF OUR
FELLOW-CREATURES,
THE
Oppressed Africans,

RESPECTFULLY RECOMMENDED TO

THE SERIOUS CONSIDERATION

OF THE

LEGISLATURE

OF

GREAT-BRITAIN,

By the PEOPLE called QUAKERS.

———————————

LONDON:

Printed by JAMES PHILLIPS, George-Yard, Lombard-Street, 1784.

THE CASE OF THE OPPRESSED AFRICANS.

WE are engaged, under a sense of duty, to bear a publick testimony against a species of oppression which, under the sanction of national authority, has long been exercised upon the natives of Africa, is grown up into a system of tyranny, and is unhappily become a considerable branch of the commerce of this kingdom: an oppression which, in the injustice of its origin, and the inhumanity of its progress, has not, we apprehend, been exceeded, or even equalled, in the most barbarous ages.

We are taught, both by the holy scriptures, and by the experience of ages, to believe that the Righteous Judge of the whole earth chastiseth nations for their sins, as well as individuals: and can it be expected that he will suffer this great iniquity to go unpunished? As the design of the institution of government is for a terror to evil doers, and the praise of them that do well, we wish it may be seriously considered, whether this has been made the rule of its administration in this land. Will it not rather be found on inquiry, that, with respect to the enslaved negroes, its benevolent purposes have been perverted; that its terrors have fallen on the innocent, while evil doers, and oppressors, have been openly encouraged?

But notwithstanding government, in former times, have been induced by what we conceive to be a mistaken, as well as an unjust, policy, to promote this evil, we are persuaded that many of the present members of the legislature, as true friends of civil and religious liberty, hold this unrighteous traffick in the utmost abhorrence. This persuasion, joined to the favourable reception of the petition of our last yearly-meeting to the House of Commons, encourages us to address you, thus freely, on this important subject; and we apprehend that the abolition of this iniquitous practice is not only required by the calls of justice and humanity, but is also consistent with found policy. For avarice in this, as in other instances, has defeated its own purpose. Africa, so populous, and so rich in vegetable and mineral productions, instead of affording all the advantages of a well regulated commerce, is scarcely known but as a mart for slaves, and as the scene of violence and barbarities, perpetrated, in order to procure them, by men professing the Christian religion.

The arguments which have been advanced by the few writers, who have attempted to justify this inhuman business, can have no weight with generous minds. Those, in particular, which are drawn from the permission to hold slaves amongst the Jews, can in no wise be applied to the practice amongst us: for, blessed be the God and Father of all our mercies,[1] who hath made of one blood all nations of men, we now live under a dispensation essentially different from that of the law; in which many things were permitted to the Jews, because of the hardness of their hearts. All distinctions of name and country, so far as they relate to the social duties, are now abolished. We are taught by our blessed Redeemer to look upon all men, even our enemies, as neighbours and brethren, and to do unto them as we would they should do unto us.

Under a dispensation so admirably adapted to promote the temporal as well as the eternal happiness of mankind, that any should deviate so far from its principles, as to encourage a practice so replete with iniquity, and in particular that this nation, generally characterized by its attachment to civil and religious liberty, should have contributed, perhaps more than any other, to the establishment and continuance of slavery, is a most painful reflection. It would surely have been more consistent with the avowed principles of Englishmen, both as men and as Christians, if their settlement in heathen countries had been succeeded by mild and benevolent attempts to civilize their inhabitants, and to incline them to receive the glad tidings of the gospel. But how different a conduct towards them has been pursued! it has not only been repugnant, in a political view, to those commercial advantages which a fair and honourable treatment might have procured, but has evidently tended to increase the barbarity of their manners, and to excite in their minds an aversion to that religion, the professors whereof so cruelly treat them.

This traffick is the principal source of the destructive wars which prevail among these unhappy people, and is attended with consequences, the mere recital of which is shocking to humanity. The violent separation of the dearest relatives, the tears of conjugal and parental affection, the reluctance of the slaves to a voyage from which they can have no prospect of returning, must present scenes of distress which would pierce the heart of any, in whom the principles of humanity are not wholly effaced. This, however, is but the beginning of sorrows with the poor captives. Under their cruel treatment on shipboard, where, without regard to health or decency, hundreds are confined within the narrow limits of the hold, numbers perish; and, by what is called the seasoning in the Islands, many are relieved by a premature death, from that series of accumulated sufferings which awaits their less happy survivors. The measure of their afflictions yet remains to be filled; being sold to the highest bidder, and branded with a hot iron, they have yet to linger on, unpitied, the whole term of their miserable existence, in excessive labour, and too often under the merciless controul of unprincipled and unfeeling men, without proper food or clothing, or any encouragement to sweeten their toil; whilst every fault, real, or imaginary, is punished with a rigour which is but weakly restrained by the colony laws: instances of the greatest enormity, even the most wanton or deliberate murder of the slaves, being only punished, if punished at all, by trifling pecuniary fines.

But a bare enumeration of the calamities of this wretched people, would exceed the limits proposed to this short address: we think it not improper, however, to give the following extract from a late author, who was an eye-witness of the miseries of this persecuted race.

'If we bring this matter home, and, as Job proposed to his friends, "put "our soul in their souls stead;' if we consider ourselves, and our children, as exposed to the hardships which these people lie under, in supporting an imaginary greatness;'

'Did we, in such case, behold an increase of luxury and superfluity among our oppressors, and therewith feel an increase of the weight of our burdens, and expect our posterity to groan under oppression after us;'

'Under all this misery, had we none to plead our cause, nor any hope of relief from man, how would our cries ascend to the God of the spirits of all flesh, who judgeth the world in righteousness, and, in his own time, is a refuge for the oppressed!'

'When we were hunger-bitten, and could not have sufficient nourishment, but saw them in fulness, pleasing their taste with things fetched from far;'

'When we were wearied with labour, denied the liberty to rest, and saw them spending their time at ease; when garments, answerable to our necessities, were denied us, while we saw them clothed in that which was costly and delicate;'

'Under such affliction, how would these painful feelings rise up as witnesses against their pretended devotion! And if the name of their religion were mentioned in our hearing, how would it found in our ears, like a word which signified self-exaltation and hardness of heart!'

'When a trade is carried on productive of much misery, and they who suffer by it are some thousand miles off, the danger is the greater of not laying their sufferings to heart.'

'In procuring slaves from the coast of Africa, many children are stolen privately; wars also are encouraged among the negroes: but all is at a great distance. Many groans arise from dying men, which we hear not. Many cries are uttered by widows and fatherless children, which reach not our ears. Many cheeks are wet with tears, and faces sad with unutterable grief, which we see not. Cruel tyranny is encouraged. The hands of robbers are strengthened; and thousands reduced to the most abject slavery, who never injured us'

'Were we, for the term of one year only, to be eye-witnesses to what passeth in getting these slaves; were the blood which is there shed, to be sprinkled on our garments; were the poor captives, bound with thongs, heavy laden with elephants teeth, to pass before our eyes, in their way to the sea;'

'Were their bitter lamentations, day after day, to ring in our ears, and their mournful cries in the night, to hinder us from sleeping;'

'Were we to hear the sound of the tumult, when the slaves on board the ships attempt to kill the English, and behold the issue of those bloody conflicts; what pious man could be a witness to these things, and see a trade carried on in this manner, without being deeply affected with sorrow?'——

Our religious society in these kingdoms, and in North America, have for many years tenderly sympathized with this unhappy people, under their complicated sufferings, and have endeavoured to procure them relief: nor has their cause been without other advocates; whose numbers we have with much satisfaction observed to increase. The expectation of many, who are anxiously concerned for the suppression of this national evil, is now, under Providence, fixed upon the wise and humane interposition of the legislature; to whom, with dutiful submission, we earnestly recommend the serious consideration of this important subject; with a pleasing hope, that the result will be, a prohibition of this traffick in future, and an extension of such relief to those who already groan in bondage, as justice and mercy may dictate, and their particular situations may admit. That so the blessings of those who are ready to perish may rest upon you, and this nation may no longer, on their account, remain obnoxious to the righteous judgments of the Lord, who, in the most awful manner, declared by his prophets, that the land should tremble, and every one mourn that dwelleth therein, for the iniquity of those who oppress the poor, and crush the needy; and who likewise pronounced a "woe[2] unto him, that buildeth his house by unrighteousness, and his chambers by wrong; that useth his neighbour's service without wages, and giveth him not for his work.'

Signed by order of the meeting for sufferings,[3] London, the 28th day of the eleventh month, 1783, by
JOHN ADY,
Clerk to the meeting.

Notes

1. Acts xvii.26.
2. Jeremiah xxii.13.
3. This meeting is composed of about one hundred members of the society residing in London, who are chosen by, and correspond with, the meetings in the country. It was instituted, and thus named, during the times of persecution, (anno 1675) in order to receive accounts of the sufferings of our members, and to solicit relief from those in power. It still continues to superintend the general concerns of the society during the intervals of the yearly-meeting.

AN
INQUIRY

INTO THE

EFFECTS

OF

PUTTING A STOP

TO THE

African Slave Trade,

AND OF

Granting LIBERTY to the SLAVES

IN THE

BRITISH SUGAR COLONIES.

By the AUTHOR of
The ESSAY ON THE TREATMENT AND CONVERSION
OF AFRICAN SLAVES IN THE BRITISH
SUGAR COLONIES.

LONDON:

Printed and Sold by JAMES PHILLIPS, in GEORGE-
YARD, LOMBARD-STREET. 1784.

Advertisement.

THE present inquiry was originally intended to have made a part of the Author's Essay on the subject of Slavery. But by the advice of those, to whom the propriety of that publication was submitted, it was suppressed, till matters should become ripe, and mens minds be prepared for the discussion. The Author is now obliged to publish it, perhaps prematurely, in defence of the principles of his work.

The Monthly Reviewers, in their Review, June. 1784, were pleased to give a criticism on the Essay, which, considering it as a composition, was perhaps full as favourable as it deserved. The writer never has published either for reputation or profit, never has acted the Author, but when his opportunities and situation pressed him into the service of his country and his king. Praise or blame in a Review could, therefore, be to him a matter only of imaginary moment: and were it not so, that impartiality, which alone can support such a work as theirs, must render it impertinent in an Author to thank them for their commendation, and vain to reproach them for their censure.

But that feeling and sentiment, which first suggested to the Author the discussion of this subject, will not suffer him to be indifferent to its success. The Author, while arguing for the abolition of slavery, is represented as a friend to the slave trade; and, while treating of a subject sufficient to soften the most obdurate heart, is censured for shewing less enthusiasm and ardour than Rousseau and Reynal have affected, when labouring only to make palatable a poison aimed at every thing of worth and dignity in human nature. It is true, in their Review of July, they have, on his remonstrance, candidly said, "they have perhaps expressed themselves without sufficient accuracy,' in representing him as a friend to the slave trade, and they have subjoined a note from his book, which enables the Reader to judge for himself. This, as far as regards his character, ought to be satisfactory to him. But the charge remains against his book; "It speaks with extreme caution of the horrid trade.' Now there is not a passage in it, that he trusts can bear such an interpretation; but several that condemn it in pointed terms. It was not within the plan of what was published to treat directly of it; but when it came in his way, it found no quarter. However, to put the matter out of dispute, he offers the following article to the public. If his plan be objected against as visionary, he shall only answer, that every thing must have a beginning; and that there are many parts of the slave coast, where the inhabitants are sufficiently polished to be capable of carrying on the manufacture of sugar, planting tobacco, and indigo; that they already have rice of a more valuable quality than that of the Carolinas.

With respect to his want of ardour and enthusiasm, as if he betrayed the interest he pretends to espouse, he answers: Indiscriminate blame never was intended. Planters are like, are not worse than, the common run of men; many would not lose by comparison with the better sort of people in Britain. It is their situation, it is the very nature of slavery, that leads to all that inconsiderate oppression and suffering which take place in the relation of master and slave. He has accordingly observed, that these causes almost universally operate more strongly in adventurers from Europe, than in natives of the colonies. Now the intention of his book was to convince and conciliate, not to inflame;— to shew that the matter's true interest was to be found on the side of liberty, and of moral and religious improvement, not in niggardly pinching, not in stripes, chains, and nakedness. But so intimately is the subject connected with sentiment, so naturally did a warmth of expression mix with every part, that the Author's great aim in every transcription has been to soften whatever could be supposed capable of offending. And after all the severity, that moderation and his regard for individuals called for in the correction, better judges, who decided ultimately on the work, thought proper to prune not only words, phrases and sentences, but whole paragraphs, so as often to leave the expression naked, and the connection obscure, rather than suffer any improper warmth to appear. After submitting this account to the Reader, that unblushing, unprincipled monster Rousseau (fee his Confessions) is welcome to possess, unenvied by the Author, all *the gloom and ardour* for which he is celebrated.

The Author takes this opportunity of observing an objection made by some pious persons to the reformation proposed by him, drawn from the ill success of his own private endeavours to instruct slaves. He offered it as a strong argument, to shew the necessity of advancing the condition of slaves, before they can be made objects of religion; or rather to shew, that civil privileges and religious instruction must go hand in hand. If this be duly weighed, the objection here mentioned must conclude greatly in favour of his plan.

This objection has given him the more chagrin; because he does not find in it that attention to the scope of the argument, which its importance requires. His aim is to prove Africans objects of religion; the advantages of which are chiefly to the slaves themselves. In conformity with the generous spirit of Christianity, and to make their masters propitious to his views, he proves even to demonstration, that every degree of liberty conferred on them would be so much gain to their present masters, and, if conferred in proportion as their faculties opened, would facilitate the reception of religion among them. Hence arises in his plan the union of liberty and religion both slowly advancing together, without any abrupt or violent change in the condition of the slaves themselves. He is clearly of opinion, that the distinction of master and slave never was meant by the God of nature to be an object of society, and the effects of the abolition of slavery in Europe confirm his judgment; but he is also of opinion, that since slavery has taken place, its strict discipline may be made subservient to the purposes of religion.

Nor is there any thing in the account of the author's own slaves to countenance this despondent conclusion. In the last nine years it is to be observed, that he had made considerable steps. He should indeed have remarked, that the principal part of his slaves were grown up when they came from Africa, and therefore never could perfectly acquire the English language, nor form any adequate ideas of any general abstract terms with which they were not acquainted in their own country, but that his few creoles were particularly sensible and acute. —Still the success of the Moravians, which he finds is much more complete, and truly pleasing to the pious mind, than he from his former information could have represented it, is a convincing proof that very considerable advances may be made among the negroes, even in their present state. And, as the pious divine, who conducts the labours of these truly apostolical preachers, observes, Christianity insensibly draws after it relaxation of slavery and personal privileges. Oppression is often unwillingly forced to draw back his heavy hand from meek and willing submission.

But whatever be the consequences, the author must continue

generally to insist on the propriety and even necessity that liberty and religion should advance slowly together. A Heathen slave is less valuable than a Christian slave; this last is much less valuable than a Christian freeman. We want every motive that can be drawn from freedom and religion to secure propriety of conduct. The negroes have two classes of friends, one that looks chiefly to liberty, while the other regards only religion. Suppose them free untutored heathens. There are crowds of unprincipled idle thieves and robbers let loose on the public. Suppose a Christian slave offering up with his master his devotions to their common Father on Sunday. See him on Monday morning, by the caprice of a boy overseer, held with his face downwards by his hands and feet, till his back be furrowed with the cart-whip, his flesh torn in pieces, and his whole body rendered one loathsome wound. While humanity gives her tear of pity, can religion smile or sanctify the horrid oppressive relation of master and slave, that makes such havock in the claims of brotherhood. But why may not both classes unite to vindicate from oppression and heathenish ignorance the ill-fated race, why grudge each other's claims, and leave oppression and tyranny to profit by their opposition?

AN INQUIRY, &c.

IT may be asked, supposing the African slave trade stopt, and the negroes on our sugar colonies made freemen, how will the measure affect the trade and interest of Great Britain and her colonies? Will not a gainful commerce with Africa be shut up? Will not our sugar colonies, if peopled with freemen, despise the rule of Britain, because they do not feel it, and join themselves to America? In this case, will not a great source of national wealth be cut off, and that nursery for seamen, on which our navy depends, be greatly contracted?

I state the argument in the strongest manner for those who favour slavery, and shall not use one expression to explain away its force. I am seriously of opinion that the sugar trade, with which that for slaves is connected at present, is of the utmost importance to the state; and that any sudden shock, that affects it, will be widely and deeply felt: and it must be confessed, that several of the sugar colonies shewed, in the beginning of the late disputes, strong signs of an unaccountable bias to the ideal empire of America.

North America is now separated for ever from the British State; and though one must continue to wish that the operation had been accompanied with less violence, and had left a less ugly fear behind it, yet neither sentiment nor policy will permit the friend of Britain to desire a reunion. While Americans remember the methods by which they acquired their independency, they must be suspicious of every thing wherein Britain is concerned. It will remind them of the circumstances of a contest, which brought both parties to the brink of ruin. No dependence can be placed in the forming any new connection with them, where they themselves shall not have the advantage, or where they can treat with other nations on the same or equal terms. Nor can any treaty be lasting, which is made with a people where a designing demagogue, working on an ignorant town committee, can prescribe to the legislature. We shall therefore have no tie over them but conveniency; and we are free to settle our trade, and accommodate ourselves in the manner that will best suit our own purposes, without taking into account how it may probably affect them. We shall by and by apply this reasoning to our subject.

We have now upwards of 200 years traded with Africa in human flesh, and encouraged in the negroe countries wars, rapine, desolation, and murders, that we might be supplied with that commodity. The avarice with which we crowded the slave ships, and the caution that self-preservation made necessary to guard against their rising during the voyage, have destroyed in almost every instance a considerable proportion. The seasoning of them in our islands has in general cut off still more; and those that have survived in too many cases, have been, to say no worse, preserved only for hunger, stripes, and oppressive labour. On the whole, we have considered the trade only as a matter of gain; and as such in any probable future state of our sugar colonies, it cannot be reckoned higher, in every possible view, than the supplying of the wants, and reaping of the labour of half a million of people.

But suppose that by establishing factories, and encouraging civilization on the coast of Africa, and returning some of our West Indian slaves to their original country, we should try to make up for our past treachery to the natives, and guard against the views of the Americans on our sugar colonies, by instructing the inhabitants in the culture of tobacco, indigo, cotton, rice, &c. to barter with us for our manufactures, and supply us with those articles, our demand for which has been so advantageous to America, and so well enabled her to set up for herself. Were Africa civilized, and could we preoccupy the affections of the natives, and introduce gradually our religion, manners, and language among them, we should open a market, that would fully employ our manufacturers and seamen, morally speaking, till the end of time. And while we enriched ourselves, we should contribute to their happiness. For Africa, in its highest probable state of culture, could not possibly interfere with the staple of Britain, so as to hinder an extensive and mutually advantageous trade from being carried on between the countries. The great difference of climate and soil must always distinguish the supplies and wants of each.

Suppose, then, (and let it be attended to that I only suppose it) the sugar colonies subdued, or incorporated willingly with America, we might carry on a much more useful and extensive trade, than hitherto has been done, in every American and West Indian article with free people in Africa, without making them any burdensome loans, or being under any uneasy alarms about them. And without attempting any monopoly, or insisting on any preference, the goodness of our manufactures, and spirit of our traders, must always continue to command the most valuable branches of that commerce. Nor need it be a vain idea to expect in time to be supplied from Africa with various valuable wines in exchange for our staple commodities, instead of paying for them in money to our more northern rivals.— How must even this distant thought of the subject warm the heart, while it contemplates, as gained to the true religion, and to legal society, not a colony, but a continent, whose barbarous manners, and brutish ignorance, have so long disgraced the human character, and sunk it in sloth and depravity well nigh below compassion!

Should it be objected, that if we abandon the African trade, our rivals will extend their share in it, by which their wealth will be immediately increased, and their sugar colonies improved to the certain advancement of their, and as certain loss of our, naval importance, I might leave the answer to the man of morality and sentiment; but I fear not to encounter it in a political view. That the African trade is in itself destructive to our seamen, is known to every person who has an acquaintance with it. Indeed a mortality among his crew in the middle passage (from Africa to the West Indies) is a pleasant thing to a Guinea captain, of which he is not often disappointed. It saves the ship a great expence in wages; for many more mariners are wanted to collect the slaves on the coast, then to navigate the ship after she is fully loaded. And it is not obscurely hinted, that ill usage, at least, has often been tried, in order to produce it; which if it has not its full effect on the passage, makes the seamen quit the ship as soon as she arrives in the West Indies. I mean not here an undistinguishing censure: however oddly it may sound; I have, in this line, known men of feeling, that were far above such vile notions of parsimony. But the greatest advocate for the trade will not say, that these last are the most numerous party.

Now if the slave trade were changed for an ordinary commerce, or mutual barter of commodities with Africa, this temptation to destroy or dissipate seamen would be taken away. Some ships would load on the African coast directly for Britain; others would load with cattle, mules, rice, pipe slaves, &c. for the sugar colonies. One great cause of an alarm in the sugar colonies from the checking of their intercourse with America, is the loss of a market for their rum. This might be most profitably exchanged, by fitting it for the African market, and giving it in return for African commodities.[1] The quantity of goods exchanged for slaves in Africa, is perhaps the least object of that commerce. The annual British exports to Africa are not estimated higher than £.500,000, including a considerable quantity that is usually exchanged with American and other foreign traders on the coast; about £.50,000 of this is returned in ivory, gold dust, &c. The greatest part of profits of the slave trade is raised on the sugar planter. It is true, slaves grow every year dearer on the coast, in proportion as the Africans become better acquainted with the value set by the white traders on their wretched countrymen. But at their highest price they have seldom, if ever, come up to one third of what they sold for in the West Indies, if valued as the goods for which they were bought were shipt in Britain. Till lately, a great proportion was bought on the coast, at a sixth part of what the planter was obliged to pay for them. It is also to be remarked, that our present trade to Africa is confined to a few tyrants, and their brokers. But were the country once civilized, every person in it, who could labour with his hands, would make a demand on our manufactures, and extend our commerce. The change then proposed here, so far from lessening our trade, and the number of our seamen, would extend the one, and preserve and increase the other in an almost inestimable proportion; and we have plainly shewn, that its effect on the trade of the new empire of America ought not to be the object of our concern.

To the objection that our quitting the slave trade would throw a profitable branch into the hands of our rivals, would improve their sugar colonies, and advance them in naval importance, we answer, that this commerce can continue in no hands longer than the negroe countries remain in a state of brutish barbarism; for when they become civilized, it must cease of course. And from our having been the most forward in this scandalous traffick, it becomes us to be the first to labour in effecting a reformation. Were the tyrants on the slave coasts made sensible, that riches consisted in the number and wealth of their subjects; instead of going to war to make prisoners, and sell them for slaves, to be carried to a distant climate, among a strange people, they would contend in encouraging the greatest possible numbers to settle in and cultivate each his own territory, and would try to intercept those sent down to the slave market from the inland parts. The only effect therefore that this consideration respecting our rivals should produce is, at once, to set heartily to the work, that they may have the less time to reap advantage from the circumstances.

But it is a notorious fact, that a considerable proportion of our African trade for the last 25 years has been actually directed to the supplying of the French colonies with slaves, and that the improvement arising thence contributed to enable them to make that formidable appearance with their navy in the beginning of the late war, which in the general opinion threatened to bring our existence, as a naval power, to an end. Now, on the supposition that our slave trade is to continue on its former footing, and to be directed, as before (perhaps, considering our superior mercantile activity in a more profitable way for our rivals, than if they were to carry on the whole trade immediately with Africa) to the aggrandisement of our rivals, I in the strongest manner insist, that the subject calls for the most serious deliberation, and the most pointed inquiries both from administration and parliament. I have long foreseen the fatal consequences of it, with an heart-felt concern for my country. And surely it deserves to be discussed, whether a branch of trade, confessedly of some importance, but confined to two or three ports, ought at the expence of every human feeling to be put in competition with our future naval superiority; or, if it must be preserved, whether it should not be confined to the demands of our own colonies. If I be asked the question, should we refuse, will not our rivals procure their supplies from other hands? I may answer by another question; if we deliberately contribute to our rivals naval importance, shall we deserve pity when we are crushed under it? But the truth is, if we were to abandon the trade, two thirds of the whole must fall to the ground for all other nations have already their shares in it according to their genius and demand.—It may perhaps not be generally known, that there are now English agents at Madrid, treating with the Spanish ministry for the annual delivery of 80,000 African slaves in the Spanish colonies.

But in the civilization of Africa we have a certain remedy against this danger. The French planters, by living as farmers on their plantations, and cultivating a fresher and more luxuriant soil than is contained in our colonies, and being less dependent than we are on foreigners for provisions and other stores, can raise sugar at two-thirds of its usual price in the British colonies; whose proprietors live generally in Europe, and require large remittances to support them, while other managers and their families must also be maintained to do their duty on their plantations, and neither cattle nor provisions are raised on them to lessen the expence. I reckon twenty-five shillings sterling per cwt. on the spot to be a very moderate saving peace price for sugar in some of the British colonies, and to be equal to about sixteen shillings in the French colonies. But such sugar is raised in the East-Indies by free people for three shillings and four-pence per cwt. Nor is there reason to doubt, that it might be raised by freemen in Africa, if not at so low a price as this last, yet surely much below even the French price. Africans, under the pressure of slavery, are the manufacturers of sugar and rum in the colonies; why may they not be equally so in their own country working for themselves? Were this event brought about by the civilization of Africa, it would be impossible to raise sugar, that could command the market, by the expensive culture of slaves. And if the French persevered, they could not, by the utmost strictness of regulation, supply more than their own country; and their trade with the sugar colonies, instead of bidding fair, as at present by our help, to engross a great share of the European and American markets, must then be confined to their home demands.

If we continue to encourage our slave trade for the supply of the French colonies, (that of the Spanish colonies is yet only ideal) such is the extensiveness and fertility of their islands, particularly Hispaniola, such the frugality of their planters modes of life, that in less than twenty years, even in spite of our enormous bounty of twenty shillings per cwt. they will worm us out of every foreign market for sugar. This ability on the part of our rivals of extending indefinitely their sugar market, which must in time draw after it a naval superiority, requires to be solemnly considered, at least as far as we contribute to it, that those methods may be embraced, that can best counteract its effects respecting us, and help to preserve our rank as a naval power. After laying all this before the reader, we may confidently conclude, that the African trade is more confined in its utility, than is generally imagined, and that of late years it has contributed more to the aggrandisement of our rivals, than of our own national wealth.

We come now to consider the probable consequences to our own sugar colonies, that may be expected from advancing the condition of their slaves. That Britain has a majority in them attached to her laws and her interest, it would be ungenerous not freely to acknowledge; and whatever prejudices existed among them against a connection with her, when compared with her rival, they have in a great measure been done away in the small islands, by their late experience of the nature of a French government. Still it is not to be concealed, that in several of them there is a strong lurking bias for the new empire of America. The conduct of Barbadoes and Jamaica, in the beginning of the late contest, marked this too strongly to admit of a contradiction; the restless emigrations from the sugar colonies thither continue to mark it. The Americans indeed have not yet been able to give any specimen of liberality of sentiment to encourage this bias, or of advantages to be gained by espousing their cause. But that individuals, who have occasion to wish for an easy method of paying debts, should delight in change, even when it promises little, needs not to be wondered at.

But supposing this bias, and the propriety of it, still it is a doubtful point, if any considerable share of West Indian propriety will be in the families, who now posses it, at that period when Britain and France shall be so weak, and America so strong in naval force, as to allow of our sugar islands being added as an appendage to the American empire. Though it may be an object of deliberation with whom they may best be connected, yet it will not be disputed that they can never think of setting up for themselves. They must ever continue to belong to some one or other naval power; and surely from present appearances no period can be assigned, when that power shall be America. Yet suppose every thing to happen as speedily as it is fondly imagined, and observe the consequences.

America, under a republican government, can never be but a disjointed unwieldly state, which nothing but common danger can possibly unite in one purpose. If the sugar islands be connected with them, it must be by conquest, when they are become superior at sea to the European naval powers. By the maxim on which America separated from Britain, no countries, between which seas intervene, can be incorporated together. The sugar colonies, therefore, can never hope to be allowed to partake of any particular American constitution. They must be governed as consquests belonging to the union. When they were first settled, it was by Englishmen intitled to all the privileges and laws of the mother country, and preserving all the rights and claims of citizens. But when subdued by an American squadron, they will be considered as a despised part of an hated people. Some American rice or tobacco planter, who perhaps has the clanking of the chains of his own famished slaves ringing in his ears, will make flaming speeches against sugar planters. He will call them inexorable tyrants over helpless slaves. He will advise to have them treated as slaves; and he will offer himself to be the instrument, because he is well acquainted with the mode.— When this desired change commences in the sugar colonies, what a fine outlet will there be for all the turbulent spirits of America in filling the departments of law, police, customs, and every civil establishment, not omitting the confiscations, that sagacious interest will discover or make. Perhaps, when too late, the indolent rule of Britain, then no more, may be an object of regret.

Again: Suppose our sugar colonies a favoured part of this empire, when will America be able to give them the same high prices for their staple, that Britain has long afforded them? As the children of Britain, their planters had the monopoly of her market. They cannot belong to America, till she has driven out every European power, and seized their colonies for herself. She will consider herself under no particular tie to give them the preference, but will supply her wants from the cheapest market.

Farther, money (the foundation of high prices) can never be in plenty in a country, that is not far advanced in manufactures. Politicians have not yet fixed the time, when the population of America shall be supposed able to manufacture for herself, far less for a foreign market. Whenever, therefore, our colonies are subjected to America, the price of sugar in them must fall one half, and every proprietor must become a bankrupt; for their opulence, their very being as planters, depends on their union with Britain. Suppose then none but freemen inhabiting the sugar colonies, they can propose no benefit by changing their protector. Nay, it must continue to be their interest to cultivate, and even maintain, at the hazard of their lives, an union with their mother country, in whose government they share, who alone can be expected to rule them with a mother's indulgence, who alone can afford them a price for their commodities equal to the expence of their culture. Yet, this being the case, why have we such exaggerated accounts of the necessity of their intire dependence on the new states? Why do they not patiently suffer some temporary inconveniency, till matters can be settled on their new foundation?

Such indeed is the growing demand for sugar in Britain and Ireland, as to call for all that will ever probably be produced in our remaining islands. Doubtless they (Jamaica especially) are capable in themselves of producing much more than they have ever yet sent to market. But such have been the consequences of the several events, that have happened within these last twelve years, that in any case it will be long before they can much exceed what they have formerly made; nor can they possibly increase their quantity so fast, as it probably will be called for. But as soon as any revolution destroys the monopoly of the British market, the British sugar colonies must dwindle into insignificancy.

One reason should ever induce West Indian proprietors to prefer a connection with an European power to one with America. Europe must ever be dependent on the West Indies or Africa for this now necessary of life, sugar. Europe is therefore the proper market for sugar, and it must be the interest of the planter to have a particular country in Europe, where he can lodge his produce, till he can send it to the place of consumption. And where trade is freest, and the merchants have most money, and give the longest credit, (in all which Britain hath the advantage) will be the best spot for fixing their staple. We might add here, that the situation of things, and the manners prevailing in America, must change greatly, before that country becomes as agreeable a retreat as Britain to the rich man or the valetudinarian. Setting therefore aside long habits of acquaintance, the sameness of laws and customs, it must also, in respect of interest, continue to be the planters wish, that Britain may ever be able to protect her colonies, and keep them united to her government. And the advancing of the condition of their slaves, or even the communicating intire freedom to them, can make no difference in the nature of the union, will rather enable the colonies to defend themselves, and do their part to preserve the connection, whereon their own prosperity depends. And it otherwise indisputably appears to be the proprietor's interest to employ only freemen on his plantation.

If it be asked how are sugar plantations to be cultivated, without the usual supplies of slaves from Africa; I answer, on old settled plantations, such supplies are only now necessary from the original ill assortment of the sexes, the oppressive manner in which they have been worked, and the niggardliness with which they have been fed. Had they been treated with humanity, and had their population, instead of being checked by every vile method, been encouraged, the slaves, brought into our old colonies, would long ago have been so greatly multiplied, as to have afforded sufficient numbers to have peopled the islands acquired by the peace of 1763. There are now sufficient numbers in the several islands to do this in the gradual manner, that will be most profitable in the end, if we begin even thus late to treat them generally like human creatures.

But I have not the vanity to imagine that any thing advanced here, or any thing, however just or practicable, that can be proposed by speculative men, will operate at once on the public. The utmost that reasoning can be expected to do, is gradually to correct and inform common opinion, and change insensibly the popular way of thinking. But suppose a statute enacted, that the present slave trade should cease after a period of three or six years, every planter would immediately set himself seriously to stock his plantation, and to give such orders for the treatment of his slaves, as would favour their health and population. This in the mean time would divert our slave trade from the improvement of the French colonies to that of our own: and the end of the period would find the several islands in a state of opulence and happiness that they never yet have experienced, and prepared for that extension of privileges, and unexcepting freedom, which is the scope of our argument. But in making this supposition, I mean not to be accountable for those barbarities, and outrages to humanity, that the shortest existence of the slave trade must in the mean time necessarily occasion.

On the supposition that the sugar colonies, either by their own choice, or the events of war, are separated from Britain, is suggested the possibility of our being supplied with sugar from Africa. Indeed the improvement of Africa is a compensation which we owe for the horrid barbarities we have been instrumental in procuring to be exercised on her sons, both in their native country, and in the West Indies: and certainly we might proceed to great lengths without affecting our sugar colonies; rather they might get many other supplies than slaves from Africa. We mean nothing hostile to our colonies by the plan. Such is indeed the nature of their connection with Britain, that nothing but unavoidable necessity should dissolve it. They were settled by Englishmen, with English money, on the faith of a monopoly of the British market. Without this monopoly they could not continue to be cultivated. On the other hand, hitherto the whole of their profits has been wealth added to the British stock. The bond therefore is reciprocal, and ought not to be weakened on one side, till it has been cancelled on the other. The colonies cannot find an equivalent for the British market; Britain will not soon find a nursery for her navy equal to the West Indian trade, should she by any revolution lose it. He who is a friend to the one must consult the interest of the other; for their prosperity consists in their union. Nor can Britain, take any step in contradiction to it without forfeiting her honour, nor the colonists without risking their possessions. They must exchange concessions; the colonists suffering inconveniencies, rather than injure the commerce and navigation of Britain; Britain sacrificing advantages that her superiority in money and manufactures may give her to preserve her colonies in a condition to supply her market with sugar. But what is mutually to be surrendered will be discovered best from the level, on which things settle naturally of themselves, if we prevent it not by our precipitation in fixing regulations, that cannot be reclaimed, before things have accommodated themselves to their new state; and much might be done for Africa, and great advantage drawn from it, without losing sight of this purpose.

I shall here subjoin an extract of a letter which I have just received from that humane intelligent sea officer, who favoured me with the letter that closes the discussion of the capacity of negroes in the Essay, and who in his late command on the coast of Africa laid himself out for information on the subject, to see what could be suggested or proposed to check or give a new turn to the slave trade. His stay on the coast was short; but did every one, according to his opportunities, apply with the like sentiment and good-will to collect facts, it would soon enable us to strike some plan out to put an end to this diabolical commerce, or at least strip it of its present horrors.

"When the Portuguese extended their discoveries along the coast of Africa, they were very assiduous in introducing the Christian religion in that part called the Grain Coast, from Cape Mount to Cape Palmas. They were at first successful; but when they emigrated to the Brazils, the negroes relapsed into their former idolatry. Many of the negroes at Goree are Mahometans, but in general they are Pagans of the religion and language of the Joliffs. The French have been industrious to teach them manners, and their language; but have paid no attention to religion. I visited all the chiefs of the negroes in our settlements from Santa Apollonia to Athera, which is upwards of 250 miles, and found the police and punishment of all crimes supported by the slave trade. Those who commit crimes or trespasses against their laws, are, at the decision of twelve elders, sold for slaves for the use of their government, and the support of their chiefs. Theft, adultery, and murder, are the highest crimes, and, whenever they are detected, subject the whole family to slavery. But any individual condemned to slavery for the crime of his relation, may redeem his own person, by furnishing two slaves in his room. Or when a man commits one of the above cardinal crimes, all the male part of his family are forfeited to slavery; if a woman, the female part is sold. While on the coast, I saw instances of this sort so truly cruel, as made my very bosom bleed. This traffick in crimes makes the chiefs vigilant. Nor do our planters, who purchase them, use any pains to instruct them in religion, to make them amends for the oppression thus exercised on them. I am sorry to say they are unnaturally averse to every thing that tends to it; yet the Portuguese, French and Spaniards, in their settlements, succeed in their attempts to instruct them, as much to the advantage of their commerce, as of religion. It is for the sake of Christianity, and the advantages accompanying it, that English slaves embrace every occasion of deserting to the settlements of these nations.

I had such a proof of this religious attention in the Portuguese of the island of St. Thomas under the Line, as I shall always reflect on with pleasure. This island was once rich, populous, and full of fair churches, schools, convents, and other pious seminaries. The bishop of Loando was joint bishop of it, and visited it annually. It is now fallen much below its former state. But there are still upwards of 15000 negroe Christians in it, instructed to read and write, who daily attend divine worship, clean and well clad. Friars of all orders, and priests of every denomination, are chosen from among them, and are instructed in divine worship and the Christian rites. And though the ecclesiastick wealth is wasting fast away, yet there still remains that good order and moral conduct among them, which religion alone teaches, or can inspire. There are circumstances in popery that a sensible man cannot approve of; but the peculiar zeal with which the Portuguese have propagated the doctrine of Christ is truly meritorious, while the listless indifference of Protestants is to us a sinful reproach.' Thus far this worthy officer.

This gentleman, during his short stay on the coasts, probably had not an opportunity of seeing those crowds of slaves that are driven down like so many sheep, perhaps 1000 miles from the sea coast, and who are generally inhabitants of villages that have been surrounded in the night-time by an armed force, and carried off to be sold to our traders on the coast. The annual exportation of slaves from Africa has exceeded 100,000. The sea coast, on which this inhuman refinement has been introduced by the European traders, could not have supplied such a number of culprits, without having been long ago depopulated.

From this account it plainly appears, that the slave trade occasions a degree of barbarous cruelty and oppression, which humanity, in its lowest state, must have revolted at, if not supported by avarice, and a lust for gain. We go on the coast, and tempt the natives, with what to them are articles of luxury, to sweep away, for the real or pretended fault of an individual, whole families in exchange, because they can supply us with no other articles that we desire to possess. But from the success of the Portuguese among them, it is clear, the Africans are capable of instruction and improvement, and that agriculture and arts might easily be introduced among them, and lay a foundation for trade, that far from wounding humanity in this high degree, might raise and improve it, and be a blessing and advantage to all concerned.

Why might not the culture of sugar, tobacco, indigo, &c. be introduced into St. Thomas's? And why might not that island send out, in time, negroe teachers and artists to instruct and improve their brethren on the continent? By stopping the importation of slaves into our colonies, you increase the value of those who are already there; you oblige their masters to use them well, and improve their condition. But while ever the slave trade continues open to supply the ravages made by oppression and famine, one great inducement is wanting for treating slaves with humanity. Without meaning to cast any reproach on masters, who, like all other bodies, consist of good, bad, and indifferent men, I affirm, that till some check or new turn be given to the slave trade, it will be found a most difficult business to advance the condition of slaves in our colonies, so as to answer the fond wishes of piety and philanthropy respecting them.

Aug. 10, 1784.

POSTSCRIPT.

THE preceding Inquiry has been so long in the press, as to give the Author an opportunity of taking notice of a curious attack made on him by an anonymous writer, which charges him with having written certain "Thoughts on the Slavery of the Negroes in the American Colonies.' These Thoughts the Author knew nothing of, and never saw them till they were in print. As far as he is the Author, therefore, of these Thoughts, the virulent abuse thrown on him by this enemy in the dark is altogether misapplied. But though from some strong traits in the style, he believes it would not be a difficult matter to trace his adversary out, he shall leave him to enjoy his uncontested victory, with his hearty prayers that he may learn and know the truth; and then the Thoughts that he gives to the publick will be very differently expressed.

But as he appeals to my knowledge of certain facts, and silence may be construed into assent, I must beg leave to set him right.

There is no law (but an old neglected one in the Bible) in St. Kitts, to confine the punishment of a slave to thirty-nine lashes. And had Moses had the cart-whip in contemplation, he would have restrained his people to a much smaller number; for that instrument, in good hands, would soon have made the poor sufferer "vile in his brother's "sight.' There is an instance in Antigua of a white man being hanged for the murder of a negroe; but in the island to which he refers, I never knew of any inquisition for negroe blood. The pickling of the wounds from stripes is not confined to negroe freemen, as he may learn, if he will make a proper inquiry.

I wish his description of the treatment of sick and old slaves were, true; but it was not quite so good in the quarter where I was best acquainted. His account of the peculium of slaves is altogether new to me; nor are "the means of even a bare livelihood' placed in the reach of four out of five slaves with whose situation I was ever acquainted.

It is more pleasing to me to communicate an account of the virtues and improvement of an honest African, that I have just met with in the late travels of Five Danish philosophers[2], originally published in German, and since translated into French, in three volumes, quarto.—Farhan, a jet black negroe, was carried a boy into Arabia, and there sold to an officer in the court of the Imam or prince of Yeman. His master gave him every advantage of education, and entrusted him, as he grew up, with the management of his affairs. These he conducted with so much propriety and address, as to attract the notice of the prince, who took him near his person, and afterwards made him governor of Loheia, a city on the seacoast. There our travellers found him ruling his people, as a kind father would his children. To these travellers he behaved with the utmost kindness, generosity, and even politeness, expressed the greatest fondness for their conversation, and a warm desire to learn and be informed of whatever was striking in Europeans. In short they, when speaking of him, call him the good Farhan, and had many sad opportunities of contrasting his behaviour with the other native Arabian governors. Here then we have an African towering above the subtile Arabian; and shall his country, by European insolence, be still depressed in the scale of reason and human excellence? It is ignorant pride that fancies a distinction to its prejudice.

Notes

1   The slave ships generally return from the West Indies in ballast, and they go out to Africa but lightly freighted. The expence therefore of carrying rum to Africa cannot be considered as high, or capable of enhancing the price.

2   Voyage en Arabie & en d'autres Pays circonvoisins, par C. Niebuhr.

THE
SUBSTANCE
OF THE
EVIDENCE
OF
SUNDRY PERSONS
ON THE
SLAVE-TRADE,

COLLECTED IN THE COURSE OF A TOUR

MADE

IN THE AUTUMN

OF

THE YEAR 1788.

LONDON:

PRINTED BY JAMES PHILLIPS, GEORGE-YARD,
LOMBARD-STREET.
M.DCC.LXXXIX.

THE SUBSTANCE OF SEVERAL
CONVERSATIONS HELD WITH

And committed to Writing in his Presence, at
September, 1788.
No. VII.

MR. [Ellison] was ten voyages to the coast of
Guinea for slaves. The first three were in the
[Upton] of Liverpool, Captains [Birch and
Pemberton]. The fourth in the [Briton] of
Liverpool, Captain [Bagshaw]. The fifth in the
[Liberty] of Liverpool, Captain [Briggs]. The
sixth in the [Friendship] of Liverpool, Captain
[Mr. Saul]. The seventh in the [Marquis of
Granby] Captain [Cobban] of Lancaster. The
eighth and ninth in the [Nightingale] Captain
[Carter] of Bristol; and the tenth in the [Mary
Anne] Captain [Saunders] of London. He
returned from his last voyage, to the best of his
recollection, in the year 1770.

No. VII.
Situation and
qualification of
the relator to give
evidence.

Mr. [Ellison] cannot positively say, in general
terms, how slaves are originally obtained; but,
if he were allowed to take his opinion from the
few instances that came within his knowledge
upon the coast, he should say first, that they
were obtained by the natives by means of
treachery or force, and that this order of slaves
was more extensive than any other.

The first reason which would induce him to

Great bulk of
the slaves at
Benin procured
by treachery or
force.

form such an opinion, may be taken from the following occurrence:

Mr. [Ellison] was lying in the [Briton] in Benin River. At the time alluded to, Captain Lemma Lemma, a great trader of Benin, was on board. This trader, happening to be on deck, observed a canoe with three people in it, crossing the above river. Upon seeing it he dispatched a war canoe, which was then lying along side the [Briton], and on board of which were five of his people, in pursuit. They presently came up with the canoe aforesaid, and, having seized her, brought her alongside of the [Briton]. The three people were then taken out of the canoe, and brought on board. They consisted of a father son, and daughter. The two latter were sold to the chief mate, Captain [Bagshaw] being then at the factory at Gatoe. The former, on account of his age, was refused. Upon this Captain Lemma Lemma ordered his people to take him into his own canoe, which they accordingly did, but laid his head upon the thwart of the boat, and in two strokes with a cutlass cut it off. This Mr. [Ellison] saw with his own eyes.

Three of the natives stolen by Lemma Lemma's people. Fate of one of them.

A second reason which would induce him to form such an opinion, would be this, That the ship was supplied afterwards with a great number of slaves by the same Lemma Lemma, and that the same Lemma Lemma

Same Lemma Lemma procures for the ship —a notorious robber.

was considered as a robber or stealer of men by the natives, for they were exceedingly afraid of venturing out whenever any of his war canoes were in sight.

A third reason would be this, That he has often heard from the slaves on board, whose language he could understand, that they had been stolen by their own countrymen, and conducted to the vessel.

Slaves on board declare they had been stolen.

Mr. [Ellison] is more confirmed in his opinion, namely, That the order of kidnapped people, or people taken by fraud, is more extensive than any other, first, because in all the voyages he has made, he recollects but two or three instances of slaves being brought on board who had any wounds upon them: So that few, in his opinion, are prisoners of war: And secondly, because in every ship to which he belonged, there were always a number of boys and girls, who had no relations on board, who, on account of their age, could never have been criminals.

Very few with wounds on board---many boys and girls — conclusion from thence.

Mr. [Ellison] is of opinion, that kidnapping, or the taking away of people by treachery, is also now and then practised by the whites. This he supposes from the following circumstance:

Kidnapping practised by the whites.

When he belonged to the [Liberty], Captain [Briggs], he was sent with two seamen in the shallop to the island of Fernandipo for yams. A musket was fired, as usual, to let the natives

Two of the natives of Fernandipo taken off by a Liverpool trader know that they were coming to trade with them. None of them, however, ventured down till the afternoon, when they were discovered to be peeping through the bushes, and approaching slyly at the same time. About eight or ten of them came at last upon the beach. They brought with them a goat, and a few baskets of yams, but would by no means venture to the boat. Upon this Mr. [Ellison] jumped into the water, and swam to them. He was immediately, on his arrival upon the shore, surrounded by a great number of the inhabitants, who came about him with their lances. One of them, an old man, informed him that two of their people, a man and woman, had been stolen from the island by a Liverpool ship's long-boat. The people now became rather tumultuous, and brandished their darts over Mr. [Ellison], giving him to understand that, unless he could bring back the two islanders and had been stolen, they would kill him: The sailors in the shallop seeing this, fired two muskets over their heads, which had such an effect upon them, that they immediately ran away, and left their goat and yams behind them. These Mr. [Ellison] and the two seamen put into their boat, and proceeded to Old Calabar. On their arrival there they related the circumstance as it happened, and, on making a proper inquiry, found the two people, who had been stolen, on board a Liverpool Guinea-man, which Mr. [Ellison], as far as his recollection goes, thinks was the Dobson. The two people being thus found out, were, on a representation made that no more trade could be carried on with the inhabitants of Fernandipo, sent on board the [Liberty] next morning. On the same day Mr. [Ellison] took them back to their own island, when he was rewarded with fowls, goats, yams, honey, and other articles, nor could the natives be prevailed upon to take any thing from him in return.

Mr. [Ellison] is of opinion that crimes either supposed or real, form a source, from whence the slave trade is supplied also. The two following facts that came under his own knowledge have induced him to think so.

Crimes also produce slavery.

At Yanamaroo, a town up the river Gambia, a black trader, who had many wives, charged one of them with adultery, and accordingly sold her to the vessel. Up the same river also some canoe boys were sold to the [Upton], who, speaking all of them good English, told Mr. [Ellison] and others, that they had been sold for theft. They were sold by their own masters. Mr. [Ellison] believes that no trial takes place, but that in such cases they are instantly upon detection brought on board.

Mr. [Ellison] says, that there is another order of slaves upon the coast, namely, of those who

Country slaves—their employment.

73

are born in bondage there. These are employed in fishing, in cultivating the ground, and in rowing canoes for their masters These are sold to the Europeans for any trivial offence, and, when their masters are in want of goods, they generally make use of some pretence to accuse and sell them.

Those who are slaves in Africa, and are employed as before-mentioned, are neither worked so hard nor treated so ill, as the slaves in the British colonies. They are more on a level with their masters. Mr. [Ellison] has seen them eating in the same apartment, and talking freely with each other. He has never seen nor heard of any instances on any part of the coast, which he has visited, where slaves were beaten or even struck. If they commit a fault, they are mostly sold.

Their slavery not so grievous as in the West Indies.

The slaves, that are purchased up the Gambia, are generally brought thither through the interior country by land. They come in droves of three or four hundred at a time. The women and boys are permitted to walk freely. The men, however, are confined; the arms of some of the latter are tied behind them. Two or three others are tied together by means of leathern thongs, or ropes of grass, at the neck. Two others are confined by means of a pole, at each end of which is a crutch to put the neck in, of the following form:

Method of bringing down slaves to the Gambia.

Their two necks being placed in the crutches, as represented in the above figure, are confined in them by leather thongs, made fast to the ends or extremities of the said crutches. Sometimes it happens that one man is seen by himself to have such a crutch upon him. In this case the pole which is fastened to the crutch, is placed behind him, and one of the servants of the black merchants uses it as a goad, and pushes him along with it, holding it in his hand, and forcing it against the back of his neck. In this manner they are driven down with skins, full of water on their backs. Almost all of them carry their own water. Others bring down wax and ivory. They are generally covered with dust, and suffer much, not only from this circumstance, but because their feet are frequently swelled with walking, and their wrists and arms cut by the pressure of the thong, which confines them. Such a body of slaves is called a *cauffle*. The traders, who drive them down, ride upon horses, some before, some behind, and others on each side of them, according as the breadth of the path will permit. Mr. [Ellison] has seen several in the cauffle lame with walking. As to the other places which he has visited upon the coast, he had never an opportunity of seeing how the slaves were brought down to them there.

When the slaves are brought down, the black traders or brokers, who are acquainted with the English, and Portugueze, and other languages, as well as the languages of the interior Africans, offer them to sale to the Europeans. The latter examine them, and refuse such as have any defect, or are at all sickly. The medium of exchange, by means of which they make their respective bargains, is called a bar in the Gambia and upon the Windward coast, but at Old and New Calabar, a copper. This bar was in Mr. [Ellison]'s time equal in value, and estimated at about 5s.

Slaves examined— medium of exchange —its value.

It is customary to lend goods, both up the Gambia, at Old and New Calabar, and at Benin, to the black traders. These, however, are obliged to leave their sons, daughters, and other relations on board, as a security for the payment of the same. Those, who are so left, are called pawns. It is not unusual with the English Captains to sail away with them. The Captain of the [Briton] in which vessel Mr. [Ellison], sailed, carried away two persons of this description.

Traders trusted with goods— leave their relations in pawn. Two pawns taken off in the _____.

Mr. [Ellison] says, that the slaves are much dejected indeed, and that he never saw them otherwise than dejected, when they were

Slaves look dejected, when brought on board. Men are put into irons.

brought on board.

The men immediately on their entrance into the vessel are put in irons, and chained two and two together. The irons are fastened to their legs, or to their wrists, or, if they are refractory, to their necks. Mr. [Ellison] has seen both their legs and wrists much chased and swelled in consequence of these irons. It was, in general, the custom in those vessels to which he belonged, to take them off when within about ten or twelve days sail of the destined port.

The slaves are usually brought upon deck at about nine o'clock in the morning, and stay up till sun-set. They are fed twice in the day, namely, at ten in the morning, and five in the afternoon. Their food consists generally of rice, yams, and horse-beans. They have sometimes two pint pannekins of water per day, but not often, and when water begins to run short, not half the quantity.

Time and nature of their meals.

It is the custom to insist upon their dancing, whenever the weather will permit, in order that they may exercise their limbs, and thereby preserve their health. Some of them however appear unwilling to do it. All such are compelled to it by a cat of nine tails, which is invariably used on such occasions.

Compelled to dance.

Mr. [Ellison] says, that the slaves, in consequence of too close a stowage, complain

Dreadful situation on account of heat.

much of heat, and that he has seen them panting and almost dying for want of water.

He says also, that the rains are frequent and violent on the middle passage, but that in those ships, in which he sailed, they never covered the gratings with a tarpawling, but made a tarpawling awning over the booms: Notwithstanding which he has seen the slaves after a rain panting for breath, and in such a situation, that the seamen have been obliged to get them immediately upon deck, fearing otherwise that they would immediately faint and die.

Mr. [Ellison] believes that in all the vessels, in which he sailed, platforms were used, and that they had windsails in the [Liberty] and in the [Friendship].

Platforms and windsails

With respect to the treatment of slaves, while on board the ships, they are used well in some, and as badly in others. The latter mode of treatment is in general productive of bad consequences, as may be seen in some of the following instances.

Cat of nine tails made and inlaid with wire.

When Captain [Bagshaw] died, his chief mate Mr [Wilson] succeeded to the command of the [Briton]. On his arrival to such command, he ordered Mr. [Ellison] to make him a cat of nine tails, and to inlay each of the tails of it with three pieces of wire. With this cat he was accustomed to flog the slaves, and apparently

Slaves flogged with it on board the ____

Women jump over-board.

for his diversion.

On a certain day, on the passage from Benin to [Virginia], while the said Captain [Wilson] was at dinner, the slaves happened to be making a noise over his head. He immediately rose up, and taking with him the wire cat before-mentioned, went amongst them. The slaves, having often before experienced his fury, were immediately thrown into consternation. Six women instantly jumped overboard. Five of them were drowned. The sixth having been taken up and saved, was afterwards by the Captain's orders hoisted up to the yard-arm, and from thence let down into the water, and this was repeated so often, that she had nearly shared the fate of the other five.

At another time, a noise being made in the mens rooms, Captain [Wilson] selected eight of them for punishment. These he ordered to be tied up by their wrists to the booms. He flogged them with the cat before-mentioned in a very cruel manner: but, not thinking this a sufficient punishment, he ordered thumb-screws to be fixed upon them; in consequence of which the thumbs of some of them mortified and rotted off, and they died.

Others tortured by thumb-screws. —Thumbs rot off—they die.

It is not unusual with the slaves, whether from a love of liberty, from ill treatment, as before described, from a spirit of vengeance, or other causes, to attempt to rise upon the crew.

Slaves frequently rise.

The True Blue of Liverpool was cut off at sea by the slaves on board, and all the white people, but three or four, were killed. These, together with the slaves, were taken up by another vessel.

Rise on the crew of the True Blue kill most of them. Rise on the crew of the Africa— three killed— eight selected for punishment.

At another time an attempt was made by the slaves to rise upon the crew of the Africa, a Bristol Guinea-man, and then lying in New Calabar River. They had already extricated themselves from their irons, and were forcing open the barricado door, when Mr. [Ellison] and seven seamen in the [Nightingale']s boat, well armed with pistols and cutlasses, got on board. They immediately mounted the barricado, and fired over the heads of the slaves; but this not deterring them from their design, they fired among them, in consequence of which one man slave was killed.

Notwithstanding this, the slaves made a second attempt, but not succeeding, went forward. Mr. [Ellison] and the rest followed them with their arms. Some of the slaves, upon seeing them advance, jumped overboard, others ran below, and others staid upon deck. Among the latter they fired again and killed two.

Being now subdued, and afterwards secured, eight of them were selected for an example. They were tied up to the rough tree, and every person in the [Nightingale']s boat, as well as every one of the crew of the Africa, flogged them till from weariness they could flog no more. The Captain of the Africa then heated the tormentor or cook's tongs, and the surgeon's instrument for spreading plaisters, and burned their flesh. This operation being over, they were confined and taken below.

With respect to the loss of slaves, Mr. [Ellison] says, that in his first voyage on board the [Nightingale], they purchased about 350, and buried 5; that in the [Briton] they purchased about 70, and buried about 100; and that in the second voyage in the [Nightingale] they purchased about 350 as before, and buried about. At this time they have taken up eight or ten dead in a morning. The rooms and platforms of the slaves were at this juncture like one continued scab; for the small pox had broken out among them, and had occasioned the prodigious loss now mentioned. In the rest of the voyages which Mr. [Ellison] made, they always buried some slaves: but how many he does not now recollect.

Number purchased and lost.—Small pox on board the ___. Dreadful situation on account of it.

Mr. [Ellison] says, that some seamen go volun-tarily into the slave trade, and for various reasons: Some, because they have been every other voyage but that to Guinea, and they are desirous of trying it: others, because they have an affection for an old ship-mate, who has perhaps shipped himself for Guinea, and they

Method of procuring seamen for the slave trade

are willing to be with him: These and other reasons induce them often to go there; but by far the greater part of them go from necessity. Some of these embark in it from want, and because the West Indiamen and others having sailed, they can get no other employ. Others are threatened by their landlords, who have purposely gotten them into debt, and are obliged to go to avoid a goal [sic]: others are taken from the goal [sic] itself, whither they have been put for that purpose, many instances of which have come under his own knowledge. Mr. [Ellison] has seen as fine seamen in the slave trade as in any other whatever.

The treatment which the seamen undergo, who are employed in the slave trade, in whatever point of view it is considered, cannot be sufficiently reprobated. Mr. [Ellison] says, that in all his ten voyages he was obliged to receive half his wages at the port of delivery, in currency instead of sterling. He asserts also, that no seaman whatever, in all the ten voyages alluded to, had any shelter or place where he could put his head during the whole of the Middle Passage, but that every one was exposed night and day to the inclemency of the weather: that the provisions on board the slave ships are not only very bad, but are dealt out so sparingly, that the crew are often put to great pain from the calls of hunger; that the very largest allow-

Are paid in currency.—have no shelter—nature and quantity of their provisions—use the gun barrel.

ance, which he himself ever had, was but four ounces of beef or pork when boiled, per day, and five pounds of bread per week; and that the smallest allowance was three pounds of bread per week, and the same quantity of beef or pork as before mentioned per day, and that they were obliged to get their water from a gun barrel, to be fetched from the mast head.

With respect to the ill usage of seamen in other points, Mr. [Ellison] gives the following particulars:

When he was on board the [Nightingale] in New Calabar River, the Phœnix from Bristol, commanded by Captain Bishop, was lying there. Captain Bishop was a very severe man, and behaved in a very barbarous manner to his crew. At one time in particular, he missed a small piece of ham. He immediately manned his yawl, and sent after the seamen who were gone to cut wood for the vessel. Immediately on their return on board, they were obliged to receive from the doctor, and to take an emetick, in order that he, Captain Bishop, might know who had eaten it. He had not however the satisfaction of punishing any of them on that occasion, for no signs of a thief were to be found.

In this and other ways the seamen of the Phœnix were ill used, and the oppression of the Captain was at last so seriously felt by

Cruel treatment of them on board the Phœnix. Case of Thomas Jones, and five others.—die at Forje

83

them, that they grew quite weary of their lives. Six of them accordingly took the yawl, and left him in New Calabar River, determined to suffer any hardships rather than stay in their own vessel. It was not long, however, before they were taken by the natives in their war canoes, and brought to Forje, a small town in the mouth of New Calabar River. Captain Bishop, on being made acquainted with their capture, ordered them to be chained by the neck, legs, and arms, and to be kept there. He ordered also that only a plaintain per day should be given them. Thomas Jones, who was one of them, an excellent seaman, and a ship-mate of Mr.[Ellison']s, became in consequence of his situation, raving mad, and, deprived of all sustenance, died in his chains. The remaining five soon shared his fate, and died also in their chains at Forje.

Mr. [Ellison] says, that on board the [Nightingale] his own ship, the seamen were also very ill used. He has seen Captain [Carter] kick them about repeatedly, and beat them with his fist, and with ropes, and with any thing that he could first lay his hand upon, on the most trifling occasions.

The gunner of the [Nightingale] was one day acting as centinel over the slaves. Captain [Carter] upon seeing him, desired him to look forward. The gunner made him no reply,

On board the ___. Case of the gunner —dies.

but said privately to himself, "I could very willingly turn my musket upon you,' or words to that effect. The Captain over-hearing him, ordered him to be tied up. He flogged him in an unmerciful manner with his own hands. In about four days afterwards the gunner died.

Mr. [Ellison] says, that in Guineamen, when the seamen were just at the last gasp, and died in a day or two afterwards, or on the same day, he has seen them beaten about, and compelled to do their duty by force nor have indulgences of any kind been granted them. On board the [Nightingale] a seaman was in so weak and feeble a state, that it was dangerous for him to go up to the mast-head to fetch the gun barrel, to enable him to drink. Notwithstanding this, he was debarred from having his water in any other way. The poor man at length, on account of extreme thirst, was obliged to attempt to go. He ascended as well as he could; but, when he had gotten up about half way on the main shrouds, he called out for help. Mr. [Ellison] accordingly with another went up to him, and by means of their assistance he came down, but was unable to get up as far as the gun barrel, neither were they permitted to fetch it for him. Mr. [Ellison] at length, after much intreaty, prevailed upon the surgeon to give him a decoction, but the sailor died in a few days.

Seamen abused when sick.— Case of another —dies.

On board the [Briton], another ship, in which Mr. [Ellison] was, the same sort of treatment prevailed. The cabin boy, who went by the name of [Paddy] was singularly oppressed. Mr. [Wilson], the chief mate seemed to take a delight in persecuting him. It happened one day, that the tea kettle, the management of which belonged to this boy, was not boiled in time; upon which the aforesaid chief mate threatened to beat him, as soon as ever the breakfast should be over.

The poor boy, on account of his former ill usage, was terrified at his threat, and betook himself to the lee fore chains. When the breakfast, however, was over, the chief mate came out of the cabin, and, not forgetting his promise, took a piece of rope out of his pocket, calling out at the same time, "Paddy.'— The boy, seeing and hearing this, and perceiving also that Mr. [Wilson] was approaching towards him, immediately jumped into the sea, which was very high at the time, and was drowned. This happened on the outward-bound passage.

At another time when the vessel was lying at Benin, James Allison, was very ill. Mr. [Wilson] ordered him down into the womens room to scrape it. The above Allison accordingly went, but, having received several bruises before by means of a rope used

On board the — Case of the cabin boy — drowns himself.

Case of James Allison—dies.

upon him by Mr. [Wilson], which bruises occasioned him to be in a feeble state, he was unable to perform the allotted task. Upon this Mr. [Wilson] asked him why he did not proceed in his work. He replied "that he was really unable.' He had no sooner uttered these words, than Mr. [Wilson] threw an handspike at him from the deck, which struck him with great violence upon the breast. In consequence of the blow he immediately fell down, and, though he began to recover a little afterwards, he lived but four days.

Mr. [Ellison] says, that the treatment of the seamen in this ship was cruel from the very beginning to the end of the voyage; that ropes and hand-spikes were in common use, and that the seamen were also kicked and beaten with the fist for only imaginary faults. He says also that he cannot now recollect any more specific instances of ill usage, but can assert with truth, in general terms, that seamen were very ill used in those ships, in which he failed in the slave trade.

General description of their treatment.

In a former paragraph it was said that the slaves attempted to rise on board the Africa, a Bristol Guineaman, and then lying in Old Calabar River. On board this vessel was a black seaman, who acted in the capacity of a cook. This man was suspected of having encouraged the slaves to rise, as before stated, and of

On board the Africa of Bristol. Case of the cook —dies.

having furnished them with the cooper's tools, in order that they might knock themselves out of irons.

From this supposition merely, and without any proof of the fact, he was ordered into the main-top: A neck-collar was there put upon him, and he was chained to the main-mast head. In this situation he was obliged to remain night and day. He had only one plaintain and one pint of water per day allowed him: nor had he any other covering than one pair of long trowsers, to shield him from the inclemency of the night.

The Africa at length, having completed her cargo, dropt down the river, in order to leave the coast. The Captain, however, conceiving the punishment, inflicted upon the cook, to have been of too short a duration, sent him on board the [Nightingale], in which Mr. [Ellison] was, to have it continued there. He was accordingly chained in the [Nightingale]'s main-top, and had the same allowance of plaintain and water, as in the former vessel. Having been in the main-tops of the two vessels for about five weeks, that is, three weeks in that of the first, and a fortnight in that of the second, and having experienced inconceivable misery in both, he was relieved by death.

The above unfortunate man was at the time of his death a most shocking spectacle; for, about three days before, he had been delirious, and had attempted to free himself from his fetters. In the struggle, the chain that confined him, had rubbed the skin from several parts of his body: the neck collar too had found its way to the bone. Hunger and oppression had reduced him to a skeleton. These circumstances contributed to make his appearance horrible. Mr. [Ellison] lent an hand to heave him out of the top into the river, and from that circumstance saw the situation he was in. His remains were immediately devoured by the sharks.

Mr. [Ellison] says, that in his first voyage in the [Upton], about 25 seamen were lost to the best of his knowledge out of about 35; and in his second, about 15 out of 35; and in his third, about 24 out of about 35 or 37. In this voyage Captain Penny, one of the delegates from Liverpool, in opposition to Sir William Dolben's Bill, was second mate. This gentleman afterwards commanded the Cavendish. In the [Briton] 35 were buried before they came to Virginia. In the [Nightingale] about 15 or 16 on the coast and in the Middle Passage. In the [Liberty] about 5. In the [Friendship] about 4. In the latter vessel several of the seamen were carried sick and lame into the West Indies.

Loss in the different voyages.

Mr. [Ellison] says, that he has seen seamen in the different West India islands, but

89

particularly in Jamaica, lying on the wharfs and other places in an ulcerated and helpless state. Some of these he had known before, and knew also that they were such as had been discharged or had deserted from Guineamen on their arrival there. Of others he enquired how they came into that situation, and to what vessels they belonged. Their usual reply was, "That they came out of Guineamen, and that they were unable to get their pay.' On asking them how they could think of leaving their ships before they received their wages, they replied, "That they chose rather to come on shore than stay on board, and be used in a barbarous manner.'

Dreadful situation of such as are put adrift in the West Indies—Fate of many of them there.

The above people he has seen begging about and driven to such distress, that he has often carried them a little provisions from his own ship. He has seen them ulcerated from the knee pan to the ankle, and in such a state, that no ship whatever would receive them. He has seen them also dying on the wharfs through hunger and disease, and instances have come before him of negroes carrying their dead bodies to Spring Path to be interred.

Mr. [Ellison] being once in a West Indiaman at Barbadoes, was accustomed to go on shore to the watering wharf. He has seen there several Guinea seamen in great distress, and in want of the common necessaries of life, with their legs in an ulcerated state, eaten up by the chicres, and their toes rotting off, without any person to give them any assistance, or to take them in. On this wharf a shed had been built, in order that the slaves in wet weather might get under it and be dry. In this shed he has seen them lying, nor had they any other place to go to, except that a negro was now and then kind enough to take them into his hut.

Mr. [Ellison] is therefore strongly of opinion, that a very considerable number of those seamen, who from cruel usage are forced to desert in the West Indies from the different Guineamen that arrive there, annually perish, after having experienced a state of misery, which no pen can be equal to the talk of describing.

THE SUBSTANCE OF THE EVIDENCE
OF

Taken from a Personal Interview with him there.

No. XXI.

No. XXI.
Situation &
qualification of
the relator to give
evidence.

Mr. [Parker] was three voyages on the coast of Africa, the first on board the [Black Joke], Captain [Pollard], from Liverpool, the second on board the [Latham] Captain [Colley], to Old Calabar, which ship he left there and went home in the [Dalrymple], Captain [Allanson], and the third on board the [O' Hara], Captain [? Zannegan]. His first voyage was made, he believes, in the year 1765.

Expedition up
Old Calabar
River. —The
natives forced
into slavery by
robbers in the
night.

Mr. [Parker] having left the [Latham] in Old Calabar River, as just stated, was received by the king of New-Town, who to the best of his recollection was called Dick Ebro. He resided with the king for about five months, during which time he had two opportunities of seeing in which way the natives in that quarter were made slaves.

The people, belonging to the king, went during his residence there up the river to trade. They went in a fleet of canoes, to the number of ten or twelve, and took Mr. [Parker] with them. In this expedition they called at the villages, as they passed them, in the day-time, and purchased slaves, but in the night made excursions on the banks of the river for the purpose of seizing and bringing off whomsoever they could find. When they came to what they considered to be a proper place, they left an armed party in their canoes, and proceeded with the rest to certain villages, which were inland. On their arrival at these, they rushed into the huts, and seized men, women, and children promiscuously, Mr. [Parker] went with them into these huts, and assisted in seizing some of the inhabitants himself. About fifty of them were so seized and carried off at different times in the course of the expedition.

During his stay at New Town he was solicited to attend another expedition up the river for the purpose of getting slaves. He complied with the requisition, and saw the same practices in the second as in the first. Between fifty and sixty more of the inhabitants were brought off in the manner before described. Having resided about five months with the king, he left him, and shipped himself on board the [Dalrymple], Captain [Allanson], as has been stated above.

Second expedition— made slaves of in the same manner.

While he was on board the [Black Joke], he saw the following circumstance: Among the slaves brought on board was a little negro girl, about two years old, who came with her

Cruelty to a child on board the —

mother. She frequently cried, and was sulky. Mr. [Marechal‡], who had just come to the command on the death of Captain [Pollard], said, on hearing the noise, he would make the child remember. He accordingly rivetted one of her little legs to a small billet of wood. In this situation she crawled about, but cried as frequently as before. On these occasions he would sometimes take her up by one arm, and holding her out, flog her with the other with a cat. Both the legs of the child began in process of time to swell. Upon this he said he would cure them. He accordingly ordered hot boiling water to be brought to him in a bucket. In this water he was going to put the child's legs. The person who brought him the bucket remonstrated with him on this proceeding, alleging that the water was too hot. The wretch however totally disregarded what he had said, and put her legs in that situation into the boiling water. The child shrieked out, as if in the greatest agony, and it appeared on taking her legs out of the water, that the nails of the toes had come off. The child lingered for about two days afterwards, when it died.

Mr. [Parker] says that it is a common practice at Liverpool, to get seamen into debt, in order that the landlords may have them in their power, and be thus enabled to force them to go to Guinea.

Method of procuring seamen for the slave trade. Ill used. Loss of them in the slave trade.

Captain [Pollard] behaved very well to his seamen, but Captains [Connelly], [Allanson], and [? Zannegan], in as barbarous a manner. The treatment which they experienced at the hand of the former on board the [Latham], was so very cruel, that Mr. [Parker] left the ship in Old Calabar River, which gave him an opportunity of seeing the expeditions before mentioned.

Mr. [Parker] does not recollect the exact mortality in the ships in which he sailed in the slave trade, but remembered the aggregate loss of seamen to have been great.

†Editor's note: Should read 'Marshall'

NOTEBOOK OF THE REV. JAMES RAMSAY

BODLEIAN LIBRARY
OF
COMMONWEALTH AND AFRICAN STUDIES
MSS.BRIT.EMP.S.2

QUESTIONS
CONCERNING THE STATE OF SLAVES
IN THE
SUGAR COLONIES
[AND] AN ADDRESS TO _____ ON THE
PROPOSED BILL FOR THE
ABOLITION
OF THE
SLAVE TRADE

TRANSCRIPTION OF FOLIOS
41V-60V [AND] 63V-65V

QUESTIONS CONCERNING THE STATE OF
SLAVES IN THE SUGAR COLONIES [f.4IV-6ov]

√[Q] Have you ever been in the West Indies.

[A] I was about two years and an half in a Man of War on that Station. I afterwards settled in St. Christopher, and continued upwards of 19 years there; leaving it August 1st 1781.

√[Q] When in a Man of War on that Station were you frequently on shore.

[A] I may say frequently and much on account of the necessity of careening¹ the Ship, and recruiting her water and stores; and the accident of breaking my thigh in the Service.

√[Q] Could you Learn much concerning the Treatment of Slaves while on the West Indian Station.

[A] I could give no satisfactory account of it; till I had been long settled in a situation, that brought it before me in every possible circumstance.

√[Q] You might have seen the Slaves chained together; you might have seen them with heavy Iron puddings² hammered about their ancles [sic], Iron Crooks rivetted about their necks, their backs furrowed by the whip, and their bodies naked.

[A] It was impossible to walk the Streets or be on the road, without meeting with someone or other object in such situations; but I was never placed in circumstances during this period that could lead me to judge, what general treatment they received, or what degree of happiness or misery they possessed.

√[Q] You often visited in families.

[A] Yes. But there I saw only Domestics dressed neat and clean for the occasion, and assiduous to please, which always gives the appearance of ease and satisfaction as well to the entertainer as the guest.

√[Q] Do you mean to infer, that Officers on the Stations are not usually in circumstances which can enable them to judge of the State of Slaves.

[A] Most positively; unless they set out with a resolution to make inquiries, and know enough of the general management of the Slaves to direct them in the search. They must attend to their food, their cloathing, their hours of labour, their punishments, their treatment when sick, their accommodations; all of which are kept out of sight, during occasional visits.

√[Q] Of whom do Domestics chiefly consist.

[A] Concubines, creoles, or such sprightly Slaves, as have been brought mere children from Africa.

√[Q] How are Domestics fed.

[A] They have a Small weekly proportion of grain and herrings; together with the Scraps from their Masters Table; which being more plentiful when they entertain company, gives them on such occasions an air of cheerfulness.

√[Q] Can a Sea Officer on the Station invited occasionally to dine at a planters house, or staying for a few days on shore be in a situation to judge of the state of Slaves in the Sugar Colonies unless he sets himself on purpose to inquire and examine into it.

[A] He may observe and remark ill treatment; because he has his own feelings to guide him in making the application for this his evidence is good. But before he can judge of what is good treatment, he must be acquainted with the whole oeconomy of the plantations, and must be able to compare what he sees with the standard of proper treatment formed in his own mind. He must examine their punishments, their work, their food, their hours of rest, their cloathing, their management when sick, and a thousand other particulars, that will not readily occur to such an occasional visitor.

√[Q] In your time was the treatment of Slaves considered usually in a moral point of view.
[A] Not usually nor to the best of my recollection within my knowledge by more than one single planter.

√[Q] Was it in any light an ordinary Subject of conversation.
[A] It was not an ordinary subject of conversation; except as it respected the character of the Planter as an easy or severe Master; as it respected the slaves feelings it was not within my knowledge considered but in the single case hinted at above.

But Negroes are brought from a state of misery and oppression in Africa, and placed in an easy happy situation in the West Indies[3]. This is an argument which no Planter dares to use before a man acquainted with the West Indies. Was it ever before heard, that men made long voyages, employed their wealth by sea, risked their healths by disease, and their lives by rebellion to go on a precarious trade, to set one half of a country against the other to rob burn murder and enslave each other, that they might coop up the captives for two or three months in a ships hold by which one half die of thirst foul air and disease, that they might sell the wretched remains to famine stripes and hard labour, on the poor chance, that perhaps one in 50 of the number lost to Africa may meet with a master, that by not using all the oppression towards him, which others his fellows meet with, gives an appearance of fellow feeling and humanity. If they are happier in the West Indies, it is because the cursed Slave trade arms them in their own country against each other and renders their situation insecure; and in the West Indies being sunk to the extremity of misery they have nothing farther to be afraid of.

But what right have we to judge of an Africans feelings or to determine for him, that 49 persons are to be murdered or rendered miserable, that the odd man may be made happy. Do Africans ever offer themselves to be received into our Ships, to escape from their wretched country. Is there not a charm in country, that makes the Greenlander prefer his native fields of ice to the polished cities of Europe. But if Africa be such a step mother, how can she bear an annual loss of 200,000 people in the prime of life, at which the slave trade and its consequences may be fairly estimated; While the West Indies, this Negroe paradice, to which to keep up the analogy they are translated, through sufferings imprisonments martyrdoms and deaths require large annual supplies to keep their numbers from decreasing. Yet little and easy labour supplies them with sufficient food and cloathing in Africa unceasing toil starves them in the West Indies. Indeed how can people be said to be happy in a country, who in many situations have not a scrap of land allotted for their maintenance that can be turned to any other culture; who have no law to secure them against the effects of avarice spite caprice or ignorance in an unfeeling master.

We must not therefore stop at gaining humanity over to our side, but go on to inquire how far commerce, and political claims may probably be affected should the liberty at which we aim ever be accomplished. And this will lead us to consider how far Negroes in a State of freedom promise to become good and useful citizens, or whether their place might not be supplied by free white labourers.

Affect not to make yourselves unhappy lest our throats be cut should you refuse to receive us; for our Countrymen whom you employ to hunt down and enslave us will not risk their lives, and travel two or three thousand miles at an enormous expence for the sole pleasure of sacrificing us in sight of your ships.

√[Q] How came you to settle in St. Christopher.[4]
[A] The fracture of my thigh was in such a place as brought on an irremediable lameness, which made a Sea life dangerous to me. My original turn was to the Church. There was a want of Clergymen in the Island; and my Commander and his friends procured me a title for orders from the Governor.

√[Q] Did you not practice Surgery there.
[A] I happened to be settled in a Quarter, where there was no Surgeon. My time was wholly taken up in giving advice to the neighbourhood. My living did not afford my family a decent maintenance, nor according to the custom of the Colony, supply me with employment. I yielded [sic] to the necessity of the case and the pressing instances of my friends and neighbours; giving way to such as attempted to settle, and in almost every case confining myself to such convenient business as freely offered.

√[Q] You said while in the Kings service, you could not judge of the State of the Slaves; nor till you had been settled in a situation, that brought it before you in every possible circumstance. Did you mean this of your practice among the Sick Slaves.

[A] I did. I visited the plantations daily. I saw their cloathes and their provisions distributed. I was frequent witness of their punishments. I attended to their hours of labour. The Sick were under my care. They frequently applied to me to intercede with their Masters. In short the whole oeconomy of a Sugar plantation was before me.

√[Q] What is the price of new or African slaves.

[A] Anno 1762 When I settled in the Island the prices were from about £36 down to £30 or £28 according to circumstances. The Ordinary average about £26 or £27 including the refuse Slaves. During the last war they rose as high as £49 for prime slaves. Lots have sold as high as £45 or £43. The increased demand for the Spanish and French Settlements, with the increased difficulty of procuring them on the coast, continues I believe to keep up the price.

√[Q] How are new slaves managed.

[A] When brought home, they have generally a small blanket (perhaps about 2 or 2 ½ yards of blue baize) given them or this made into a jacket. They are fed on rice or Maize, or bonanas [sic] and other Island provisions sometimes on flour, under the eye of the overseer and his wife. After becoming a little acquainted they have their allowance raw, and either join some family, or mess by themselves.

√[Q] When are they considered as seasoned, or when may their labour be depended on.

[A] This indulgence depends on the Manager's disposition. Three years is the time calculated, when from ⅓ to 2/5 and ½ may be expected to have died. It is certain that those plantations that usually purchase slaves have almost constant demands for them; and that few at the end of any period of time appear to be added to their list.

[Q] Do African Slaves usually leave posterity.

[A] Our Planters having the choice of the Slave Market generally prefered [sic] Males. This of necessity kept the demand open for new supplies, and discouraged population.

√[Q] Are African Women fruitful.

[A] Not in Colonies; though from no natural cause. But they are transplanted at an improper time. They have no opportunity of accumulating around them little family conveniences. Their diet is poor and scanty. They generally fall into the hands of the principal slaves, who have each from two to three or four wives, to some one of which they must be drudges. Their hard and incessant labour hurries on infirmities and old age. In my time no encouragement was given nor indulgence shewn. To come to calculation perhaps there remains not one Creole in the Colonies for 12 Africans that have been imported.

√[Q] Did the planters in your time favour the population of their slaves.

[A] Never but in one case to my knowledge, except from Accident. In all solemn discussions of the subject, the decision was given in favour of buying before breeding. One planter, by good treatment, plenty of food, comfortable hutts [sic] and great attention encouraged population. In about six years he increased his gang from 160 to 180. On his death, in about 8 they were reduced back to 157.

√[Q] What are the accidents that favour population.
[A] The plantation being under the care of a discreet married man whose wife attends of her own accord to the situation of pregnant women and nurses; where the most is made of the proportion of food which the owner allows to be distributed, and where there is less hurry than usual in conducting the plantation work.

√[Q] What care is taken to supply the Slaves with provisions.
[A] A few scraps of broken worn out land are divided among them. Sometimes they have a fallow field to plant yams or potatoes in. Some part of the year they have an allowance of flour or imported grain, sometimes of yams.

√[Q] What allowance have they in crop time.
[A] On many plantations nothing but a weekly Allowance of six herrings. Their Scraps of Land and the Cane juice is supposed to support them.

√[Q] Can the Slaves in their present situation be well or regularly supplied with provisions from their grounds.
[A] In no respect. The Principal Slaves generally appropriate the best of the provision ground. Weakly slaves are thrust out, or have their roots stolen from them. Sometimes the seasons are unfavourable and the land yeilds [sic] nothing.

√[Q] What accidents prevent population.

[A] The Manager being a Batchelor without a proper family, or a raw giddy lad; excessive exertions required of the Slaves without method Cloathing food rest or indulgence.

√[Q] Are not males prefered [sic] to females.

[A] Managers generally prefer them; because there are fewer interruptions to their labour.

√[Q] Is the defect in population in any degree owing to scanty food.

[A] This is one principal cause. If the Slaves were permitted to supply themselves with food from the lands they cultivate, they would enjoy greater plenty than when it is brought from a distant quarter of the globe at a great price. The Sugar islands are in general healthy; they may be said to be all sea coast; it is only necessary to support their inhabitants from the proper soil to assimulate [sic] them to it and make them healthy.

√[Q] Are you acquainted with Mr. Spooner's Nicholatown plantation.

[A] It was situated in my parish. I was intimate with the former proprietor. I had the care of it for sometime, and was occasionally called in.

√[Q] Is there any circumstance in its situation that should render it unhealthy.

[A] I knew it nine years before it came into his possession. Then it had no such character. It lies on the windward side of the Island which is reckoned the most healthy. The Negroe huts are in a similar situation with those of plantations noted for healthiness.

√[Q] Supposing it unhealthy, how do you account for it.
[A] It may be considered as a new settled plantation stocked chiefly with African males, which must need frequent supplies. When it came into his possession, it was subjected to another plantation at a distance; which, if my memory deceives me not was supplied with grass from it.

But its chief disadvantage was the frequent change of Managers it having had five changes, all but one man, batchelors, two of them young lads, within the first eight years. These could give the Slaves no assistance, for they themselves had no conveniencies about them. They were to recommend themselves by the quantity of work performed; but had not time to think of affording any encouragement. That Gentleman has not been in the West Indies since 1760 or 1761; and knows the state of things there only by reports.

√[Q] What attention is paid to pregnant women.
[A] None deserving of the name was paid in my time.

√[Q] Is their situation made comfortable.
[A] It was not an object of consideration; except where there was a manager's wife, who of her own accord might pay some attention to them.

√[Q] Are they supplied with necessaries adapted for their situation.
[A] Never but as the case above.

√[Q] Have they any indulgence when nurses.
[A] They are in general excused grass picking.

√[Q] What care is taken of the young Children or what allowance of food is given them.
[A] I knew one planter, who gave their mothers an allowance for them from the Birth; but in general no notice is taken of them till they are able to run about, then some I think give them what is called half allowance; but as well as I can recollect in general they must be in the grass gang which is about 5 or 6 years old to have a regular allowance.

√[Q] What cloathing are they allowed.
[A] I have been trying to recollect; but cannot with certainty say that I remember to have seen them or their Mothers for them receive any before they were put to work.

√[Q] What attention can or does a Batchelor Manager pay to pregnant women or young Children.
[A] Except where a Surgeon is Manager; there is hardly anything done or indeed within his power; labour is the only thing that connects him with the Slave; whenever they complain, the Batchelor thinks he does his duty in sending for the Surgeon.

√[Q] What is the ordinary weekly allowance of flour or other imported grain.
[A] From 1 ½ lb to 3 or 4 lb per week. The most usual proportions may be from 2 to 2 ½ lb per week. Very few go so high as 4 lb or even 3 lb.

√[Q] Is this allowance given regularly.
[A] No, want of foresight often occasions scarcity.

[Q]Is it sufficient for him.
[A] It is not sufficient in one plantation out of five.

[Q] What follows.
[A] The more discreet shift as they can; many skulk away into the mountains, where they plunder the provision grounds, or fall to eating a sweet sort of clay which palls their appetite. They sooner or later are seized by the hunters who are in search of them, or comeback of themselves emaciated and sick. Then follows Iron puddings about their ankles, crooks about their necks, whipping and chains.

√[Q] Is there not a colony law, that condemns run aways to death who have been 6 Months out the Master being paid a price out of the Island treasury.
[A] Yes. But I never knew it put in practice in my Neighbourhood. A late President was noted in my time for paying his public taxes with his run away Slaves heads. Perhaps he might in one or two Instances have done so; but the particulars never came to my knowledge. He was remarkable for not feeding them.

√[Q] Were there any Masters, who did not give their Slaves any allowance of imported grains.
[A] About 40 years back, the custom was to allot annually a certain proportion of the caneland for the growth of provisions, and to have occasional supplies from England. The making of rum on which the intercourse with North America greatly

depended, was not then general. Since that time the distillation of rum has become general, and the arable ground has been in a manner confined (except in a very small proportion) to the growth of the Sugar Cane. This made them almost entirely dependent on foreign supplies especially of provisions, and had extended their intercourse with North America at the breaking out of the late war to a very disadvantageous degree; the American's obliging them to pay only a certain proportion of rum, and about 4/5 parts in money for their lumber and provisions. But several planters lessened or took away their slaves provision grounds without seeing the necessity of giving them imported grain in exchange. Many of these remained in 1762 at the time I settled there. In short the allowance then of such food was neither general nor sufficient. The Gangs were heartless and inefficient, and frequent recruits were necessary from the slave Markett [sic].

√[Q] Is there any difference in the Slaves favour from being supplied with Island or ground provisions rather than with grain from Europe or North America.
[A] Much. In the one case he has it fresh and may harvest in plenty as Nature meant it to be used (except when hunger obliges him to snatch it before it is ripe) in the other, the high price, and long carriage forces the planter to deal it sparingly out, and it often is damaged or becomes musty.

√[Q] Had any alteration taken place in the general treatment of Slaves about the time you settled; from this circumstance of turning the whole attention to the Sugar Cane or any other.
[A] My observation of the old planters was, that when they

did punish it was with severity; but there appeared more care and attachment to their slaves in general. When it became frequent for planters to abandon their property to the management of others, the support of their families in Europe [became – overwritten illegibly] their chief object, to which their plantations became only a secondary consideration. No attachment could be expected from their new masters. They, the Slaves, were considered as mere instruments of labour; and every symptom of sensibility of their degraded situation was interpreted into an act of rebellion. Hence the whip the chief instrument of government was kept in constant exercise, and the allowance of food was scanty and irregular.

√[Q] What checks are there on a harsh or cruel Master or Overseer.
[A] Censure which he never hears; perhaps an instance of an Overseer losing his place.

The Author is happy in the reflexion, that such a poor instrument has been made the means of agitating this important question, and of forcing Planters to attend to what is both their interest and their duty, on which even very good men among them from a persuasion of any reform being impracticable, were but too apt to shut their eyes.[5] He has the pleasure of repeated information that his writings have produced good effects on men, by whom both he and they are execrated and affected to be despised. The planters as a body are worthy and sensible, and only wanted to have their feelings awakened. Doubtless they will now see that their interest and their slaves advancement are connected, and go on to make their situation still more easy and comfortable, till, they shall in time become worthy of one common law and common faith.

This however has been objected to him with all the virulence of malice, without attempting to bring the charge home in a single instance. Had malice or resentment guided his pen he needed not to have been at any loss for objects or provocation. Yet in return for this fault thus forged for him he has been loaded by men, who hardly knew his person, with every crime, and every vice, that could render him odious to his country, and make him be abhorred by his friends. He is an apostate a Traitor a Hypocrite, Covetous, profligate, profane, Cruel in a degree, that even Guinea Captains have thought it necessary to instruct their Council to warn both houses of parliament against him.

Thus in highly civilized states liberty is more generally equal, than in those not so far advanced. Civilization naturally produces liberty. This is apparent from the present struggles in France. The Monarch has the undiminished Authority of Louis ·14· and an army ready to enforce it. Yet is he obliged to condescend to reason where the other would have used a Letter de cachet; and the people at present dare refuse consent to measures which from the former would have been received as gifts.

√[Q] When are the Slaves called out in the morning to work.
[A] The plantation bell rings about 4 o'clock. They assemble according to the seasons of the year so as to be in the field about dawn; or from a little before 5 to a little before six.

√[Q] When do they go to breakfast.
[A] About 9 they sit down in the field, and those eat, who have brought any mess with them; the rest sit down listless, or skulk

about the edge of the Cane field, and if they can evade the watchman's eye break and suck a cane.

√[Q] When do they leave off field work.
[A] On some plantations at 11 on others at noon.

√[Q] Do they go immediately home.
[A] They are obliged to go in some situations perhaps two miles right out to search for grass to be hand picked for the cattle. When they have collected this bundle, they then go home to dinner, if they have any; the rest must steal canes which is the general substitute for food.

√[Q] What interval is allowed for this.
[A] From 1 ½ to 2 ½ hours. This according to their hour of dismission brings about 1 or 2 o'clock. The list is called over. The absentees are noted; the bringers of small bundles or bad grass are whipped. They are then turned into the field, where they labour till near Sun set, and are then dispersed to search again for grass.

√[Q] Might not both bundles of grass be picked at once and the time and space travelled [sic] over in the search be saved.
[A] Some planters gave an extra hour at noon for two bundles. This enabled them to work the Slaves in the field till twilight, and to dismiss them at once home without obliging them to wait an hour or two after dark to be called over by list with their bundles of grass. But the two bundles and the late hours had grown into a custom, which always requires an effort to break through; and there could be no pretence used for the attempt,

except the ease of the Slave, which in my time was not very generally consulted.

√[Q] You say they have scraps of land allotted them for the growth of provisions; what time is allowed for tilling it.

Have you examined the slaves' provision ground.

What care is taken of it.

[A] Some discreet Managers give them now and then an afternoon to themselves. (In Jamaica the law gives them Saturday afternoon but I have reason to believe it is not always allowed.) But it is expected that they spend Sunday in their own grounds; and on some plantations, the Overseer superintended the work.

√[Q] You say the calling [sic]⁶ of grass is protracted till an hour or two after dark. When do the Slaves go to rest.

[A] Grass is called [sic] when the Overseer can find leisure perhaps generally between 7 & 8. The Slaves then go home and prepare their Supper. They may be able to go to sleep about 11 till the bell at 4 o'clock calls them up.

√[Q] Is it ever usual besides this ordinary labour to work half the gang all night in grinding time.

[A] I have known an instance of it. It was pretty general to have a Mill gang who wrought by day with the gang, and one night in rotation attended the Mill so as to be two days and a night without sleep.

√[Q] Are they not often made to carry out Dung in Baskets and bring home bundles of Canes on their heads.

[A] On all plantations ill supplied with Cattle, which again are in general plantations much involved in debt this is their employment.

√[Q] Might not cattle do this.
[A] This is their employment, where a proper number is kept.

√[Q] Might not a great proportion of Cane land be opened by the plough.
[A] All level lands might; and a great proportion of the hanging lands with this precaution in the rainy season, that the Negroes follow the plough and form it into holes for receiving the plant, to prevent the rain from washing it away.

√[Q] Might not much of what could not conveniently be thus opened be more advantageously cultivated in provisions and grass, which if the slaves must use the Hoe would be easier labour.
[A] Most certainly and save the immense sums that are annually required to [support – corrected illegibly] the starved Cattle and Slaves.

√[Q] What care is taken to feed the cattle besides the cane tops in Crop time, and grass hand picked by the slaves.
[A] A few scraps of land taken from the slaves' provision ground and a few ranges or walks between the Cane fields; perhaps on the whole not one acre for 8 or 10 head of Cattle.

√[Q] What Treatment do the Slaves generally meet with.
[A] On the conclusion that a Slave obeys only because he

cannot help himself; a spiteful Jealousy is entertained of all he does; and the rod is held continually over him to keep him to his work. He is hated as a rival, he is suspected as an enemy, he is treated as a brute.

√[Q] What are their usual punishments.
[A] Whipping, Iron rings about their ancles [sic], Iron Collars about their necks, chains, dungeon, stopping the plantation allowance of provisions.

√[Q] What are the crimes most prevalent among them.
[A] Absence from work, eating the sugar cane, no or small bundles of grass, purloining the Manager's poultry, robbing the boiling house or rum Cellar.

√[Q] In cases of theft is the thief only punished.
[A] Sometimes the whole gang have their allowance stopt in hopes of their discovering the Culprit.

√[Q] Is torture ever used to compel a discovery.
[A] I once saw an instance of a negroe on suspicion of having stolen some poultry hung up about eight or ten feet from the ground, the weight of his body being supported by his hands tied behind his back with a rope passed over a beam. He was kept suspended in great agony for many hours, but no discovery was made.

√[Q] Is ever melted wax used, to give pain.
[A] Either that or Gum is often threatened, and has been sometimes used, but I believe not often.

√[Q] Is ever pickle used.

[A] I have heard Managers speak of their using it; and though I was seldom present; yet I believe it is generally used after severe flogging to prevent gangrene.

√[Q] Is not severity of punishment reckoned indispensable, independent of the Master's particular disposition.

[A] Taking planters generally they are on a footing with other people, and as capable as any of being influenced by benevolent considerations; but a slave is not an object of Sympathy. He is only supposed to feel when he can be made to smart; and no appearance of a fault must be passed over without correction, lest authority be lessened.

√[Q] Can you give any instance to illustrate this.

[A] A Gentleman sent out a man to be an Overseer on his plantation. He had not been arrived from England two months, before he complained that one of the slaves had used some threatening expression to him. The Manager refered [sic] the decision to the Attorney. I happened to call in when the Affair was discussing. The one accused, the other positively denied. No proof was adduced. The Culprit was stripped naked and tied down to a ladder, and the Accuser was ordered to take his satisfaction of him. The Attorney was an easy humane man. To avoid the scene I retired with him and Dr. Grainger who happened to be present to the other side of the house. When the Attorney thought that the culprit had received a full number of Stripes, his back being all one lacerated wound, he went forward and asked the plaintiff if he did not think the punishment sufficient. Bending over the wretches wounds he replied, a few more stripes he thought would do him good. The Attorney with a curse bid him go on; and the driver continued to whip, till the overseer expressed himself avenged *

√

* Here was a man punished to extremity without proof merely to preserve discipline against the inclination of both Manager and Attorney. The Accuser was just arrived from England; therefore not to be supposed as hardened by the customs of the Colony. In short arbitrary undefined power, not the depravity of the Master is answerable for all the evils and suffering of Slavery.

[Q] Is there much difference between the treatment of Slaves under the care of the owner and under the care of a Manager.
[A] Only in a few particular Instances. The Owner wishes to accumulate, the Manager to shew his ability and both generally at the poor slaves expence. Many Managers are discreet sensible men of education perhaps on the whole on a footing with their employers. The chief circumstance that operates against them is that they hold their places at another person's will, that they must recommend themselves by immediate exertions, that they have no lasting interest in the prosperity of the plantation, and therefore look not forward to what may affect its state 20 years hence.

√[Q] Is it ever the practice to wash their stripes with brine.
[A] Frequently when the correction has been severe; in some cases to enhance the Smart, in others to prevent a mortification.

√[Q] Does the Cramp ever follow severe whipping.
[A] A Drunken Overseer flogged a poor wretch, I think for

bringing too small a bundle of grass severely. It happened to be rainy weather. He turned him out to work. He was seized with the locked Jaw and died in about two days.[7]

√[Q] What was done to the Overseer.
[A] The Attorney finding him a worthless drunkard took that opportunity of discharging him.

√[Q] Is dismembering of Slaves ever practiced.
[A] A little before my time two instances happened in St. Kitts. One of the wretches was alive in my time. I believe I have seen him. About the time of the capture of the Island I observed by advertisement, in their newspaper and other information, that three or four instances of slitting or cutting off ears had happened; one of which was the cause of enacting a law, which fixed a fine on the master, who should thence forward be guilty of that offence.

√[Q] How are they punished for the usual faults of Absence from work small bundles of grass breaking of Canes and theft.
[A] By the whip, confinement in the dungeon working in chains, iron rings about the Ancles [sic] Iron Crooks riveted round the neck; stopping of the Allowance of grain.

√[Q] Can any regulations secure general good treatment or can any law prevent a Slave from being cruelly and unreasonably treated by a Maser or overseer.
[A] The minimum of Cloathing and food may be ascertained. The hours of labour may be fixed. The extent of the Overseer's power to punish may be defined. But it is in the Master's power

to render his Slaves lives miserable every hour by a thousand nameless stratagems, that spite only can think of, in which no regulation can interpose. While Slavery continues good treatment can only be made to prevail generally, by giving a turn to sentiment, and making severity infamous.

The Danes take from a Master, that behaves cruelly to his slaves, the direction of his Affairs, and appoint him a Manager.

√[Q] Were you ever on board a slave Ship.[8]
[A] When I served in the Navy we retook a Guinea man. The Privateer had taken out the prime slaves, and abandoned the Ship, and refuse slaves. I went on board to give directions concerning the Sick. As well as I can recollect there were 7 or 8 Negroes dangerously ill of fluxes[9], and of the whole number left, which I think were about 100, there were very few that were reckoned valuable.

√[Q] Did you make any observation on the Slaves brought to the Islands sick.
[A] I had frequent opportunities. My brother in law was a Guinea Factor[10]; and curiosity led me to attend the sales.

√[Q] In engaging for the Sale of a Cargoe of Slaves, does the factor make an agreement for the whole.
[A] The Cargoe is generally divided into three sets; the healthy well assorted or prime slaves; the Puny, or second days sale; and the diseased or refuse slaves. The factor engages for a certain average on the first; and sells the other two for as much as he can.

√[Q] Do you not understand that only healthy Slaves are put on board on the Coast of Africa.
[A] Most certainly. Only such can have a chance of enduring the Voyage. But sometimes they can purchase only a bad assortment. Many of these independent of their state of health must be thrown out of the average number.

√[Q] Of whom do the refuse slaves consist.
[A] Of those who have fallen sick during the passage.

√[Q] The hardships of the passage then are answerable for the Refuse Slaves.
[A] Undoubtedly.

√[Q] What proportion do they bear to the whole.
[A] This depends on the length of the passage, or whether any Epidemic has got among them. I have understood that there have been particular instances of nearly the whole cargoe perishing, sometimes one half, sometimes a third, a fourth, a fifth; I believe seldom less than a tenth are refuse. I generally observed a very large number, but did not ever reckon them.

√[Q] Who generally purchase Refuse Slaves.
[A] Poor people or overseers.

√[Q] At what price.
[A] Perhaps from £8 or £10 to a Crown.[11]

√[Q] Do many of them recover their health.
[A] There are instances where a considerable proportion recover;

others where almost all die. I am sure I reckon the loss very moderately when I suppose that one in three recovers.

√[Q] From your observations and information, what proportion do you estimate dies in the voyage and of the refuse Slaves.
[A] I estimate a full fourth. I imagine it to be more frequently above than below this rate.

√[Q] Do you mean to say, that you consider the Voyage accountable for so many deaths.
[A] I do.

√[Q] Describe the condition you have seen the Refuse Slaves in at Sales.
[A] Naked, emaciated, and unable to support themselves.

√[Q] Are not some slaves kept on board; because too ill to be brought on shore.
[A] So I have understood in conversation with the Captain.

√[Q] What becomes of them.
[A] I cannot tell.

√[Q] What proportion of the prime or healthy new Slaves are lost in seasoning.
[A] I know only in general, that the number out of any lot of new slaves, which lives to become useful, is very small; and the plantations, which purchase slaves frequently, continue to have frequent demands. Robertson makes the loss 4 out of 10. Long from ⅓ to ½ of the whole. Trusting to these estimates I never

made any calculation; but I believe they are within the truth.

√[Q] From what do you judge this.
[A] From particular instances of plantations, and considering what large numbers are introduced, without sensibly increasing the lists.

√[Q] What is the usual time of seasoning.
[A] The above authors make it three years. The time depends upon the good sense and forbearance of the manager. In my time, they were, I believe, placed much earlier in the task or holeing Gang; which is the hardest work.

√[Q] To what do you ascribe the great loss of African Slaves.
[A] To chagrin, to poor and scanty diet, the greatest part brought from another quarter of the globe, to incessant labour, to want of cloathes and other necessaries; to want of encouragement, to the pretence of feeding then with grain from North America or Europe, instead of the provisions of the Colony. Perhaps to some lasting impression made by the confinement during the Voyage.

√[Q] Do Africans leave posterity frequently.
[A] Few leave posterity. I have tried to recollect instances of their doing this; but almost every instance is on the other side.

√[Q] To what cause do you place this.
[A] The same as the mortality that prevails among them. Especially want of rest want of necessaries want of indulgence.

√[Q] Have you made any estimate of the proportion of Creoles from the number imported.

[A] One can but conjecture; but it can hardly be so much as one Creole for 12 Africans; the colonies would otherwise have been overstocked. In Hispaniola, it has been actually calculated and found to be 1 to 6.

√[Q] Do you imagine, this disproportion has been always as great.

[A] I believe formerly when they were better supplied with Island provisions, there were more children born; because I found where any old settled plantations were more carefully managed than others, they continued to be tolerably well supplied from the births. Where they were ill managed they annually decreased, and wanted annual supplies; But these plantations had been all settled, before my time, and their Slaves were chiefly creoles.

These Strictures on the usual treatment of Slaves have been denied combated, and after all have been acknowledged to be true, but not in the extent which the author is supposed to have meant them. Now the candid Reader will observe, that here no extent is hinted at. The reasoning here used supposeth that one single oppressor in a community ought to be an object of police; and the warmest advocate for the planters humanity will not restrict ill treatment to either single or few characters in any of our colonies. The fact is, Planters are not worse than other men. Many would not lose by comparison with the better sort of people in Britain. But in my time, though the treatment of Slaves might now and then be discussed as far as it respected the Masters character as an easy or severe Man even as we might argue whether he was bald or short. Yet the feelings or happiness of the slaves was never taken into account nor was the Subject ever treated in a moral point of view. Planters are as ready as other men to shew sympathy and act with benevolence; but the poor slave was not then considered as an object of either. He was a mere tool or instrument of labour, to be used at the caprice or discretion of his owner; Sympathy did not comprehend him, benevolence did not extend to him. That this was really the case is proved from the various points wherein the best Masters, to almost a man, were negligent of their slaves in direct contradiction to morality and common sense.

√[Q] Do you ascribe much respecting healthiness to difference of situation.

[A] Not much in St. Christopher. Were the negroes to draw their support from the lands they cultivated, instead of being nominally fed with imported grain, I believe they would soon agree with any situation there. But they are not fed cloathed or worked, with any respect towards their situation.

√[Q] Is there not a disproportion of the Sexes.

[A] Only among the new or African slaves; and unless their treatment be greatly changed, no planter can afford to buy them with a view to their posterity.

√[Q] Have you estimated the general proportion of Creole and African Slaves in the Colonies.

[A] Going according to the latest returns that I have met with, and comparing one circumstance with another, I reckon the number of Slaves in all our colonies exceeds 450,000, of which I judge above 350,000 must be Creoles, where the Sexes are properly mixed.

√[Q] Are these 350,000 Creoles sufficient to send the present usual crops of Sugar to Market.

[A] Most certainly. If only a proper selection of lands were made for the growth of the Sugar Cane, three Slaves might produce at least two Hhds.[12] There are several in St. Kitts that occasionally produce more; one I know that produces in common as many Hhds almost, as it contains Slaves of all ages. But an ordinary crop is about 160,000 Hhds. This at the rate of three slaves to two hhds requires only 240,000 slaves.

√[Q] If assisted with Cattle could not still fewer Slaves send the same quantity of Sugar to Market.

[A] Of this there can be no doubt, when it is considered, that the Land whether loose and gravelly, or clay and stiff is opened with a garden hoe, that Dung is carried out, and Canes brought to the mill on Negroes heads.

√[Q] What is the usual proportion of Slaves for the cane land of a plantation.

[A] The proportion varies. But the most usual is about 3 Slaves to about 2 Acres; one half of which is planted, and the other is taken off or made into Sugar annually. So that 3 Slaves cultivate one Acre, and take it off.

√[Q] What is the usual proportion of Sugar for the quantity of land in culture.

[A] It varies according to the seasonableness of the weather and the goodness of the land, from near 3 Hhds per Acre to 1 ½ per Acre; in many cases to 1 Hhd per Acre. Here I mean the Number of Acres cut off, equal to half the plantation.

√[Q] What is the least proportion, that must be made, to pay expences.

[A] A plantation must be in particular circumstances to support itself on Hhd and an half round per Acre of the canes cut, which is usually half its quantity of Caneland.

* I say this from my knowledge of particular plantations.

* It requires extreme care to prevent those, that exceed not 1 ½ Hhd from going back.

√[Q] What is the least quantity of Sugar to be made per Acre, that will pay the expence of culture.

[A] It takes in common 3 Negroes to cultivate one Acre. The current expences where the Crop is 2 Hhd around per Acre is £9 per hhd or £18 · per Acre. Three Slaves if rented and insured would cost annually £36. Both these Articles are £54. Two Hhds and an half would hardly amount to this sum; for a Hhd of Sugar and its rum is not worth more in the colonies than £21.

√[Q] Do you mean that 2 ½ Hhds per Acre on half the Cane land do not pay the expence of culture.

[A] Yes, if we suppose the slaves rented from another man, without supposing anything for the return of lands buildings and other stock, which are usually reckoned to be double the value of the slaves.

√[Q] But as this is a larger proportion than most plantations make how can the planter support so losing a kind of culture.

[A] They never in my time calculated. But were satisfied with supporting the plantation with what must be supplied to keep matters agoing with paying of interest money, and spending the balance, and in most cases adding to their debts in hopes of some favourable year. The value of the Slaves was thrown in to the aggregate, and the Crop was a return for the whole property taken together.

√[Q] What reason have you for fixing the proportion between creole and African Slaves.

[A] The life of an African Slave exceeds not 15 years. Before 1784 the trade had been checked near 6 years. One third of all imported before that time had died in the seasoning or before 1781. To suppose 150,000 in the Colonies at the end of 1777 when the trade was checked is a large proportion. They would be 100,000 in beginning of 1781· and 75,000 in the beginning of 1784. Since that time the trade has been chiefly turned to the supply of the french [sic] and Spaniards. Hardly so many have been left in our Colonies, as to make an increase of 25,000.

√[Q] In renting a plantation stocked what was the proportion of rent.

[A] About £10 per hhd on a Medium Crop or a plantation stocked for about 100 Hhds £1000 in some cases £1200.

√[Q] What would the Slaves on such a plantation amount for rent & insurance.

[A] To a £1000 at least.

√[Q] When there is nothing left for returns of lands & other stock.

[A] Nothing in this view of the matter.

√[Q] What proportion do they bear to the Slaves.

[A] Of 2 to 1. Or if the slaves be worth £10,000 the lands & other stock are worth £20,000.

√[Q] We are left to suppose, that the lands and Stock rendered productive by three Slaves are double the value of these slaves. At what rate are Slaves reckoned in this case.

[A] This estimate was made when Slaves were reckoned about £50 or £60· each. At £60 which is now too low an Estimate the Slaves will be £180, the lands etc. we will reckon only £300· both together £480. Supposing the Slaves to belong to the planter they must be ensured at 5 percent. The Account will stand thus, Current Annual Expences on 2 Hhds the labour of 3 Slaves £18. Interest of value of Slaves & lands at 6 percent the lowest colony Interest £28. Insurance of three Slaves £9· in all £55. But two hhds of Sugar with their rum make only £42. Hence a loss of £13. It is to be remarked that the Number of plantations which give 2 Hhds round is very small. St. Christopher does not produce such a proportion taken all together perhaps not once in ten years. If we consider the other Islands either by the number of Negroes they maintain or the quantity of land they have in tillage, they produce not one hhd per Acre.

√[Q] What is the inference you draw from this.

[A] That hardly a situation can be imagined for a plantation where in Slaves purchased at the present high price can return their price expence and loss in seasoning, and insurance And that only the most select portions of a plantation should be planted in Canes.

√[Q] Have you made any estimate of the value of a new Slave, when seasoned and put to work.

[A] I have made various estimates. A lot of 10 Slaves will cost £450. Allow only £10 each for expence of feeding physic and taxes, and £90 for the interest of the 3 years seasoning. But at this time 4 are dead; so that 6 working slaves are worth £640. Allow the lands they occupy to be worth only as in the case before £600. The interest of both these sums at 6 percent (throwing out the £40) is £72. The insurance of 6 Slaves worth £100 each at 5 percent is £30 · both £102.

They produce 4 Hhds of Sugar worth, after paying Current expences, £48. Here is a loss on the purchase of 10 new Slaves of £54 per Annum.

√[Q] What must cane land produce to be worth the cultivation.

[A] If a Master has slaves, and has nothing in which he can employ them (if such a case can be imagined) perhaps 1 Hhd per Acre with its rum may pay the extra expences of cultivating that acre. But if the putting it into Canes obliges him to import grain from Europe or North America to feed his slaves, or to support his cattle in a state just above starving by hand picked grass, which ruins them and wears his slaves out, then no lands, that give not at least 1 ½ Hhd per Acre should ever be put in canes. It is to be observed that this is only ½ Hhd for a slave, which is a poor return to pay Current expences insurance and interest on the Capital.

√[Q] Do the Sugar colonies produce at the rate of 1 ½ Hhd.
[A] The ordinary Crop of St. Kitts is about this proportion;
but no other island I believe produces 1 Hhd at an average of 7
years.

√[Q] From what circumstances do you judge this.
[A] An Ordinary crop is 160,000 Hhds from the whole. St.
Kitts frequently gives 16,000 Hhds and employs from 22,000 to
24,000 Slaves. At this proportion 240,000 Slaves would send a
Medium crop to Market. But the colonies contain upwards of
450,000 Slaves, which ought to cultivate Annually and cut off
300,000 Acres of canes. Either a much small [sic] number of
Slaves must be employed in the culture of the cane, or the land
must be much less productive than 1 Hhd per Acre.

√[Q] We are to conclude the Culture of the Sugar Cane to be
very unproductive.
[A] Most undoubtedly as a Manufacture, never was national
property more absurdly laid out. The planter reckons his property
60 millions. His whole returns in every West Indian commodity
of Sugar Rum Coffee Cotton etc. cannot be estimated so high
as 250,000 Hhds. Muscovado Sugar worth in the Colony £17
per hhd or £4,250,000. The Current Expences are £9 per Hhd
or £2,250,000. The Slaves are reckon'd £40,000,000. Insurance
at 5 percent on this is £1 Millions. In these two Articles so much
of the whole produce is consumed, as to leave only 1 Million for
Interest on the Capital.

√[Q] Still the Question returns, if so unprofitable how can the planter go on at this rate.

[A] I might answer that they do not go on, but every year backwards. They become more and more involved; and yet because no body can purchase, they continue nominal possessors; but are in fact Slaves to their creditors.

√[Q] Certainly some draw very large revenues from their plantations.

[A] I acknowledge it. Though not one plantation in ten would bear the test of calculation, yet large plantations like large manufactories can stand out best with small profits. The Number of planters is small. A few of the most capital stand for a sample, and give the whole an air of opulence. They stand their own Insurers. The Annual expences of their plantations are reduced to a low rate, and all beyond that, and now and then an occasional supply of slaves is spent in their personal expences. Now and then, there is by the rise of Sugars a profit on Shipping them to Britain.

√[Q] On the whole we are to conclude, trusting to your calculations and observations, that no planter can better himself or improve his property by purchasing new slaves.

[A] There can no doubt be made of this, if the planter has profit for his object.

√[Q] What is a planter to do, if his plantation be under-handed.

[A] Turn his Domestics into the field who are generally numerous, idle and useless, and supply their places with a few free mulattoes, negroes and white people. Throw out all cane lands, that produce not a hhd & half per Acre or ¾ Hhd in ratoons.[13] Make more use of Cattle, and plant artificial grass for them and provisions for the slaves in the lands saved from the cane.

√[Q] Would not this lessen the crop of Sugar.
[A] Perhaps not. The smaller quantity would have more manure, would be better dressed, and be more certain in its returns; by standing the weather better. 240,000 Acres good land might surely be selected out of 4,000,000 which our colonies contain, ½ of which put annually into canes & well dressed might produce 200,000 Hhds.

√[Q] To what particular points do you ascribe the general unprofitableness of Sugar plantations.
[A] To the keeping too great a proportion of their land above what they can work and manure well in the sugarcane; never changing their crops, feeding their Cattle with hand picked grass, refusing to supply their Slaves with Island provisions, but pretending to feed them with imported grain from Europe and North America, wearing their slaves out with incessant labour, without food rest cloathing or encouragement

√[Q] Are any foreign Sugars every [sic] introduced into our Islands.
[A] In my time there was annually about 600 Hhds smuggled in. The returns of some little trade especially for Slaves with the Danes.

√[Q] Do not small plantations support themselves.

[A] They did very well while the planter lived on them and supplied himself and slaves with provisions from the land, and raised only sugar to furnish him with what they did not produce. But now since they have been worked as a manufacture, and made to produce only Sugar and rum, every necessary being paid out of them and brought from a distant quarter of the Globe, perhaps the planter himself conducting it at 3 Miles distance, they have in general gone backwards, and are become ruinous possessions.

√[Q] Are Slaves necessary as Domestics.

[A] They are generally but unprofitably used as such; families entertaining from 20 to 60 upwards, whose whole work might be better done by 3 or 4 free hired Servants.

√[Q] Could such be procured.

[A] In every Island there are numbers of free negroes and mulattoes and poor white people who are kept poor and wretched for want of employment; to whom such service would be an advancement.

√[Q] Are Slaves necessary as Handy craftmen.

[A] By no means. White people might be procured; and on the whole as cheap; because they are not bought at a high price.

√[Q] Do Creole Negroes degenerate.

[A] I never did observe it, nor ever heard it supposed; but the contrary; they priding themselves in the Antiquity of their family.

But if planters will turn their useless domestics into the field, will buy up the slaves of poor white people, will throw out of culture all such cane land as pays not for the tillage, which in St. Christopher in particular, though our richest spot is above a ¼ of the whole, if instead of pretending to feed their slaves with grain purchased from North America or Europe, they will cultivate Island provisions for them, if they will supply their cattle with artificial grass. Then half the present number of Slaves may send more than the present produce to market.

√[Q] Was not this always the case.

[A] No, it has chiefly grown up within these last 50 years. Before that time a Number of small planters lived in affluence on their plantations amidst their slaves. They and their slaves were in general plentifully fed with Island provisions. Such a proportion of sugar was raised as procured them foreign necessaries which the Island did not supply.

Within this period a desire of accumulating and extending possessions appeared. This raised the price of land; above what any produce but sugar was deemed capable of repaying. The first high price was I think about the Year 1750. It was £45 per Acre and was exclaimed against as exorbitant. In 20 Years it rose to £200, in some cases to near £300 per Acre. Then was the provision and grass lands seized for the Cane, every expence was put on the Sugar, and the whole labour was imposed on the slave. In the year 1724 the cane land of St. Kitts, in quantity about 22,000 Acres, was in the possession of 360 families; at present the whole number exceeds not 110.

√[Q] What is the annual value of a Slave's labour.

[A] In some very few cases, it may rise to near £20; but in general it exceeds not £10 nay often it falls below it.

√[Q] Are not the current expences to be deducted from these sums.

[A] Certainly. Suppose a slave to produce a Hhd of Sugar with its rum worth £21; this leaves only £12 to pay for his insurance and rent and the interest of the capital which he makes productive. But if he were rented from another, the rent and insurance would be £12, which would leave nothing as a return of the lands & buildings etc.

√[Q] Taking into account the great price expence of Seasoning interest of money and mortality among African Slaves, that they seldom leave posterity, that their labour is not productive; that according to your report, there are more slaves now in the Colonies, than are equal to the work even in its present disadvantageous manner of conducting it without proper tools or the Assistance of Cattle; or if more were wanting, that the Domestics might be turned into the fields, their place being supplied better with a very few white or free people, you are of opinion, that the slave trade is not necessary for the Sugar colonies in their present state.

[A] I believe the Slave trade to have become the ruin of the Sugar Colonies. Had they never imported any, the colonies would now have been inhabited by multitudes of white free people instead of a few overgrown planters with their slaves. But as it is, Were the Slave trade stopped a constant unprofitable drain for the planters' money would be stopped. The necessity of taking care of the present stock would preclude any call for supplies. If any plantation was really underhanded, supplies might be got in the slaves of poor people, who are kept idle and lazy by depending on their work, but must be diligent to accommodate themselves, if that support were taken from them.

√[Q] How have fortunes been accumulated in the West Indies.
[A] I believe hardly by any Gentleman who has bought and stocked a plantation with a view to profit. Those have made fortunes who have themselves laboured to raise them, or who have had some gainful trade or profession, which has enabled them to allot the returns of the plantation for its improvement. But one seldom hears of a man living in Paris conducting a manufactory in Norwich; yet in this situation must every planter be supposed, who assists not in person in improving his plantation.

√[Q] Is the labour of Slaves cheaper than that of free men.
[A] That may be easily decided; for supposing them rented and insured from another there is not one plantation in three on which their labour makes any rent return or interest on the land and stock occupied by him. His insurance and rent cannot now be reckoned so little as £12; But if he produces a Hhd of Sugar, which he does in very few cases, £12 is all that is left of the Sugar and rum of this Hhd after paying the current annual expences; so that even in this case the planter has no returns for his land and other stock. This will be still stronger if we consider a slave one with another, as producing only half a Hhd value after paying annual expences £6.

A free man is neither insured nor is he recruited at an enormous

Expence from the slave market. He lives to work from Generation to generation in his posterity and for a little better food and cloathing does twice the work of a slave.

√[Q.] Whence then arises the ordinary returns of Sugar plantations.

[A] The slaves generally belong to the planter. His whole plantation is considered as making one subject of revenue. He becomes his own shipper, sometimes the merchant or factor, and often as at present has the advantage of a rise in the home market. If he be lucky enough to employ a humane considerate manager, he has not the otherwise usual annual demands made on him for cattle and slaves, which chiefly eat into his profits.

√[Q.] You do not mean to say that every planter treats his slaves ill.

[A] Far from it. Some are in many respects easy and indulgent to them. But I mean to say, that it is not a principle of duty that procures good treatment to the slave. He was not in my time considered as an object of Sympathy; nor were his feelings taken into account.

√[Q.] In what particulars was this inattention of the Master to the claims of the Slave chiefly shewn in otherwise easy and good men.

[A] In their Slaves incessant labour, or rather keeping them under the Overseers lash 16 out of 24 hours; besides the time necessary for the preparation of their food, which hardly leaves 5 hours for sleep.

In thrusting in the Egyptian task of grass picking into the hour of weariness and rest.

In allowing them only Sunday to work their spots of ground.

In the parsimonious manner in which they are fed and cloathed.

In the extent of the Overseers power, and the Slaves belonging to the best Masters, being exposed without remedy to their caprice, their resentment, their lust, in the absence of their owner.

√[Q] Is plantation work in itself hard.
[A] Not necessarily so, if the Slaves were assisted by Cattle and proper Tools. It is the unceasing ill supported labour that wears them out.

√[Q] Are white men capable of it.
[A] Most certainly. White men labour as hard in the West Indies as negroes at particular trades. The French in the Neutral Islands wrought with their own hands. White men cleared Barbados, Nevis and St. Kitts, which is much harder work than the present culture of them.

√[Q] But this labour destroyed them.
[A] There is no record of its having been so fatal to them as the settling of the Neutral Islands on the peace of 1763 has been to the Negroes.

√[Q] Do you know any particular Instance of mortality.
[A] On a particular plantation in Dominica, after expending near £40,000, and placing on it 240 Slaves, almost all seasoned

in less than eight years, the slaves were reduced under 100, and in a year or two more the residue of the Slaves was taken off and the plantation was abandoned.

√[Q] Perhaps this plantation was particularly unhealthy.
[A] No. It had many advantages and was well supplied according to the ordinary rate with necessaries and provisions.

√[Q] Was such loss usual.
[A] More or less according to the circumstances; but in general not much below this; in some instances above it.

√[Q] How might this be discovered.
[A] By comparing the present lists of Slaves in the several colonies with the number originally in them, making allowance for the ordinary proportion of births which has been brought by the French in Hispaniola to calculation and is found to be one in 30 while the Deaths are two in thirty.

√[Q] Supposing the Slaves brought to such a State of improvement, as to be capable of making a proper use of freedom; how would it affect the Masters interest to grant them liberty.[14]

√[Q] What encouragement is there for Masters giving their Slaves opportunities of improvement.
[A] I might answer the advantage resulting from a reflexion on their having done their duty by helpless fellow creatures thrown by providence for this purpose to their power. But in a worldly view. By feeding their slaves better by working them more

judiciously, assisting them with cattle and proper instruments of labour to raise them from their present degradation into brutes, by opening their minds, and shewing them their connexion with futurity, by putting the means of acquiring the conveniencies of life within their reach, they would change a forced into a willing conscientious service. They would double their labour, and lessen all their expences.

√[Q] Supposing the Slaves etc., see above.

[A] This may be discovered by a reference to the third head of this evidence. If there appears, that the expence of the Slaves absorbs almost the whole returns of the plantation; leaving nothing for the lands or other stock. Had the Master no property in his slaves, half his present returns would be more profitable than the whole. He would save the expence of recruits, which with all its attendant charges of interest money physic and provision cannot be reckoned less than 1/5 of the Annual returns of the Sugar Colonies. Half the present Number of Slaves, working as freemen would be sufficient, to send the present produce to market.

√[Q] Would the public reap any advantage from granting liberty in this case to Slaves.

[A] Undoubtedly. The quantity of productive labour would be increased and the demand on the manufacturer would be doubled. A free man would work to feed himself plenteously and cloathe himself warmly; his cottage would be better furnished with utensils. The Colony would be placed in a state of security against foreign attacks.

√[Q] How may such an event be brought about.

[A] The good sense of the planters being now awakened to the advantages of good treatment, there needs only a few general laws to be enacted in the colonies to guard against particular abuses. The gradual spreading of information, and public opinion will do the rest. Planters will see the advantage of resigning the care of their Slaves, and the expence of the recruits of their labourers to the labourers themselves

√[Q] What is the usual annual Allowance of cloathing.

[A] A Wollen Cap from 1 ½ to 2 ½ Yards of Coarse Woolen; perhaps an Osnaburgh petty coat for the Women.[15]

√[Q] Is this sufficient.

[A] No. The evenings and mornings require warm cloathing.

[Q] Are they well or decently cloathed.

[A] Not in general nor from their masters allowance.

√[Q] How are the cattle supplied with food.

[A] A few ranges or walks between the cane fields, and perhaps a few Scraps of broken land are put in Artificial grass. In crop time they are supplied with cane tops. For all the rest, they depend on hand picked grass.

√[Q] How is it procured.

[A] When the slaves quit the fields at noon and in the Evening, they are sent off to pick grass, for which they must wander often two miles right out to find some shady spot in the Ravines towards the mountains.

√[Q] Is it not often taken from them.

[A] Yes. There is a law that forbids any slave without a ticket to go into another plantation. No tickets are ever issued, and the Slave is at the mercy of every man he meets with. He is glad to get away with the loss of his bundle; though he is sure of being flogged by his own overseer for wanting it. This is the cause of much whipping and frequent running away.

√[Q] You consider this grass picking as a great hardship.

[A] It certainly is, if on no other account, by being deceitfully purloined from the Slaves proper hours of rest.

√[Q] Can you give instances of plantations that have increased from the births.

[A] Mills Nicholatown plantation was under an easy Manager who had a tender careful Wife. In 1773 the Slaves were 210 in 1781 – 234. Mr. Molineux's plantation continued from 1763 increasing from I think about 192 or under 200 to 217 in 1773. In 1774 it had lost 5 in number old worn out slaves probably the remains of some African lots. In 1779 it contained 213. About this time the Manager lost his wife, and in 1781 the Number sunk to 203.

Mr. Madan's plantation in 1765 contained 158 – in 1781 · 172 – and it continues to increase under the Management of a careful Surgeon.

Lord Romney's plantation [sic].

Mr. Crooke's plantation under his own care in 1766 contained 157, in 1772 · 180. In 1781 left chiefly to Overseers it had fallen back to 157. In 1 Year under this last management the expence of Physic was 10 times that under the former.

G. W. Thomas plantation in 1762 contained about 200 Slaves.

Being hard worked, it required annual recruits, and might be considered as settled with Africans, with the Males in an over proportion. In 1763 it had a new manager, and in 1781 had received no supplies from that time. Its numbers were in 1765 183 · 1766 182 · 1781 · 164. Becoming more healthy the smaller number did the work equally well, and sent more Sugar to Market. As the same manager continues on it and the Africans must be now worn out probably it begins to increase.

√

From this plantation may be estimated the effects of the Abolition of the Slave trade where Africans abound. From the over proportions of Males, they will at first decrease. But becoming more healthy under better treatment, and assisted by cattle, and improved instruments of Agriculture, the work will be better done, perhaps more Sugar will be made, and at length they will begin to increase from the births.

But in general to expect Children to be reared is to demand bricks without straw. Scanty food, incessant labour, want of necessary accommodations afford poor encouragement.

√[Q] Can you instance particular plantations where inattention has produced loss of property and made the slaves decrease in number.

[A] It would be an invidious task; but it is only necessary for me to begin on either side of the place where I lived, and point out how the situation of every plantation was combined with the management that took place on it

Jo Holiday	1765	274	1781	232
B. Spooner	.	198	.	206
D. Mathews	.	486	.	448 probably had some recruits
Cuningham	.	364	.	341
Fleming	.	153	.	132
Estridge	1773	334	.	306
Ja Phipps	1774	204	.	104

9600	6400	61440	84000	106000
	21	169600	42000	53000
	6400	231040	8400	10600
	128		134,400	169600
	134 400[16]		6144	

648

320

1024.000

64000[17]

√[Q] Is it usual for slaves to go off and hide themselves in the mountain.

[A] In every plantation in proportion to their severe treatment, and scantiness of food, numbers run away, and keep out in the woods, or hire themselves to work in the provision grounds of other slaves. There is generally a reward given for bringing them back.

√[Q] Is there not a law to condemn them if absent 6 months.

[A] Yes, but I never heard of its being put in force, except by one man, who was said to set off his run away Negroe heads against his public taxes; the Country paying a price for every Slave executed by this law. Perhaps one or two instances might have happened to give occasion for the remark; but I cannot ascertain the fact.

√[Q] Is it not necessary to keep hunters constantly out after runaways.

[A] Almost every plantation keeps two or more of the most trusty Slaves out searching for runaways, which on different plantations amount from 1/10 to 1/5 of the whole working Slaves.

√[Q] When brought home how are they punished.

[A] They are severely flogged, have iron rings of 10 or 12 lb hammered round their ancles, iron crooks or collars riveted round their necks. They work chained 4 or 5 together. At night they are thrust into the Dungeon a place of 10 or 12 feet Square with no opening for air but a small hole cut in the top of the door.

√[Q] How are they supplied with food.

[A] They have generally some scanty allowance of grain, most frequently of horse beans;[18] which they may eat raw or scorch in the embers.

√[Q] Are there instances of their having been found dead in the morning.

[A] I have heard of one well attested instance, which from my knowledge of the discipline of the plantation, I most firmly believe. But in general they soon drop off and make new supplies necessary.

√[Q] May ever any signs of happiness be discovered among them.

[A] They will seem cheerful and sing; but it is as often the indignant expression of suffering as of joy. Feign Wretches with the Drivers whip threatening over them, and let any Man's heart tell him what happiness he can feel, who is in this situation 16 out of 24 Hours. Add to this, Wearied limbs, a naked back, an empty stomach, the insults of an unfeeling boy Overseer, and the happiness of a Slave may be imagined.

√[Q] Is there any care taken to instruct or improve the Slaves.
[A] No. One or two owners have ordered their slaves to be baptized; but I never knew any care taken to instruct them.

√[Q] Is no attention paid to their improvement.
[A] Sometimes a well disposed Negroe belonging to a humane Master will learn his prayers, and here and there one in the colony will perhaps get himself taught to read & write. Sometimes the middling sort of people will be at pains to instruct a favorite; but nothing is done that on the whole deserves the name of encouragement.

I leave this calculation as it stood in the first Edition;[19] because it answers my purpose sufficiently. But brought down to the present time, the unprofitableness of forming new, or of supporting old settlements from the Slave market is much more glaring. A Lot of 10 New Slaves will cost £450. Long tells you, they take three years to be seasoned, and in that time from one third to one half die. Robertson makes the loss in seasoning two out of five or four out of ten. Writers on the planters side affirm that it costs from £6 to £8 per Annum to support a slave.

The Colony Interest of money is from 6 to 10 percent. Allow only £10 on each slave purchased as the expence of supporting him till seasoned, or £100 on the lot. Allow only for three years Interest. 20 percent or £90 and that only four out of the ten die We have then 6 Seasoned slaves worth £640. The Slaves in the colonies produce not at the rate of more than half a Hhd of Sugar per head. Allow them to produce a Hhd each, which with its rum is worth in the Colony £21. The 6 Hhds made by the 6 Slaves are worth £126. The current expence of the plantation are £9 per hhd or £54. Insurance of the 6 Slaves worth £640 at 5 percent is £32. The interest of their value at 6 percent is £38. These three sums make £124. There are 40 sh²⁰ left for the returns of the lands and stock occupied by them, which are at least worth £640. If the quantity of Sugar produced be less, there is a proportioned immediate loss without taking the lands etc. into account.

Suppose only 16,000 Slaves annually imported into our colonies, and that the proportion that die in seasoning is only four out of ten; for 9600 Seasoned Slaves the planter has incurred a debt or an expence of £1,024,000, and an annual charge of 169,600, and has only added to his income £134,400 without taking in to account that Lands & other property which these Slaves occupy to the value of a Million make no other return.

√[Q] How are the slaves treated when sick.
[A] Differently according to the feelings of the Manager, and the situation of his family.

√[Q] Is not a Surgeon employed.
[A] Yes on many plantations by the year. In this case he is at

once sent for; and if medicine will recover the sick man, he is in no danger. If the Surgeon is only called in occasionally, it is often too late to help him.

√[Q] Is there a Nurse for the sick.
[A] Yes, on every plantation; on some indeed she is both Doctor and Nurse.

√[Q] How are the sick supported. What necessaries are provided for them.
[A] On well managed plantations where the manager has a wife and where the Sick are few they are in general well cared for, and supplied with broth and comfortable messes. But as this is in a manner voluntary in the manager, he having no allowance for it, in plantations, where through severe pinching treatment the number of sick is large, and perhaps only a young lad overseer, who has neither the means nor the thought.
the sick are left wholly to the Surgeon and Nurse, if they recover to be turned into the field, if they die to be thrust into a hole.

√[Q] Have they no particular diet.
[A] I have attended a wretch in a fever, and seen a few raw horse beans standing by him for his food.

√[Q] Are they allowed any extraordinary cloathing while sick.
[A] Nothing but what they happened to before possessed of.

√[Q] What is their general state of health.
[A] Where encouraged good, free from disease.

√[Q] Of what nature are their ordinary ailments.

[A] Those that may be ascribed to excessive, or rather incessant labour scanty crude ill prepared diet, and eating of dirt (a sweet clay found in the mountain.) to depression of Spirits and harsh treatment.

√[Q] Are the sick most numerous where the treatment is bad.

[A] There is not a single exception. The very difference between the proportion out of equal numbers, that can be brought into the field, where they are well or ill treated, will more than double the work, that can be forced out of them by excessive exertions.

√[Q] How are pregnant women treated.

[A] It depends on the Manager's having a tender hearted Women to his wife, if there be any attention paid them.

√[Q] Who delivers them.

[A] Almost every plantation has a midwife.

√[Q] Do the mothers or children frequently suffer through their ignorance.

[A] I believe very seldom. It is an observation, that a greater proportion of white women die in childbed than of Negresses, and more negroe children than white. Both may be accounted for. The White women are over nursed; the negresses are left to nature. But the Negroe children kept in a cold damp dark cottage, not sufficiently cloathed, are seized with the locked jaw, which carries many of them off within the first nine days.

√[Q] Has there been no remedy found for this.

[A] Yes but how is a new thoughtless lad to put it in practice. Plunging the child in cold water as soon as born, and wrapping him warm up is found to be effectual.

√[Q] What allowance have nurses.
[A] On many plantations only an ordinary allowance on some few an extra.

√[Q] What attention is paid to the Children.
[A] Hardly any till they be old enough to be placed in the grass gang.

√[Q] Have they no allowance before.
[A] Not generally. On particular plantations they have.

√[Q] Do Slaves live to grow old.
[A] Not in general. Grey headed negroes are rare.

√[Q] How are they treated.
[A] On one plantation where an easy Manager had suffered them to accumulate, they were nominally liberated to save the Island taxes, and continued to have the plantation allowance being employed in keeping the fences in order.

[Q] Are Slaves in general well cared for.
[A] By no means. They are considered as instruments of labour without the analogy being carried so far as to keep them in good order or fit to execute the work.

[Q] To what do you ascribe this.

[A] Not to any particular depravity in the Master; but to absolute inattention to the necessity of considering them as possessed of feeling.

√[Q] Do many of the best masters consider them in any other light, than how to make the most of their Animal Strength.
[A] This was their general estimation in my time; and as such according to the disposition of their Master they met with mild or severe treatment but morality never was the object.

√[Q] Have you ever attended to the natural capacity of Negroes.
[A] I have carefully observed them, and I am convinced, that taking their depressed situation into account, they shew no signs of inferiority to Europeans.

√[Q] Could you perceive, that though they might feel as other men, yet they could not reason.
[A] Far from it. They are as capable of being influenced by moral reasoning as any person of their degree of information. If I allowed of any difference, I should be apt to give it in their favour.

√[Q] Have you any reason to suppose that Slaves if freed would not work.
[A] There has not within my knowledge been yet a fair trial. Most of those hitherto freed have been concubines or favorite Domestics, little accustomed to labour. In their present state, it would be wrong to hold out freedom to them. They must acquire a higher degree of improvement to be capable of using it properly.

√[Q] But having attained this state of improvement you have no doubt, of their making a proper use of freedom.

[A] This fact may be proved by the testimony of persons acquainted with North America, where Numbers have been freed, and behaved soberly and diligently. A Savage will not willingly work but to satisfie some present craving. But to suppose that any who are civilized will not endeavour to support themselves by their industry is to deny them the attributes of our common nature.

√[Q] Have you any reason to suppose that foreigners will smuggle Slaves in to our Colonies.

[A] I have reason to believe the contrary. Our Planters ever since the return of peace have complained of the high prices of Slaves, and except in the extremity of want have refus'd to purchase, and transfered them to the French. Slaves are smuggled into Hispaniola from Jamaica 10, 12 percent cheaper than the French themselves can import them immediately from Africa. Times must change greatly to induce the French to smuggle into Jamaica.

√[Q] Do not planters give their managers very good and judicious orders concerning the treatment of their Slaves.

[A] I dare say they will read well. But they are constantly interpreted by the custom of the Colony, and are understood to mean send home a great crop, and draw no bills on it. I have been obliged to help a Manager in framing a letter of apology, when his absent Master reprimanded him for running into expence.

√[Q] What is the usual situation of free Negroes.
[A] Often poor and sufficiently disagreeable; often ill treated by the White people and insulted by or injured by neighbouring great mens slaves.

√[Q] To what do you ascribe this.
[A] To their want of a protector, to the want of having their station allotted them, and employment given them in the community; to no care having been taken in freeing them that they should be such as have a trade, or be put in a way of supporting themselves.

√[Q] Do not some do well, and gain an honest living and raise families.
[A] Frequently where well disposed, and agreeably situated, and put in a way of industry.

√[Q] Are they in general barren.
[A] I might in general answer No unless some particular reason were assigned.

√[Q] Would not this be their general Case, if they were farther advanced in civilization.
[A] We cannot doubt of this, if we allow them to possess one common nature with our selves, But it is brought to proof, in the many instances of their discreet behaviour [sic], who have been brought forward in society, and been trained up to be useful, and have then been left to act for themselves.

√[Q] Has any attention been shewn to the improvement of

Slaves by Masters.

[A] Nothing within my knowledge. Some Masters expressed a prejudice against it; all, even the best (if I made one exception) talked as if it were a business in which they had no concern.

√[Q] Some Slaves were certainly taught some principles of religion.

[A] The only thing within my knowledge deserving of notice on this subject is that Mistresses, and especially young growing up women usually taught their sempstresses and attendants their prayers; and that some of those who had by any means attained their freedom, contrived to attain some general knowledge of Christianity. But really the whole hardly deserves to be taken into account.

But Gustavas Vasa is a well known instance of what improvement a Negroe is capable. He was kidnapped when about 11 Years old perhaps above 1000 Miles in land. He continued a slave for many years till he by his industry bought out his own freedom. He has learned to read and write; and in vindication of the rights of his colour has not been afraid to contend in Argument with men of high rank, and acuteness of parts. But the extent of his abilities appeared very clearly, when Government resolved to return the Negroes lately to Africa. Those to whom the management of the expedition was committed, dreaded so much his influence over his countrymen, that they contrived to procure an order for his being sent ashore. In particular, his knowledge of the scriptures is truly surprising, and shews that he could study and really understands them.

√[Q] Do not Slaves fare better for the good orders sent out by their absent masters.

[A] If they appoint them more cloathes or a more plentiful Allowance of food than others probably they may receive them. But I never heard of orders to forbid the Slaves from being kept under the Overseers lash from dawn till late at night; from being harassed with grass picking from being obliged to work for their own food on Sundays; from being punished at the caprice of the Overseer.

√ Population will never florish where there are no adequate means of maintenance. This is the case of free Negroes in general. They have no rank in society. They have no employment except perhaps it be huckestering [sic][21] which they can apply. The little patches of land usually allotted to plantation slaves when made free are not sufficient to keep them employed. They are seldom taken into families or otherwise noticed; but are left each to his own exertions without assistance without encouragement.

[Q] Are there not laws in some Colonies to check the freeing of Slaves.

[A] In Barbados and I think in Grenada the law lays a fine on the Master who frees a slave.

√[Q] Have you had any opportunities of comparing the price of new Slaves in our and the French colonies.

[A] I have known instances where after the prime Slaves were sold to our planters, the Merchants from St. Eustatius have bought for Hispaniola, the remainder at a price, which the factor could not have got in the island; and as they must have been transshipped, and smuggled in at a risk, and passed through perhaps two more hands before they came to the French planter, their price must have been very considerably advanced.

√[Q] How could the French afford this.
[A] The Staple articles in Hispaniola are low in price. The Slaves were bought either with them in barter or Spanish dollars, on which a considerable profit had been gained in trade and the French planters living frugally generally on their possessions could afford to be expensive in their Settlement.

√[Q] How is the gang usually employed in crop time.
[A] Some planters of method will allot only a sufficient Number for the making off of Sugar and employ the rest in some other useful labour. But I have known instances where almost in similar circumstances 200 Slaves have been set to do what was done by 100 on another plantation.

√[Q] Did not this make it easier for the more numerous gang.
[A] Not sensibly. It is not the quantity of work done, but the time they are kept drawling at it, that wears out the slaves; and this want of method in the case of Sugar making, obliges them to hurry the Slaves in more disagreeable circumstances at other times.

√[Q] Is it not the planters interest on the whole to treat his slaves considerately.
[A] Most undoubtedly, I never knew or heard of but one instance (and that is not likely to be repeated and indeed the Slaves were there well cared for and supported) where hurrying

of the slaves did not both ruin the gang and make a bankrupt of the Master. But a hasting to be rich, a restlessness under debt, caprice, passion, resentment often silence the still voice of slow working providence.

√[Q] Do Slaves suffer in their healths from travelling by night to dances on distant plantations.
[A] Some certainly do; but not in any numbers to deserve to be taken into account. I cannot charge my recollection with three instances within my own knowledge.

√[Q] What does the custom arise from.
[A] A general law of the colony forbids dances. The Slaves therefore meet by stealth, or perhaps a good natured Master overlooks it. This draws numbers together, who are willing to forget themselves for a few hours.

√[Q] Are Negroe women careless of their children.
[A] African poor wretches, that have no friends no necessaries often seem not to know what to do with their infants; but one can see a complaining anxiety in their looks, that throws the blame on their condition rather than their want of feelings.

Perhaps there may be instances, where women having opportunities of prostituting themselves to sailors acquire an unprincipled negligence of their offspring. But no neglect can in general be charged to them. It lies wholly with their masters, who put them not in circumstances to be either Mothers or nurses.

AN ADDRESS TO _____ ON THE PROPOSED BILL FOR THE ABOLITION OF THE SLAVE TRADE

[f. 63v – 65v]

If there were not something very particular in the case of him, who wishes to arrest your attention on this Subject, he would not have brought himself forward in a cause, which is certain to be charged with some selfish design, or at best some ill informed Enthusiasm, for aiming at unhinging established customs, and breaking up what is called a profitable commerce. But, though not unwillingly made an instrument in the hands of providence for the agitating of this important question, he has been impelled by situation and circumstances to act in the character, which he has assumed. The whole plan of this iniquity has been subjected to him; and his very adversaries in this proposed reformation have obliged him to search it to the bottom; and made what at first was mere observation, a matter of absolute certainty, and clear demonstration. He has only to blame himself, that while in the midst of the scenes, which he wishes to lay open, he did not commit every event and every observation and every name to paper; in order that reference might have been had to times and facts. For could he represent before the public but one half of what was daily within his observation; there could be but one voice informing the decision: As things are, some credit must be given to the Veracity of the Relator; but luckily for his purpose all the great points have other supports, and need not be rested on his testimony.

It would be an endless labour to run over all the pleas offered in favour of the present Slave trade: Many of them indeed are so trifling and so contradictory each to the other as to be undeserving of any reply; I shall consider it therefore as it affects our Trade, our Seamen, our Sugar Colonies, as our conduct in it may have an influence on other Nations that use the trade, and on Africa, and on the Guinea traders; and last of all I shall examine the morality of it; and rest the issue on the consciences of those by whom the point must be determined.

1. The importance of the Slave trade to the commerce of the Nation has been greatly exaggerated; The exports have been raised to upwards of two Millions. But this sum will not bear Calculation. The annual purchace [sic] of Slaves is within 40,000. Their average price is within £18 per head. The whole amount is £270,000. Of this a full third consists of Venetian & East Indian goods (see Clarksons Impolicy).[22] The annual demand then made by the slave trade on the British Manufactures is within half a million. In the most prosperous time of the trade it did not greatly exceed this even including the wood trade. Now if we take into account, that the Wood trade with Africa, notwithstanding the checks received from the Slave trade makes at present a considerable Additional demand on our Manufactures and that by abolishing the Slave trade, the Africans would be forced to find other staple Articles than slaves to barter with us for Commodities which they have now got a relish for, and that their Country abounds in natural wealth, well adapted for such an exchange; instead of this pitiful quantity which is now exported, and which cannot in any probability be increased; for the supply of Slaves as the country is wasted, becomes every year more difficult and yet it prevents them from applying to any other employment we may look forward to a commerce that may indefinitely be extended; till every manufacturing hand in Britain be employed in the

supply of Africa. This is the real state of this trade; which proves, that it is not of that consequence, which may not be made to yeild [sic] to weighty considerations. But when it is discovered, that this trade is carried on in a shuttling way, at which a Jew pedlar would blush, that damaged goods, false measure, and every possible fraud (See Newtons thoughts)[23] are imposed on the unsuspecting African, we should take shame as a people, that such a trade should find among us a single Advocate.

Wood trade [Inserted note by Ramsay.]

If the freight and employment of so many ships be taken into account I answer, that little can be drawn from this circumstance in favour of the trade. Admit of the Guinea traders charge of £8 p. head of freight on all Slaves as the return of the Ships employed; this on 40,000 is £320,000. The trade employs about 5000 Men. In the Navy £52 per Annum is not sufficient for each Mans wear and tear per Annum. But Guinea Ships are in the Nature of Armed Ships; and from their proportion of Officers must be equally expensive. The wear and tear of 5000 Men will then be £260,000. This admits of a balance of only £60,000 to supply the trade with new Ships; and to make good the interest of the slow returns of the trade. For the Expence of the out fit is immediate; and the accounts perhaps cannot be settled till two or three years afterwards. If the fact be also, that Ships in this trade (See Clarksons impolicy) on account of the Stench, Nastiness and ordure of the Slaves which consume the beams and planks do last above half the time of other ships, there is little that can be urged on this head with the public for a continuation of it. The State of our Woods requires not the quick consumption of Shipping; but a steady attention to their preservation. Therefore in our Manufactures and Shipping we risk nothing to be put in competition with the great point to be gained by the abolition of this trade in bloodshed; and we prepare the way for an innocent and much more advantageous traffic with an immense continent.

But this trade is a Nursery for Seamen. This I from my own knowledge can contradict. It forms not but destroys Seamen. And this destruction of Seamen is a strong argument for the abolition of it. Mr. Clarkson has clearly proved, that it causes an annual loss of at least 2000 men and that in general ill usage received and the disorders caught in this trade draw almost the whole Number of those who engage in it either from the sea service or from their Country. In particular that the comparison of actual deaths in the same number between the African and New foundland trade is as 200 in the first to 10 in the second. If therefore we have any regard to the lives of Seamen, we ought to abandon a branch of trade which dissipates them in so unprofitable a manner.

But this Trade is the support of the West Indian trade, which will be ruined, if it be abolished. Let us first inquire in to the Circumstances of the West Indian trade; and then we shall be best able to determine. In all our Sugar Colonies making but a very small allowance for the extraordinary Number of Slaves, which this present alarm will introduce among them, we may estimate the Slaves at about 475,000 and the free people including free Negroes and Mulattoes about or perhaps a little above 100,000. Suppose them both to amount to 600,000. The highest average of Exports to the West Indies is set down by Lord Sheffield at about £1,200,000 or 40 sh each Man. The outward and home freight may be estimated perhaps nearly as high as £600,000. Let both articles be esteemed of the highest importance; we are only concerned with the effects, which the stopping of the slave trade will have on them. If the same quantity of produce comes home, and the same number of consumers of our Commodities remain abroad, we shall find no diminution of our trade by the proposed abolition. Not to insist on the fair conclusion that may be drawn from the flattering description which planters give of their treatment of their Slaves, that it is impossible for them to decrease under such management, we can apply to multiplied instances in the several Islands, where good treatment has uniformly been followed by an increase from the Births. And if good or proper treatment, as may reasonably be expected shall become the general practice, on the abolition of the slave trade, then upwards of a Million of money which is annually expended by the planters to keep up their gangs from the Slave market, will be turned from a trade, which while it is destructive of our Seamen, and on the whole unprofitable to the state, is a disgrace to human nature. But it has been repeatedly laid before the public and proved even from the concessions of writers on the planters side, that so high is become the price of new slaves, such is their expence and loss in seasoning, so unprofitable is their labour, that no lot of Africans can ever turn out profitable to the owner. They never can repay the cost incurred on their Account before they become useful.

The public are dinned with the Sugar Colonies as if they were some great national object. They will be surprised to be told and yet it is a fact, that 240,000 Acres of ordinary good land, kept in good heart, and onely [sic] one half of it or 120,000 acres cropt annually would send more sugar to Market than all our Colonies at present produce. But these 240,000 Acres may be cultivated even in the present slovenly way without the

Assistance of Cattle or farming machines by 360,000 Slaves of all ages, without forcing them to any exertions, that will waste or prevent their increase from the births. This number leaves a reserve of at least 100,000 Slaves to supply any casual diminution till things have begun to run smoothly in the new channel. And when we take into account the immense numbers of useless slaves apart of these 360,000 that are kept about families even as far as 50, or 60 in one house, whose places if they were turned into the field might be much more cheaply supplied by a few white servants or free Negroes and Mulattoes, and reckon the number of Slaves held by poor white people, who are kept in a starving idleness depending on their labour, and if they were to sell them to plantations might be made industrious and easy in their situation, we shall have another large number to answer contingencies; or even to extend our plantations, if such a plan, which I much doubt, was otherwise proper or necessary. To explaine my doubt, I am, after a very serious and comprehensive investigation, decidedly of opinion, that from this time forth, no new land can be profitably cleared, built and stocked for a sugar plantation which is to be cultivated by Slaves brought from Africa at their present advanced price, or indeed at any price, at which they can possibly be imported. For proof I propose an investigation of the success of settling Dominica, St. Vincents, Grenada and Tobago, in more favourable circumstances than any new settlement will hence forward know

There is therefore no danger to be dreaded to our Sugar Colonies from an abolition of the Slave Trade; but every advantage is to be expected: An immediate advantage is the saving of a Million of money to them in the injudicious purchace of new slaves. But I will come nearer the point. During the late war this trade was stopt about six years, without any warning of or preparation for it. This was before the necessity or profit of good treatment was generally understood, or I may say thought of. For I most solemnly affirm, that at this time, whatever a few individuals here or there might do or think of it, as a matter of general attention, the treatment of slaves was an untouched subject. Every master or Overseer of Slaves treated them, rather used them, as he would do any other instrument of labour according to his particular disposition, without considering himself accountable in a moral point of view for his method being harsh, unfeeling, or cruel: The planters are now, or ought to be, prepared for the event: Let the trade therefore be strictly prohibited for six years: From experience we know the consequences can be fatal neither to our trade nor our colonies. After this trial, the friends of humanity may leave it to Parliament; taking every circumstance into consideration, to determine whether to persevere, or return to this trade of oppression and murder.

Here state the throwing out useless Cane land encouraging of population better feeding etc. [Inserted note by Ramsay.]

We will now state the case. Supposing the Slave trade abolished, we immediately shut up an alarming drain of our Seamen; we put an end to a commerce which is at best precarious and on the whole a losing branch, We save an annual million of money to the planters. On the other hand by drawing off the Africans from this vile business, which arms village against Village, brother against brother, and a father against his children, we force them to cultivate their country and raise numberless articles to exchange for our manufactures in a trade which will be a real nursery not the grave of our Seamen. Instead of supplying a few starved wretched slaves in our sugar colonies with a few mean articles, our trade thither will be more than doubled to supply the wants of an annually increasing multitude of well cloathed well fed labourers. The increase to be expected in this branch, supposing it to be only 20 sh on each annually, which is a moderate estimate, would make rich amends for the loss of the export of goods to purchase slaves in Africa. By a judicious selection of our best lands for the growth of the Sugar Cane, manuring and working it properly, we should have more certain and better crops, from a smaller quantity and less proportion than at present of labour, and have lands reserved for the growth of provisions and the support of cattle to lessen the annual outgoings. Our planters May have an increased revenue, and save two thirds of their present out goings in the recruiting and feeding of their slaves and cattle. These are not visionary advantages. The Planter will not, cannot dispute them.

But it is objected that other nations will seize on our part, and extend this trade if we abandon it: In the name of common sense, what is that to us, if we have proper reasons for giving it up. Let them judge and determine for themselves. It is a fact, that the French traders with all the helps of immense bounties cannot extend this branch in proportion to their demands; and that our Traders smuggle in Slaves into Hispaniola ten percent cheaper, than the French can bring them from Africa. Now if ours be but a precarious trade, what must theirs be but certain loss. Nor do the French planters themselves make any invidious advantage by the bargain. Adventurers only attempt the settlement of plantations in hopes of being more lucky than their neighbours. Old planters continue to buy because they have been accustomed to buy, and because living on and managing their own plantations, they can lay out that money however unprofitably in stocking them which our planters spend in Europe at a distance from their plantations. But it is a general complaint among them that Sugar plantations are unprofitable possessions. Government only holds out this encouragement to them on Account of making the trade a nursery for their navy; and it winks at our smuggling in of slaves; because it saves their seamen from being consumed on the coast of Africa.

If it is suggested, that on our abandoning so large a part as perhaps two fifths of the whole African trade, that other nations, the French in particular, will purchase their slaves cheaper, and therefore draw great advantages from it; this argument also will be found fallacious. The price of Slaves has been gradually increasing on the coast every year; and when all circumstances are taken into account it is surprising not to find it higher. To traverse a country perhaps three thousand miles up and down, to wait the issue of a predatory war, or a conspiracy for kidnapping, to travel incumbered with a few bulky commodities, to have taxes to pay to every petty tyrant, through whose territory they march, to have their wretched bargain to support on the journey, and be able to sell them each for £16 or £20 worth of damaged goods wanting in measure, false in appearance, will not allow of any possible deduction from the Adventurers profit. We therefore may positively affirm, that Slaves cannot possibly become cheaper unless the African Slave brokers shall resolve at their own certain loss to supply the French Market with them.

But it is farther said if Africa must be robbed of her inhabitants by every violent and base method why may we not continue to hold our share of the plunder. To this may be answered, we are accountable for our own conduct; let other nations see to theirs.

Yet what means this excuse? Only this: I see a parcel of fellows have fallen on a lonely house and are robbing and murdering the inhabitants and carrying off the bounty I will go and come in for my share, and rob murder and plunder as much as they. Are we never to do what is proper; because we are not sure that others will imitate us? Is this accursed trade never to be broke up; because we are jealous of the French nation? Is no state to hearken to the moaning of humanity because All others cannot at once resolve to listen to its dictates? But Africa will be the better, Africa will be improved. If we withdraw ourselves from this business of blood to cultivate a fair exchange of merchandize. Civilization will gradually extend itself, and produce all its happy effects on their lives, their industry, and manners: But when our Neighbours shall see, that instead of an alarming mortality among our Seamen, and an immense drain of the planters money for slaves, that a better trade to Africa florishes, that our Slaves in our Sugar Colonies multiply from the births, and their produce is increased, that their demand for the goods of the Mother Country is doubled and the planters are out of debt and easy in their circumstances, then will they eagerly run to share in the same advantages.

But we owe a Justice to our Guinea Traders, who have embarked their property in this traffic, and must suffer if it be given up: That several worthy men have been concerned in this trade, and have without thought been guilty of barbarous oppression and multiplied murders in the course of it, is with real sorrow to be acknowledged. It can only be said, they had never examined the nature of this commerce, and went into it, and acted as others had done before them in it, as a thing of course, for which no account was to be given in this world or the next: But no man concerned in this trade can now pretend ignorance of the oppression and cruelty attending it. To set aside the suffering of wretches shut up for seven or ten weeks chained together, or crowded on each other amidst foul air, stench, ordure, disease, and every loathsome exhalation; they must know, that though all come under their power in a state of health; yet from their confinement, sometimes one half hardly ever fewer than one eighth part die in this short time, and perhaps double this last proportion, though landed alive never recover to become useful, and that full one third of those whose healths are not sensibly impaired are also lost in the seasoning; and that they are answerable for all this waste; and therefore they are base murderers and felons in the due and proper sense of the word. Examine the trade in this point of view, and we should as soon think of giving a recompence to a highwayman shut up in a jail for the robberies and murders he might have committed if at liberty as to a Leverpool [sic] Trader for not continuing to bribe the Africans to rob murder and kidnap each other, that he may get slaves to be confined, suffocated, and consumed by disease in the middle passage, that he may sell the wretched remains to labour, to chains, hunger and stripes.

But allow this Slave trade to be a nursery for seamen, allow that the West Indian Trade depends wholly on it and must rise and fall with it, or even as some of its Rodomontading advocates affirm, that the whole British trade must be crushed if any thing affects it, still if it cannot be carried on without the basest treachery in the very intercourse with the brokers by short measure, alarming imposition and tricking fraud; if kidnapping, every sort of violence and murder lie indispensably connected with it, then is it to be given up with all its profits; unless we as a nation be willing to renounce our claim to humanity and justice. But its advocates allow it requires regulations, though it must not be abolished. Who is to see these regulations enforced? This Trade finds, or makes, unfeeling Savages of almost every man, who continues any length of time in it. Who is to come between a Brute in power, and the helpless wretches submitted to his lawless passions? Can a few general regulations prevent him from tormenting them in a thousand ways every hour of their existence?

But suppose this trade regulated, and the regulations complied with by Leverpool Captains. How is a British act of Parliament to be enforced 1200 Miles inland in Africa? Or can we pretend, by regulating the stowage of the helpless wretches on board our ships, to express a fellow feeling with them, when we encourage by this trade, their countrymen and neighbours to murder and enslave them? While we receive them in to our ships we are guilty of all the murders, that are committed in the kidnapping and enslaving of them throughout the continent: We set them on to fight, to lie in wait for and destroy each other: every helpless wretch who falls lame or sick in the march, and is left to be devoured by the lion or tyger is murdered by our sword is the victim of our Avarice. No regulation can extend here, no arrangement can prevent these Crimes. The trade must be abandoned, that is connected with them. The North American provinces were but lately considered as essentially necessary to the very being of Great Britain in a much more important degree than the Slave trade now is; yet because it was discovered, that no man should be obliged to contribute to the safety of the State of which he was a member, except he consented to the tax by his representative, it was strenuously argued that they ought to be emancipated: Gracious Heaven! how much stronger is the poor African's pleas! I seek no communication of privileges, I ask for no indulgence: Allow me only to possess my own cottage and family in my own country: Bribe not the blood thirsty tyrant to surround the peaceful town in dead of night with flames, that he and his blood hounds may see to seize on the fugitives. Set not the insidious kidnapper to watch at the fountain with his dogs to intercept the unsuspecting villager: Do not encourage him to way lay the lonely traveler in the path: Allure not the husband with your intoxicating liquors to accuse his innocent wife of a crime, which condemns her to exile and slavery: Surely these are not great things which I ask: Surely they may be granted to that common relation which we all bear to one great and good Creator. But are we indeed refered to a common relation? or carries not that common relation some important claims with it? And shall human nature plead in vain before a British Senate? Shall a few interested traders be heard, and their extravagant claims founded on murder, and stained with innocent blood find Advocates, and helpless Africans pleading only not to be injured, not find a Protector? It cannot be. Every senator will hasten to understand that he may plead their cause. He will rejoice in giving a vote, which shall wipe away this infamy from his Country, and pave the way for the future civilization and happiness of Africa. He will obey that heavenly voice which now echoes from every corner of his country, and cries aloud to him to cause to cease the oppression, the murder, the exile, the Slavery of our helpless Country: And that Gracious Providence which sees and approves, this glorious struggle in the cause of humanity will richly make up every imaginary loss, by the increased prosperity and happiness of the state: Every man who gives a vote in favour of the abolition of the

Slave trade, helps to save his country from divine vengeance, and to draw down success and blessings on every public undertaking.

Notes

1. 'Careen, *v*,' to turn (a ship) over on one side for cleaning, caulking, or repairing; to clean, caulk, etc. (*OED Online*, Oxford University Press, 4 Apr. 2000). Hereafter cited as OED.

2. 'Puddings, *n*,' 4. *naut.* a. A wreath of plaited cordage placed round the mast and yards of a ship as a support; a dolphin. b. A pad to prevent damage to the gunwale of a boat; a fender. c. The binding on rings, etc., to prevent the chafing of cables or hawsers. (OED)

3. This paragraph and the three following have a single line drawn down the centre of them.

4. Also known as St. Kitts.

5. This paragraph and the two following have a line drawn down the left half of them.

6. 'Call, *n*,' 2. b. *spec.* The reading aloud of a roll or list of names; a roll-call; *v.* 3. To utter (anything) in a loud voice; to read over (a list of names) in a loud voice; 4. a. To summon with a shout, or by a call; *hence* to summon, cite; to command or request the attendance of, bid (any one) come. (OED)

7. 'Lock-jaw,' popular name for trismus, or tonic spasm of the muscles of mastication, causing the jaws to remain rigidly closed; a variety of tetanus. (OED)

8. The following questions and answers are very similar to those posed in ff.6-7r of the notebook (not reproduced here).

9. 'Fluxes, *n*,' an abnormally copious flowing of blood, excrement, etc. from the bowels or other organs; a morbid or excessive discharge. *Spec.* An early name for dysentery. (OED).

10. 'Factor, *n*,' an agent. (OED) A Guinea Factor was an agent based on the Guinea coast (where most of the slaves were shipped from).

11. In f.6v he gives the figure 'from £6 or £8 down to a Crown'.

12. 'Hhds', an acronym for hogshead.

13. 'Ratoon, *n*,' a new shoot or sprout springing up from the root of the sugar-cane after it has been cropped. (OED)

14. This question has a cross drawn across it, but it is then repeated below.

15. 'Osnaburgh' was a type of linen which was often used for women's petticoats.

16. Ramsay was multiplying the numbers in this figure. He leaves out the 'os' in 128,000, and places the 21 to the left of where it is conventionally placed.

17 Cf. the additions represented here with Ramsay's description in f.57r. (included below).

18 Horse beans, also called fava or broad beans.

19 See additions listed above.

20 'sh', an acronym for shillings.

21 'Huckstering,' petty trafficking; sordid dealing; haggling. (OED)

22 Thomas Clarkson, *Essay on the Impolicy of the Slave Trade* (1788).

23 John Newton, *Thoughts on the African Slave Trade* (1788).

SCRIPTURAL RESEARCHES

ON THE LICITNESS

OF THE

SLAVE-TRADE,

SHEWING ITS CONFORMITY

WITH THE PRINCIPLES OF

NATURAL AND REVEALED RELIGION,

DELINEATED IN THE

SACRED WRITINGS OF THE WORD OF GOD.

BY THE REV. R. HARRIS.

SEARCH THE SCRIPTURES, FOR IN THEM YE THINK YE HAVE
ETERNAL LIFE. JOHN. C. 5. V. 39.

LIVERPOOL:
PRINTED BY H. HODGSON, POOL-LANE,
M.DCC.LXXXVIII.

TO The WORSHIPFUL the MAYOR, RECORDER, ALDERMEN, BAILIFFS, And other MEMBERS of the COMMON COUNCIL Of the ancient and loyal BOROUGH and CORPORATION of LIVERPOOL, The following SCRIPTURAL RESEARCHES On the licitness of the SLAVE-TRADE, Are most respectfully inscribed BY Their most obedient And most humble Servant, RAYMUND HARRIS.

PREFACE.

UNWILLING to incur the displeasure of every friend to justice, religion, and humanity, I hasten to inform the Reader, who has cast an eye on the Title-page, that, in attempting to establish the licitness of the SLAVE-TRADE, nothing is farther removed from my thoughts, than to set up as an advocate for injustice and oppression: I am as much at enmity with both, as the most sanguine advocate for African Liberty may be. I am well apprized, that acts of violence and oppression, however authorized by numbers, however firmly established by long use, and a kind of traditional inattention to the sufferings of persons in an abject condition of life, can never change the criminality of their nature. Whatever is essentially incompatible with the sacred and inalienable rights of justice and humanity, can claim no place in the catalogue of virtues, even of the lowest rank; it must be for ever branded with every mark of infamy and guilt.

FAR then from attempting the least encroachment on the rights of Virtue, my sole drift in the present Tract is to examine with the utmost impartiality, the intrinsic nature of the SLAVE-TRADE: that is, whether the Trade itself, prescinding from every other incidental circumstance, which may have rendered the practice of it hateful, or even criminal, be in its own nature licit or illicit.

Now, it being evident in the first place, that the intrinsic morality or immorality, licitness or illicitness of all human pursuits is essentially inherent to the pursuits themselves, and not at all depending on our habits or ideas of *Right* and *Wrong*, which are but too often influenced and darkened by prejudice, interest, and other passions; and, it being equally evident on the other hand, that the declarations of the Written Word of God are so many incontrovertible decisions, by which we are to judge of the intrinsic licitness or illicitness of such facts as are registered in the Sacred Volumes; it follows necessarily, that, one of those facts being undoubtedly the SLAVE-TRADE, no arguments can be so forcible and conclusive, towards evincing the inherent lawfulness of it, as those Oracular decisions of the Word of God, which give a positive sanction to the Trade itself.—It is then by enforcing these unerring decisions only, the surest guide to direct our judgements in forming a just estimate of the merits of the present Controversy, that I mean to vindicate the licitness of the SLAVE-TRADE; not by pratronizing such crying enormities and abuses, as are said to be perpetrated in this most ancient commercial pursuit.

SHOULD the sanction of divine authority appear evident in favour of the SLAVE-TRADE, from the testimonies I shall produce in the series of my Researches, I shall consider myself perfectly disingaged from the most distant obligation of answering such objections, as are not grounded on the same divine authority: an authority of that irresistible weight of conviction, that every person, who has any pretensions to Religion, must immediately assent to, however plausible or ingenious the opposite arguments may appear, when viewed through the scanty light of mere human reason and sense.

THE scope of the following Researches being evidently to try the merits of the present Controversy by the Sacred Canons of the Written Word of God, I can expect conviction only from such persons, as are not so far destitute of every sentiment of religion and good sense, as to disbelieve the divine authenticity of those Sacred Writings, in which the Finger of God has left in indelible characters the visible impression of his Wisdom.

Now, as these Sacred Records contain transactions relative to the SLAVE-TRADE, as practised in all the three religious Dispensations that have appeared in the World since the formation of the first of men to the present time, I shall, accordingly, divide my Scriptural Researches on that Trade, into three separate Parts: in which I shall successively prove, that the SLAVE-TRADE is perfectly consonant to the principles of the Law of Nature, the Mosaic Dispensation, and the Christian Law, as delineated to us in the Sacred Writings of the Word of God.

I HAVE prefixed to the whole a few positions or *Data*, which, I trust, will be found unquestionably true, and exactly conformable to sound reason; in order, that I may not be interrupted in the sequel with unnecessary repetitions of general principles, nor be in the least constrained to enter into a formal confutation of arguments, which do not immediately affect my subject, and that the Reader may see at one view the very fundamental principles of those inferences, which I draw in vindication of the SLAVE-TRADE from the Scriptural passages I have selected in the course of my Researches, out of a greater number of the same import I could easily produce.

THE Scriptural passages are literally transcribed from the

Protestant Vulgar Translation of the Bible; which, being the most generally received in these Kingdoms, will, of course, have a greater weight of authority than any other with the major part of my Readers. The Edition I use is that which was published in London by John Bill and Christopher Barker in the year 1669.

WITH respect to composition, I can pretend to neither elegance nor style: a Foreigner, unacquainted with the least element of the English Language till the twenty seventh year of his age, can have no claim to either: if he can but arrange his periods with a tolerable degree of grammatical accuracy, and express himself with sufficient clearness, method, and perspicuity, he has reason to expect every indulgence from the native candour of an English Critic.

DATA

I. THAT the Volume of the Sacred Writings, commonly called the HOLY BIBLE, comprehending both the Old and the New Testaments, contains the unerring Decisions of the Word of God.

II. THAT these Decisions are of equal authority in both the Testaments, and that that authority is the essential veracity of God, who is TRUTH itself.

III. THAT, as there can be no prescription against the authority of God, whatever is declared in any part of the Scriptural Records to be intrinsically good or bad, licit or illicit, must be essentially so in its own nature, however contrary any such declaration may be to the received opinions of men for any length of time.

IV. THAT, as the Supreme Legislator of the World is infinitely just and wise in all his decisions respecting *Right* and *Wrong*, and is no ways accountable to his creatures for the reasons of his conduct in the government of the World; so it must be a degree of presumption highly criminal in any creature to refuse assent to those Decisions, only because he cannot comprehend the hidden principles of that impartial justice, which characterizes every decision of God.

V. THAT no person can be supposed to acknowledge in fact, that the Holy Scriptures are the infallible Word of God, unless he acquiesces without reserve in every scriptural Decision, however incomprehensible the reasons and motives of those Decisions may be to him.

VI. THAT every person, who professes to acknowledge the Holy Scriptures to be the unerring Word of God, must consequently assent to every Scriptural Decision without reserve, only because he believes them to be the declarations of God; who, being TRUTH itself, can neither err himself, nor lead any one into error.

VII. THAT, if one or more Decisions of the Written Word of God give a positive sanction to the intrinsic licitness of any human pursuit (for instance, the SLAVE-TRADE), whoever professes to believe the incontrovertible veracity of the Written Word of God, essentially incompatible with the least degree of injustice, must consequently believe the pursuit itself to be intrinsically just and lawful in the strictest sense of the word.

VIII. THAT no advantages whatever attending the prosecution of an unlawful pursuit, nor any abuses whatever committed in the prosecution of a lawful one, can so far affect the pursuits themselves, as to render the latter intrinsically criminal, or the former essentially just.

IX. THAT, as no private or national advantages whatever can alter the inherent turpitude or a pursuit essentially unlawful; so no arguments whatever, built solely on the strength of those advantages, will ever justify the SLAVE TRADE, till the same be proved essentially just and lawful in its nature.

X. THAT, as no abuses or malepractices whatever, committed in the prosecution of a lawful pursuit, can ever alter the intrinsic licitness of it; so no arguments whatever, built solely on the strength of those abuses, will ever evince the intrinsic deformity of the SLAVE-TRADE, any more than that of any other lawful pursuit, where abuses are committed, unless the same be proved essentially unjust and illicit.

XI. THAT, if abuses and malepractices, committed in the prosecution of a lawful pursuit, can be checked and prevented by Legal Authority, the private and national advantages arising from that pursuit, and the inconveniencies attending the suppression of it, joined to its intrinsic licitness, ought to have a very powerful influence towards not abolishing the prosecution of that pursuit.

XII. THAT, if abuses and malepractices, though evidently subject to the control of the Legislature, are to be considered as sufficient arguments to suppress the SLAVE-TRADE, without any regard to its intrinsic licitness, every other branch of Trade, in which abuses are committed, ought, on the same account, to share the same fate.

SECTION I

Scriptural Researches on the licitness of the Slave-Trade, shewing its conformity with the principles of the Law of Nature delineated in the Sacred Writings.

I. THAT period of years, which elapsed from the day on which *God created Man in his own image*[1], to the day, on which He gave his Laws to the Children of Israel on Mount Sinai[2], is generally called the period of the Law of Nature. The exact duration of this period is a matter of controversy among the Learned. Archbishop Usher, whose chronological accuracy in the computation of scriptural years is much admired, reckons 2513 years between the Creation of the World and the promulgation of the Mosaic Law. But be this as it may (for no difference in computation can affect the subject of my present Researchers), it is evident from the tenour of the Sacred Records, that, between the creation of Adam and the promulgation of the Mosaic Law, the Dispensation of the Law of Nature, commonly called Natural Religion, or the Religion of Nature, was the only true Religion in the World.

II. SIMPLE as the principles of this Religion may appear, directed chiefly to worship one, Supreme, Eternal, Being, the Creator and Governor of all things, and to chuse and act in exact conformity to the inward dictates of sound and unbiassed reason in every transaction of life, where *Right* and *Wrong* were left to choice of Man; it would be exceedingly difficult, as well as perfectly extraneous to my present subject, to digest those principles into a regular Code of those particular laws and duties, which constituted the whole system of that Religion.—I have not engaged to display the whole frame and structure of Natural Religion: I am to shew no farther, than that the principles and laws of that Religion, as far as we find them delineated in the Sacred Writings, not only never forbade the SLAVE-TRADE, or hinted the most distant opposition to the prosecution of it; but that, the same being frequently exemplified in the constant and uninterrupted practice of some of the most faithful observers of the laws and principles of that Religion, under the visible protection of God, whose favourites they were, the laws and principles themselves were in perfect harmony with the practice of the SLAVE-TRADE.— Two very singular instances of this kind, verified in the conduct of two of the most distinguished Characters within the above period of the Law of Nature, ABRAHAM and JOSEPH, will, I flatter myself, be sufficient, without mentioning others, to justify my assertion, and set the present Controversy in the clearest light of Scriptural conviction.

ABRAHAM.

III. IN every place of Scripture, where mention is made of the Venerable Patriarch, he is uniformly represented as a perfect pattern of every virtue. The strongest faith in God[3], the firmest reliance on his promises[4], and the readiest and most unreserved obedience to his commands[5]; the most sympathizing humanity to every fellow-creature[6], the strictest justice and integrity in all his dealings with men[7] and the utmost disinterestedness of heart[8]; infine, the greatest love of peace and harmony[9], together with every other religious, domestic, and social virtue[10], are the distinguishing characteristics of his person.

IV. OWING, no doubt, to these exalted virtues, he is frequently represented in Scripture in familiar intercourse with God[11]; who, in innumerable places of Holy Writ, styles himself emphatically *The God of Abraham,* as the most acceptable person he had on earth: he calls him *His Friend*[12], and makes the most exalted panegyric of his virtues, when, appearing to his son Isaac after the death of his Father, he speaks to him in the following remarkable and comprehensive words: *In thy feed shall all the nations of the earth be blessed; because that Abraham obeyed my voice, and kept my charge, my commandments, my statutes, and my laws*[13].

V. NOR is his unimpeachable character, as a righteous man, less conspicuous in the Writings of the New Testament; where, among many other testimonies of his irreproachable life, the Son of God himself, who always speaks of him as one of the most faithful servants of his Eternal Father, rebukes the Jews for having so far departed from the rectitude of Abraham's conduct, as not to be entitled to the appellation of his Children; for, *If ye were Abraham's children,* says he, *ye would do the works of Abraham*[14].

VI. Now, it is very remarkable, that among the *works* of Abraham, the very faithful, obedient, humane, just, disinterested, righteous, and virtuous Abraham, who constantly obeyed the voice of God, kept his charge, his commandments, his statutes, and his laws, and found such acceptance with him, as to be admitted to the familiarity of his friendly intercourse; it is very remarkable, I say, that there should be found among his *works* the practice of dealing in human flesh, the practice of purchasing with money those of his own species, and making them *Bond-Slaves*[15], without the least intimation being ever given by any of the inspired Writers, that his conduct in this particular, where the natural rights of justice and humanity are said to be so essentially interested, was ever reproved, or even discountenanced in the most distant manner by any private or public intimation of God's displeasure !

VII. AND what can we reasonably conclude from this uniform silence of the inspired Writers? but that the practice of purchasing slaves was never accounted in the sight of God a violation of any of the laws of the Religion of Nature. For, is it credible, or, rather, is it possible for any one to believe, consistently with the ideas we ought to entertain of the infinite holiness of God, in whom dwelleth essentially the fulness of justice, that he would style himself *The God of Abraham,* in preference to any other; that he would vouchsafe to honour him with the appellation of *His Friend*; that he would bless in his seed all the nations of the earth[16]; that he would declare he had obeyed his voice, kept his charge, his commandments, his statutes, and his laws, without excepting any one; or that Jesus Christ would have ever commended his works without any restriction whatever, if the SLAVE-TRADE, so publickly and so constantly practised by Abraham, had been an iniquitous, unnatural pursuit, essentially opposite to the sacred laws of Nature, to the natural rights of justice and humanity?

VIII. THE force of this powerful inference, considered even as a mere negative argument in favour of the intrinsic licitness of the SLAVE-TRADE, carries such an irresistible weight of conviction, that it amounts, in my opinion, to a positive approbation of it: it being otherwise impossible to reconcile the justice of God with his own scriptural decisions concerning the essential impartiality, and eternal unchangeableness of its nature.

IX. THAT this positive approbation, this sanction of Divine Authority in favour of the SLAVE-TRADE, so visible in the conduct of God, eye-witness to every transaction of Abraham's life, is not a bare conjecture, or a mere negative inference of a passionate advocate for slavery, but the real intent and meaning of the Written Word of God, will appear evident to the most zealous advocate for African Liberty, who, divesting himself for a moment of every prejudice, that the love of humanity may have created in his mind, will dispassionately examine with me the striking circumstances of the following Case. It is that of a BOND SLAVE in the service of Abraham; which, as related in the Sacred Writings, contains such interesting particulars, that, I flatter myself, it will evince to demonstration, that the SLAVE-TRADE has the indisputable sanction of Divine Authority, even when attended with circumstances not of the most pleasing complexion to the eyes of humanity.

X. THIS very decisive fact is thus literally related in the xvi[th] Chapter of the Book of GENESIS.

    1. Now Sarai Abram's wife bare him no children: and she had an hand-maid, an Egyptian, whose name was Hagar,

2. And Sarai said unto Abram: behold now, the Lord hath restrained me from bearing: I pray thee, go in unto my maid: it may be, that I may obtain children by her: and Abram hearkened to the voice of Sarai.

3. And Sarai Abram's wife took Hagar her maid, the Egyptian, after Abram had dwelt ten years in the land of Canaan, and gave her to her husband Abram to be his wife.

4. And he went in unto Hagar, and she conceived: and when she saw that she had conceived, her mistress was despised in her eyes.

5. And Sarai said unto Abram: my wrong be upon thee: I have given my maid into thy bosom; and when she saw she had conceived, I was despised in her eyes: the Lord judge between me and thee.

6. But Abram said unto Sarai: behold, thy maid is in thy hand; do to her as it pleaseth thee. And when Sarai dealt hardly with her, she fled from her face.

7. And the Angel found her by a fountain of water in the wilderness, by the fountain in the way to Shur.

8. And he said: Hagar, Sarai's maid, whence comest thou? and whither wilt thou go? And she said: I flee from the face of my mistress Sarai.

9. And the Angel of the Lord said unto her: return unto thy mistress, and submit thyself under her hands.

10. And the Angel of the Lord said unto her: I will multiply thy seed exceedingly, that it shall not be numbered for multitude.

11. And the Angel of the Lord said unto her: behold, thou art with child, and shalt bear a son, and shalt call his name

Ishmael; because the Lord hath heard thy affliction.

XI. Enough have we for the present to observe on this portion of Hagar's history, without proceeding to relate the treatment she received in her Master's house some time after her return. — Here we have a Hand-maid, called soon after a *Bond-woman* by God himself[17]; born in Africa, for she was an Egyptian by birth, and, consequently, an *African Slave*, labouring under every natural disadvantage attending the condition of a Bond-slave; bought by a stranger, transported from her native Country into a distant land, the Land of Canaan, where Abram dwelt; that is, transported from Africa into Asia: separated for ever from her dearest relations, friends, and acquaintance, and obliged to wait at hand, and work for the advantage of her Masters.

XII. THE sterility of her Mistress seemed rather to flatter Hagar with the prospect of meliorating her condition, by becoming her Master's wife at the solicitation of her Mistress: but the event proved the contrary, and disappointed all her hopes; for not only she did not obtain her freedom by becoming his wife, but finding she was with child by her Master, and being, on this account, not quite so respectful to her Mistress, as the latter expected in quality of Abram's principal wife, she was so roughly handled by Sarai, with the permission of Abram, that, unable to bear her treatment, she fled from her house, left her service, and took refuge in the desert. What the correction was, that Sarai inflicted on Hagar, is not particularly specified in the Sacred History: the Hebrew word used upon the occasion, and rendered by the Translators *dealt hardly*, has such an extent of signification, as may easily convey the idea of a very cruel and oppressive treatment, which, in the actual state of Hagar's pregnancy, must have rendered her affliction much more intolerable and oppressive.

XIII. EVERY circumstance attending the wretched situation of this poor African Slave, who, though legally married to her Master, is kept still in bondage, and forced, as it were, out of his house and service in the condition she was in, through hard usage and severity, though charged with no other crime, but being not quite so respectful to her husband's first wife as she had been before her marriage, seems to excite compassion, and justify her escape. —Were Hagar's case that of any African female slave now in the West-Indies, and were the same to be tried before a jury composed of some of the present advocates for African Liberty in this Island, one might decide almost to a certainty in whose favour the verdict would be given: the Slave would most probably be declared free, and both Master and Mistress severely reprimanded, if not also condemned in a heavy precuniary mulct: no other verdict would be consistent with the principles they so publickly avow.

XIV. BUT did Hagar obtain the same favourable sentence at the impartial Tribunal of God, when she pleaded her Cause before the Minister of his justice, whom he deputed to represent his Person? Did he approve of her conduct in leaving her Master's house, and quitting his service? Did he hint the most distant reflection on the proceedings of Abram or her Mistress Sarai? Did he signify to her, that her quality of Abram's wife, or the severity of Sarai's treatment, even in her actual state of pregnancy, emancipated her from her bondage, rescinded the original contract of her purchase, or that that contract had been illicit and contrary to his laws, or that she might, on this account, consider herself as no part of Abram's lawful property, but at full liberty to dispose of her person as she thought best?—NO:—on the contrary, her conduct was condemned by the Representative of God, who ordered her in his name *to return to her Mistress, and submit herself under her hands*; though at the same time he assured her, that *the Lord had heard her affliction*.

XV. WERE all other scriptural evidences wanted in favour of the SLAVE-TRADE, this Decree alone of the highest Court of Justice possible, this solemn Sentence of the Supreme Judge of *Right* and *Wrong, Who is no respecter of persons, but, in every nation, he that feareth him, and worketh righteousness, is accepted with him*[18], and who, in the case before us, had an intuitive and comprehensive knowledge of every particular circumstance attending the claims of both the Parties, must convince every impartial Reader, that the licitness of that Trade is evidently warranted by the Written Word of God; who, by the very act of deputing an Angel, on purpose to command the fugitive Slave to return to her Master's house, and submit herself under the hands of her Mistress, declared her to be her Master's indisputable property, and the original bargain or contract, by which he had acquired that property, to be just and lawful in its natural: that is, that the SLAVE-TRADE, even when attended with circumstances not altogether conformable to the feelings of humanity, is essentially consistent with the sacred and inalienable rights of justice, and has the positive sanction of God in its support; however displeasing those circumstances may be to his fatherly Providence, as they appear to have been in the Case of Hagar;

who, in alleviation of her sufferings and affliction, was promised the honour of being the Mother of a numerous progeny, branched out afterwards into twelve powerful kingdoms[19].

JOSEPH.

XVI. WHOEVER has the least acquaintance with the principal human Characters exhibited in the Sacred Records, must readily acknowledge, that the character of JOSEPH, great grand-son to Patriarch Abraham, is one of the most amiable, most upright, and instructive. He is there represented in every vicissitude of fortune, acquiring in every station by his wisdom and virtue favour with God and man[20]. His virtue suffers no diminution whatever, but shines with greater lustre, in passing from the condition of a slave to that of Governor of all Egypt. His fidelity to God, and to his Master Potiphar, is assailed by strong temptations, which, in spite of youth and interest, he resists with the most exemplary fortitude[21]. Thrown into the horrors of a dungeon through the artifice of a false woman, whose honour he preserves at the expence of his own, his integrity and prudence soon render him conspicuous even in that dark recess[22]. Favoured with the divine spirit of prophecy, and called in his Prophetic Character into the presence of Pharaoh, the wise and extensive plan he forms to save the Kingdom from the miseries of impending famine, raises him to that height, where his abilities and virtues are eminently displayed in the public service, and answer the purposes of the Providence of God in favour of his chosen People[23]. Enabled by despotic power to retain his unnatural brethren in that Egyptian bondage, to which they had once consigned him, and gratify revenge by every accumulation of disgrace, he not only generously forgives them the outrageous treatment he had received, but he even effaces the very remembrance of those injuries which had produced his adversity; and, without recriminating his adversaries, without retaliating their injuries, he extenuates in some measure the guilt of a crime, which, by the interposition of Providence, had proved subservient to a happy issue[24].

XVII. Every feature of this most amiable Character is so perfectly finished, so exactly conformable to the model of the strictest virtue, that the whole Piece is one of the completest portraits of righteousness and humanity, that has ever been exhibited to the World in any stage of Religion. Christianity itself can produce but few exemplars, that will contend with him for superiority; especially, when it is considered, that Joseph's innocence and virtue, from his youth to his decrepit old age, retained, in the very heart of infidelity itself, the same uniform lustre and firmness, though beset at different periods by such strong temptations to infidelity and vice, as are the inseparable attendants of extreme adversity and prosperity. In a word: every step of Joseph's conduct in every stage of his life met the approbation of God, and was especially directed by his protecting hand; for, in the language of the inspired Writer, *The Lord was with him: and that which he did, the Lord made it to prosper*[25].

XVIII. Now, if we examine the history of this eminent Personage, as described in the Sacred Records, we shall soon find a second very remarkable instance of the licitness of the SLAVE-TRADE, as practised, not only without control, but under the visible protection of God, by one of the strictest professors of the Religion of Nature, the laws and principles of which were the invariable rule of his conduct: a man in high favour with the Almighty, the framer of those very principles and laws; and who, in the inscrutable order of his fatherly Providence, chose him the instrument and promoter of his glory[26], imparted him the divine spirit of his wisdom[27], led him, as it were, by the hand, in every step of his life[28], and prospered whatever he undertook[29]. An instance, attended with circumstances of that singular nature and tendency, as seems not only to fix the subject of the present Controversy in the best point of view, but to ascertain, beyond the power of reply, the inherent lawfulness of the SLAVE-TRADE

XIX. THE fact, with all its attending circumstances, is thus described in the XLVIIth Chapter of the Book of GENESIS

13. And there was no bread in all the land; for the famine was very sore: so that the land of Egypt, and the land of Canaan fainted by reason of the famine.

14. And Joseph gathered up all the money that was found in the land of Egypt, and in the land of Canaan, for the corn which they brought; and Joseph brought the money into Pharaoh's house.

15. And when the money failed in the land of Egypt, and in the land of Canaan, all the Egyptians came unto Joseph, and said: give us bread; for why should we die in thy presence? for the money faileth.

16. And Joseph said: give your cattle; and I will give you for your cattle, if money fail.

17. And they brought their cattle unto Joseph: and Joseph gave them bread in exchange for horses, and for the flocks,

and for the cattle of the herds, and for the asses; and he fed them with bread for all their cattle, for that year.

18. When that year was ended, they came unto him the second year, and said unto him: we will not hide it from my Lord, how that our money is spent; my Lord also hath our herds of cattle; there is not aught left in the sight of my Lord, but our bodies and our lands.

19. Wherefore shall we die before thine eyes, both we and our land? Buy us and our land for bread, and we and our land will be servants unto Pharaoh: and give us feed, that we may live and not die, that the land be not desolate.

20. And Joseph bought all the land of Egypt for Pharaoh: for the Egyptians sold every man his field; because the famine prevailed over them: so the land became Pharaoh's.

21. And as for the people, he removed them to cities, from one end of the borders of Egypt, even unto the other end thereof.

22. Only the land of the Priests bought he not; for the Priests had a portion assigned them of Pharaoh, and did eat their portion which Pharaoh gave them; wherefore they sold not their lands.

23. Then Joseph said unto the people: behold, I have bought you this day, and your land for Pharaoh: lo, here is feed for you, and ye shall sow the land.

24. And it shall come to pass in the encrease, that ye shall give the fifth part unto Pharaoh, and four parts shall be your own, for seed of the field, and for your food, and for them of your housholds, and for food for your little ones.

25. And they said; thou hast saved our lives: let us find grace in the sight of my Lord, and we will be Pharaoh's servants.

26. And Joseph made it a law over the land of Egypt unto this day, that Pharaoh should have the fifth part; except the land of the Priests only, which became not Pharaoh's.

XX. THE transactions related in this portion of Joseph's history, afford us a considerable number of very pertinent reflections on the SLAVE-TRADE: the following appear to me very remarkable.

1. Here is a whole Nation of free and independent Africans, one only description of men excepted, inhabiting the richest, the most populous, and the most civilized part of Africa, or, perhaps, of any other part of the Globe at that period, all made SLAVES in one day by a most explicit, deliberate, and formal contract.

2. Allowing, the Kingdom of Egypt at that time to have extended no farther than it does at present; that is, 600 miles from North to South, and 250 from East to West, it must have contained, on the most moderate computation, as many inhabitants, at least, as the Kingdom of Great Britain does at this present time; Egypt was then the Emporium of the whole world, where all arts and sciences, commerce, agriculture, and polity flourished in a degree of perfection and refinement, superior, perhaps, to that of any part of Europe in our days. Accordingly, the number of Africans purchased by Joseph in one day, at the very moderate price of one year's maintenance per head, including their land, amounted, at least, to seven or eight millions of persons: a number not unequal, perhaps, to all the purchases of the kind ever made by English Merchants since the commencement of the GUINEA-TRADE .

3. The happy condition of these Africans, prior to Joseph's

purchase, is a circumstance worth observing: it differed in every respect from that of most of their present countrymen purchased by our European Merchants. The latter are generally Slaves, or Captives, in their native land; the former were all free and independent subjects: those, when purchased by our African Merchants are in a state of absolute indigence and poverty; whereas the latter were all people of property, and, indeed, of landed property; for it is very particularly specified in the scriptural account that *the Egyptians sold every man his field*; that is, his landed estate.

4. The circumstance of transporting Slaves from their native soil into a distant Country, is also very obvious in the conduct of Joseph, subsequent to the purchase he had made; for, *as for the people*, says the Scripture, *he removed them to cities, from one end of the borders of Egypt, even unto the other end thereof:* by which expedient he deprived them of every prospect of ever re-enjoying their respective paternal Estates, and the places of their nativity. And is it not more than probable, that, in the execution of so extensive a plan, as removing so many millions of inhabitants of every age, sex, condition, and rank, infants at the breast, young children, old and decrepit people, infirm and delicate, from one end of the borders of so extensive a Country as Egypt, even unto the other end thereof, many must have inevitably perished in passing through the scorching sands of a Country desolate with famine, and parched up, as it were, by an uninterrupted drought of six consecutive years, whatever wise regulations we may naturally suppose were made by Joseph to accommodate such an extraordi-

nary number of Slaves?

5. This numerous multitude of free and independent Africans, become now by contract menial Slaves to Pharaoh, are immediately sent by Joseph to cultivate their Master's Estates throughout all Egypt, for *the land became Pharaoh's*: so, that we may consider them with the utmost propriety, as so many Slaves, transported from their native place, and sent by their Master, or his Steward or Overseer, to work in his different Plantations, merely for their keep; for all the land was the property of Pharaoh, and the portion of the yearly produce of it, which they were allowed, is said to have been given them only *for seed of the fields, for their food, those of their housholds, and their little ones.*

6. The last and most interesting circumstance, in my opinion, attending this singular transaction, is the manner in which Joseph proceeded to effect his purchase. For, in consequence of that prophetic spirit, with which the Almighty had especially favoured him, and by which he foresaw the wonderful fertility of the land for seven years to come, and the extreme sterility of it for as many years after, he engrossed all the corn that grew in Egypt during the first seven years of plenty, and laid it up against the time of impending famine[30]. When this began to rage in the Land, he opened his stores, and made the Egyptians pay ready money for their corn: being entirely drained of cash, for *Joseph gathered up all the money, that was found in the land of Egypt*, he refused to supply them with bread, unless they gave all their cattle in exchange; which, accordingly, they did, for such proportion of corn as would keep them one year: being now reduced to the

last extremity, and entirely destitute of provisions, as well as of every means of procuring them, save their lands and persons, he availed himself of this favourable opportunity to effect a purchase, for which he had gradually paved the way: a bargain was accordingly concluded between him and Pharaoh's subjects, by which he bought all their lands and persons for as much corn, as would keep the latter the space of one year; which, from the circumstance of giving them feed, wherewith to sow the land, appears to have been the last of that septennial dearth. So, that, even taking advantage of the extreme indigence of his fellow-creatures, when able to relieve them, in order to reduce them to the condition of Slaves, was not deemed by this righteous, and inspired Man, *with whom the Lord was*, an infraction of those sacred laws of Nature, which were the invariable rule of his conduct.

XXI. How far Joseph's conduct in every stage of this remarkable transaction, so favouruable to the SLAVE-TRADE, may appear equitable or otherwise to the present humane advocates for African Liberty, through the feeble light of mere human reason and sense, I know not: this however is most certain, that there is not so much as one JOT in the Sacred Writings of the Word of God, that seems to disapprove in the most distant manner any one part of his conduct, either in this or in any other transaction of his long and holy life[31]. On the contrary, in every place of Scripture, where this eminent Personage is introduced, whether before or after this transaction, he is constantly represented as one of the most faithful and acceptable servants of God, under whose particular protection he lived and thrived[32]; by whose immediate direction he acted[33]; and who did nothing whatever, but the Almighty *made it to prosper*[34]. The very transaction, we are speaking of, when rehearsed by one of the inspired Writers[35], a Man according to God's own heart[36], is so far from being taxed with the least intimation of guilt in any one circumstance attending it, that the whole process, without any exceptions whatever, is there represented as the effect of that divine Wisdom, with which he was inspired from above.

XXII. A FURTHER scriptural evidence, that the conduct of Joseph in purchasing so many millions of his fellow-creatures, and reducing them to the condition of Slaves, met the entire approbation of God, and was therefore perfectly consonant to the sacred laws of Nature, is that remarkable declaration of the Word of God, registered in the First Book of CHRONICLES, c. 5. v. 1—3, which assigns the true reason for transferring the right of Primogeniture, or First-born, from the Family of Reuben, eldest son of Jacob, to the Family of Joseph; which, as it is expressly mentioned in that place, was Reuben's incestuous conversation with Bilhah, his Father's concubine[37].—But is it credible, consistently with the essential justice of God, that he should deprive Reuben's children of their Primogeniture or birth-right, for having once transgressed one of the Laws of Nature, and yet should at the same time, even in preference to Judah the Messiah's progenitor, give it to those of Joseph, who, by the very act of enslaving so many millions of his fellow-creatures, and using them as he did, must have necessarily incurred the horrid guilt of reiterated transgressions of several of those sacred Laws, if, what is so confidently asserted be true, that the SLAVE-TRADE, or the purchasing of Slaves, is an iniquitous unnatural pursuit, and a crime of the blackest die in direct opposition to every principle of Nature? How could any one in such chimerical supposition reconcile the visible partiality of God's conduct with his own Scriptural declarations of the eternal and immutable rectitude of his justice?

XXIII. ONE evidence more, drawn from the same scriptural source of conviction, will, I hope, be sufficient to evince the irreproachableness of Joseph's conduct in the transaction now before us. Every body knows, who knows any thing of Scripture, that the speeches made to their Children by the holy Patriarchs of old, prior to their departure from this world, called in the language of Scripture *Blessing the Children*[38], were so many prophetic declarations of the Word of God, predicting to them the future events that should distinguish them and their families, and entailing upon them and their posterity that portion of happiness or misery, to which their moral or immoral conduct entitled them. This being an undoubted truth, let us now examines with an attentive eye some of the most material circumstances of that solemn Blessing, which Jacob bestowed on Joseph and his Brethren a little before his death[39].

1. This Blessing was bestowed on Joseph and his Brethren about ten years after Joseph had enslaved all the inhabitants of Egypt, excepting those of the Sacerdotal Order[40].
2. Jacob in this Blessing reproaches Reuben, his eldest son, with the infamy of his incestuous crime in the strongest terms; and declares, that, in punishment of it, *he should not excel*, but should be as *unstable as water*.
3. Simeon and Levi are branded by the holy Patriarch with

being *Instruments of cruelty*; he abhors their counsels; calls their company dishonourable; curses the fierceness of their anger, and the cruelty of their wrath, *because in their anger*, says he, *they slew a man*; meaning Shechem the Hivite and his father Hamor, together with all his male subjects, whom *they slew with the sword*[41]; and, as a punishment of their barbarous cruelty, he declares they should be divided and scattered in the land of Promise.

4. When the Holy Patriarch comes to bless his son Joseph, he expresses himself in the following emphatic and divine strain. "Joseph is a fruitful bough; even a fruitful bough by a well, whose branches run over the wall. The archers have sorely grieved him, and shot at him, and hated him: but his bow abode in strength, and the arms of his hands were made strong by the hands of the mighty God of Jacob: from thence is the Shepherd, the stone of Israel; even by the God of thy father, who shall help thee, and by the Almighty, who shall bless thee with blessings of heaven above, blessings of the deep that lieth under, blessings of the breast, and of the womb. The blessings of thy father have prevailed above the blessings of my progenitors: unto the utmost bounds of the everlasting hills, they shall be on the head of Joseph, and on the crown of the head of him, that was separate from his brethren'[42].

In these prophetic and beautiful expressions, exhibiting in the most pleasing colours the personal character of Joseph, and the blessings entailed on his posterity, literally fulfilled afterwards, we can perceive nothing but what necessarily supposes in Joseph the greatest innocence of heart, the most unimpeachable rectitude of conduct, and the most gracious acceptance with his Creator. No part of his conduct is here branded with disgrace, with the least appearance of the smallest guilt, or with the most distant intimation of reproof.

BUT, were the SLAVE-TRADE as criminal in its nature as it is pretended, were it a pursuit hateful in the sight of God, and an atrocious encroachment on the sacred rights of justice and humanity, would Jacob, or, rather, would God, who spoke by his mouth, have overlooked the atrocity of a crime big with such an accumulation of guilt? Would he have engaged his word to be his help and protection, and to bestow such a plenitude of blessings on the crown of his head, as soon almost as he had concluded that Slave-contract we are speaking of, and at the very time he was keeping in bondage so many millions of his fellow-creatures? Would God, I say, or could God, without a most glaring opposition to the essential rights of his own justice, have acted thus in the case of Joseph, and at the same time rebuke his brethren Reuben, Simeon, and Levi in the severest terms, and inflict a lasting punishment on them and their posterity (though the former had only one accusation against him, and the two latter pleaded in justification of their violent proceedings the revenge due to their sister Dinah, and the honour of their Father's house[43]), had not Joseph's recent conduct in reducing so many millions of free Africans to the abject condition of Slaves, as well as every other transaction of his life, been perfectly agreeable to the invariable tenour of those sacred Laws, of which he alone was the Author and Judge?

To every one of these questions there is but one direct answer; which, as it must necessarily be in the negative, must of consequence evince to the meanest capacity, that the SLAVE-

TRADE has the indisputable sanction of God in its support.

XXIV. I WILL not conceal, or even disguise, in favour of the Cause I have espoused, what, I apprehend, will be objected to the argument I have just enforced, from the Scriptural account of Joseph's extensive purchase of African Slaves. —It will be objected, I presume, that Joseph's purchase was not a forcible purchase; that the Egyptians, whom he bought, offered themselves of their own accord, and desired he would buy them at a certain price[44]; and that, of course, the free and voluntary cession they made of their liberties and persons justified Joseph's conduct, and rendered his contract just and valid, without injuring the natural rights of justice and humanity; which being far otherwise in the usual practice of the SLAVE-TRADE, in which persons are sold and bought without their consent, the inferences drawn in vindication of that Trade from the practice of Joseph, can have no weight of conviction in support of the SLAVE-TRADE.— No one, I trust, will tax me with partiality to my Cause from the statement of this argument against myself: I have given it, I think, all the weight it is able to carry: how much it will weigh in the scale of sound and unprejudiced reason, will soon appear from the following considerations.
XXV.

1. I can by no means allow, that Joseph's purchase of Pharaoh's subjects was not a forcible purchase in fact, and in strictness of language. It is true, the Egyptians themselves, without any apparent explicit proposal on the part of Joseph, desired him to buy them for bread: but did they ever think of making that offer, whilst they had any bread to eat, or any means left for buying or procuring

it? Did not Joseph himself, prior to that offer, pave, as it were, the way to it, by engrossing all the corn in the land of Egypt, and by selling it to them for money and cattle, till they had neither money nor cattle to give in exchange? —Let us hear how they address themselves to him: their petition will best explain, how far their offer may be called voluntary on their part. "They came unto him the second year, *says the sacred Writer*, and said unto him: We will not hide it from my Lord, how that our money is spent; my Lord also hath our herds of cattle: there is not aught left in the sight of my Lord, but our bodies and our lands. *Wherefore shall we die* before thine eyes, both we and our land? Buy us and our land for bread, and we and our land will be servants unto Pharaoh; and give us seed, that *we may live and not die*, that the land be not desolate.'

Is this the language of persons, who freely, voluntarily, of their own accord, and without any compulsion whatever, offer themselves to sale? Is it not evident from the very words of their own address, that, finding themselves reduced to the last extremity of indigence, and seeing nothing before their eyes but inevitable death or slavery, they were forced, through dread of the former, to submit to the latter? And can there be a more forcible contract, than that which is made only through fear of death, only to avoid inevitable death? – The cession then made by the Egyptians of their liberties and persons, was neither in fact, nor in strictness of language, nor, indeed, in conformity with the Scriptural account of the circumstances attending it, a free and voluntary cession. Had not therefore Joseph had better grounds in the principles of his Natural Religion, of which he was a most strict observer, to assure himself of the justice of his contract, the cession of the Egyptians, forcible in the strictest propriety of the word, would never have rendered his Contract just and valid in the sight of God.

2. But even granting, for a moment, that the Egyptians did really make a free and voluntary cession of their liberties and persons; I do not see, upon what principle of reason their cession could justify Joseph's conduct and make his purchase lawful, if, as it is so confidently asserted, the SLAVE-TRADE be essentially unjust and illicit in its own nature. For, if to purchase those of our own species be highly criminal in itself, be an unjust invasion on the rights of justice and humanity, and directly opposite to the Sacred Laws of Nature, how is it possible to conceive, that any cession whatever of the party to be purchased should make that just and lawful in the sight of God, which by his unalterable eternal laws is essentially the very reverse? Can human agreements dispense in the laws of God? Whatever is essentially unjust and illicit to purchase, must be as essentially unjust and illicit to sell. —The objection then grounded on the pretended voluntary cession of the Egyptians, however plausible it may appear at first, is utterly inconclusive and ill founded.

XXVI. I could easily produce a greater number of distinguished Characters within this period of the Law of Nature, whose uniform manner of acting, with reference to the present subject, would afford me an additional number of arguments in vindication of the SLAVE-TRADE. But as the Sacred Book, where those great Patterns of every religious and social virtue are exhibited, is in every body's hands, and, as I have sufficiently demonstrated, I think, from the Scriptural account of two of the most eminent Characters within the same period, that the SLAVE-TRADE has the indisputable sanction of Divine Authority, and is in exact conformity with the principles of the Law of Nature, as delineated in the Sacred Writings of the Word of God, I shall now proceed to demonstrate in the subsequent Section, that it is equally conformable to the principles of the Mosaic Law.

SECTION II

Scriptural Researches on the licitness of the Slave-Trade, shewing its conformity with the principles of the Mosaic Law delineated in the Sacred Writings.

I. THE Mosaic Law, called also the Written Law, and the Mosaic Dispensation, succeeded the Dispensation of the Law of Nature: not, as if, by the publication of the former[45], the latter had been totally abrogated, or suffered the least relaxation in any of its laws, which are of perpetual obligation; but because the Almighty willing to establish a Covenant with his Chosen People, the Children of Israel, added to the former obligations such other statutes, Laws, and ceremonies, as were to distinguish them from every other Nation in the World. This Law is very frequently called, even in Scripture, the Law of Moses[46], and Moses is said to have been the Law-giver or the Legislator of the Children of Israel; not because it was framed by him, but because the Almighty delivered it to them through his ministry, and he committed it to writing. How long this Law was in force from the first promulgation of it, has been the subject of much inquiry among the Learned: but, without entering now into a critical discussion of this controverted point, we may safely venture to fix that period, without either advantage or prejudice to the Subject of our Researches, to the time of the Apostles Council held at Jerusalem, in which the Law of Circumcision and other Legal observances were, by an express Decree of that Council, declared unnecessary to Salvation, and consequently of no further obligation[47]. This Council, according to the computation of Archbishop Usher, was held in the Year of the World 4055; and as the Law was promulged in the Year 2513, according to the chronological computation of the same Author; it follows, that the Law of Moses, or the Mosaic Dispensation, continued in force 1542 Years.

II. Now, before I proceed to shew, that the Laws and principles of this second Divine Dispensation of Religion, not only never prohibited the SLAVE-TRADE, but gave, on the contrary, a positive sanction to the prosecution of it; I judge necessary to apprize the Reader, that the arguments I mean to enforce in vindication of the SLAVE-TRADE, as confined to this second period of true Religion, shall be entirely grounded on such written laws and principles of internal moral rectitude, as constituted the true morality of that Religion; and not on such Legal observances and practices, as were peculiar to it, and constituted only the ritual, typical, or ceremonial part of its frame. The following decisive instances of the former sort, will, without producing others, be sufficient, I hope, to establish my assertion beyond the power of reply.

EXODUS.

III. It is singular enough, that the very first Law, or *Judgement*, in the Scripture language, enacted by God himself immediately after he had delivered the Ten Commandments to his People, should be respecting the SLAVE-TRADE; and that also with the additional circumstance of not restraining them from purchasing their own brethren, their own flesh and blood! "These are the judgements, *says God to Moses,* which thou shalt set before them. If thou buy an Hebrew Servant, six years he shall serve, and in the seventh he shall go out free for nothing. If he came in by himself, he shall go out by himself; if he were married, then his wife shall go out with him. If his Master have given him a wife, and she have borne him sons and daughters; the wife and her children shall be her Master's, and he shall go out by himself.'[48]

IV. HERE, it is evident in the first place, that, however limited the time was of the Slavery of an Hebrew, he was yet in the strictest sense of the word a true and real Slave for the time; for he was his Master's property, bought for a certain price; and his Master, on this account, had an undoubted right and power to sell him again to another person before the expiration of that time. But, were the SLAVE-TRADE, or the purchasing of those of our own species, and dealing in human flesh, a pursuit of that heinous and crying nature, as to be essentially unlawful, essentially incompatible with the principles of reason, nature, and true Religion, would God, Justice and Sanctity itself, have authorized the practice of it with so positive, so manifest, so explicit a sanction, I do not say for the space of six years, but even for a single moment, at the very time he was making his Holy Covenant with his chosen People, and teaching them the very principles of true Religion?

AGAIN: the Hebrew, thus bought by his Brother, and reduced to the condition of a Slave, under the express sanction of God, was a Child of the Circumcision: now, Circumcision, under the Mosaic Dispensation, was a solemn, religious Rite answering that of Baptism in the Christian Law: it was a token of the Covenant between God and his People[49], as essentially requisite in every male person, who hoped for acceptance with God[50], as is Baptism in the Covenant of the New Law. If then, notwithstanding the prerogative of Circumcision, which made the professors of the Mosaic Law true Children of God, true believers, and members of his Church, a free circumcised Israelite was still subject to the law of human bondage or slavery, and that even under the dominion of one of his own Communion and Church; from what maxim or principle of true Religion and justice does it follow, that a Slave, once admitted into the Covenant of the New Law, acquires by his admission a right to his emancipation from human bondage? that is, a right to deprive his Master of his property?

IN fine; it is manifest from the very letter of the Law just quoted, that, even in the Case of an Hebrew reduced to the condition of a Slave for a limited time, the Master's purchase of that Slave was so essentially just and lawful in every part of it, that, though, by an especial ordinance of God peculiar to that People only, the Slave was to be released from bondage in the seventh year, or the year of the Jubilee; yet the right of property, acquired by that purchase, was declared by God to be so vested in the Master, that, if the Master had given a wife to his Slave, that is, if the Slave had married a wife during the time of his servitude with the consent of his Master, both she and her children, if he had any by her, became the Master's property for ever: in which Case, it is worth observing, that the Slave thus emancipated, though a member of the true Church, was ordered to *go out by himself,* and leave his wife and children behind.—A separation this between husband and wife, father and children, well deserving the particular attention of every religious and humane advocate for African Liberty! — And can any one after this entertain the most distant doubt on the licitness of the SLAVE-TRADE, so positively, so unequivocally, so strongly authorized by this written ordinance of the Word of God?

LEVITICUS.

V. THE farther I proceed in my Scriptural Researches, the stronger the evidences appear to me in favour of the SLAVE-TRADE. Indeed, I have every encouragement given me in this Sacred Book of LEVITICUS to advance a step farther, and maintain, that the SLAVE-TRADE, has not only the sanction of Divine Authority in its support, but was also positively encouraged (I had almost said, *commanded*) by that Authority, under the Dispensation of the Mosaic Law. The following plain and explicit words of one of the laws respecting that Trade, and registered in this Book, can admit of no other construction.

> "Both thy bond-men and bond-maids, *says the Supreme Law-giver,* which thou shalt have, shall be of the heathen that are round about you; of them shall ye buy bond-men and bond-maids. Moreover, of the Children of the Strangers that do sojourn among you; of them shall ye buy; and of their families that are with you, which they begat in your land: and they shall be your possession. And ye shall take them as an inheritance for your children after you to inherit them for a possession; they shall be your bond-men for ever'[51].

VI. If there be meaning in language, or sense in words, here is certainly a Law enacted by Divine Authority, which does not only give a most positive and unexceptionable sanction to the licitness of the SLAVE-TRADE, but seems farther to lay, as it were, an injunction on the Children of Israel to prosecute that Traffic under no other restriction whatever, but that of confining their purchases of perpetual Slaves to the heathen round about them, and the Strangers, that sojourned among them; for the words of the Law-giver evidently imply more than a mere permission or leave: He does not say, speaking of the Heathen and Sojourn-ers, *Of them* MAY *ye buy bond-men and bond-maids,* but, *of them* SHALL *ye buy bond-men and bond-maids.*

AGAIN: the words of this Law, and they are the words of God, do expressly declare, that Slaves thus purchased from the Heathen and Sojourners among them, shall be the *Possession,* that is, the real and lawful property, of the purchasers: a property so strictly their own, that they shall bequeath it to their Children at their death, as a part of their just and lawful inheritance, a part of their paternal estate, an estate for ever, for *they shall be your bond-men for ever, s*ays the Law: that is, an hereditary estate with all the emoluments arising from it; and, consequently, with all the children born from them, agreeably to the tenour of that Law of EXODUS, which has been explained in the IVth Number of this SECTION; for otherwise the children of a Heathen Slave or a Stranger would have enjoyed a privilege, which an Hebrew Slave was denied, though a Slave only for a limited time.

VII. FROM this most decisive, most explicit, and irrefragable authority of the Written Word of God, visibly encouraging the prosecution of the SLAVE-TRADE, and declaring in the most categorical language that words can devise, that a Slave is the real, indisputable, and lawful property of the purchaser and his heirs for ever, it necessarily follows by force of consequence, that either the SLAVE-TRADE must be in its own intrinsic nature a just and an honest Trade, and by no means deserving those harsh epithets and names with which it is so frequently branded and degraded; or, that, if it does still deserve those odious names and epithets in consequence of its intrinsic turpitude and immorality, the Almighty did so far forget himself, when he made the above Law, as to patronize a manifest injustice, encourage a most criminal violation of his other laws, and give his sacred sanction to what humanity itself must for ever abhor and detest.—As there can be no medium betwixt these two unavoidable inferences, and the latter is one of the most daring blasphemies that the human heart can conceive, I leave the religious Reader to judge for himself, which side of the Question is the safest to embrace.

JOSHUA.

VIII. THE prudent and well concerted stratagem of the inhabitants of Gibeon, with all the circumstances attending its final issue, of minutely described in the IXth Chapter of this Sacred Book, will, when viewed in its proper light, add no small weight of authority to the justice of the SLAVE-TRADE. The Scriptural account of this entertaining transaction, long as it may appear to some, cannot well be contracted, without injuring its beautiful texture: the following is a literal transcript of it.

V. 3. And when the inhabitants of Gibeon heard, what Joshua had done unto Jericho, and to Ai,

4. They did work wilily, and went and made as if they had been Ambassadors, and took old sacks upon their asses, and wine-bottles, old, and rent and bound up:

5. And old shoes, and clouted upon their feet, and old garments upon them: and all the bread of their provision was dry and mouldy.

6. And they went to Joshua, unto the Camp of Gilgal, and said unto him, and to the men of Israel: we be come from a far country; now therefore make ye a league with us.

7. And the men of Israel said unto the Hivites: per-adventure ye dwell among us, and how shall we make a league with you?

8. And they said unto Joshua: we are thy servants. And Joshua said unto them: who are ye? and from whence come ye?

9. And they said unto him: from a very far country thy servants are come, because of the name of the Lord thy God; for we have heard of the fame of him, and all that he did in Egypt,

10. And all that he did to the two Kings of the Amorites, that were beyond Jordan, to Sihon King of Heshbon, and to Og King of Bashan, which was at Ashtaroth.

11. Wherefore our Elders and all the Inhabitants of our country spake to us, saying: take victuals with you for the journey, and go to meet them, and say unto them: we are your servants: therefore now make ye a league with us.

12. This our bread we took hot for our provision out of our houses, on the day we came forth to go unto you; but now behold, it is dry, and it is mouldy.:

13. And these bottles of wine which were filled, were new; and behold, they be rent; and these our garments and our

shoes are become old, by reason of the very long journey.

14. And the men took of their victuals, and asked not counsel at the mouth of the Lord.

15. And Joshua made peace with them, and made a league with them, to let them live: and the Princes of the Congregation sware unto them.

16. And it came to pass at the end of three days, after they had made a league with them, that they heard that they were neighbours, and that they dwelt among them.

17. And the Children of Israel journeyed, and came into their Cities on the third day: now their Cities were Gibeon, and Chephirah, and Beeroth, and Kiriath-jearim.

18. And the Children of Israel smote them not, because the Princes of the Congregation had sworn unto them by the Lord God of Israel: and all the Congregation murmured against the Princes.

19. But all the Princes said unto all the Congregation: We have sworn unto them by the Lord God of Israel: now therefore we may not touch them.

20. This we will do them; we will even let them live, lest wrath be upon us, because of the oath which we sware unto them.

21. And the Princes said unto them: let them live (but let them be hewers of wood, and drawers of water unto all the Congregation), as the Princes had promised them.

22. And Joshua called for them, and he spake unto them, saying: wherefore have ye beguiled us, saying, We are very far from you? when ye dwell among us.

23. Now therefore ye are cursed, and there shall none of you be freed from being bond-men, and hewers of wood, and

drawers of water for the house of my God.

24. And they answered Joshua, and said: because it was certainly told thy servants, how that the Lord thy God commanded his servant Moses to give you all the land, and to destroy all the inhabitants of the land from before you, therefore we were fore afraid of our lives, because of you, and have done this thing.

25. And now, behold, we are in thine hand: as it seemeth good and right unto thee to do unto us, do.

26. And so did he unto them, and delivered them out of the hand of the Children of Israel, and they slew them not.

27. And Joshua made them that day hewers of wood, and drawers of water for the Congregation, and for the Altar of the Lord, even unto this day, in the place which he should chuse.

IX. THE following observations seem to arise spontaneously from the circumstances related in this interesting portion of Scripture.

1. The Gibeonites were in the number of those inhabitants of the Land of Canaan, who, by the express command of God, were to be utterly proscribed, and driven out of the Land, by the Children of Israel: *Thou shalt make no covenant with them, nor with their Gods*, said the Almighty to his People; *they shall not dwell in thy Land*[52].

2. To ward this impending doom, of which they were well apprized, as appears from their reply to Joshua, they had recourse to a stratagem, which, for want of Joshua consulting the divine Oracle, succeeded to the utmost of their wishes; for they made a league, and a treaty of peace

and amity with Joshua and his People; and by virtue of this National Treaty, which was confirmed to them with the solemn sanction of an oath, and never annulled, but rather ratified in the sequel by God himself, they were exempted from the general doom, and became in every sense of the word free allies and friends to the Children of Israel.—Indeed, the sentiments of Religion and humility, so visible both in their first address and their reply to Joshua's charge, and their not joining in the general league of the neighbouring Kings, who all combined *with one accord* to fight against Israel[53], speak a sense of repentance, which might have induced the Almighty to reverse his sentence, and suffer their stratagem to succeed.

3. As soon as this was discovered, we find, that the Gibeonites were all consigned by Joshua to perpetual Slavery, *unto this day*; that is, with all their posterity; notwithstanding the sentence of proscription, the only one that the Almighty had pronounced against them, and was to be executed by Joshua, had been entirely reversed; notwithstanding they had every claim, by virtue of the recent Treaty they had so solemnly concluded with him and his People, to all the privileges and franchises of free Allies.

X. To say, that the sentence of death pronounced against the Gibeonites in several places of Scripture[54], was afterwards changed by the Almighty into that of perpetual and hereditary bondage or slavery, is to advance what is never to be found in any part of the Sacred Records; from the whole tenour of which it appears manifest, that the perpetual bondage, to which they were consigned with all their posterity, was the sole act and deed of Joshua, suggested apparently by the Princes of the

Congregation of Israel, who, prior to Joshua's curse upon them, in order to silence the murmurs of the multitude, had declared their intention of employing the Gibeonites in the servile occupation of *hewers of wood, and drawers of water unto all the Congregation.*

Now, had Joshua's sentence of perpetual bondage been only a commutation of that of death, to which the Almighty had condemned the Gibeonites, had it not been lawful in itself, on other accounts, to reduce the innocent as well as the guilty to the condition of Slaves; the sentence of perpetual bondage pronounced by Joshua, ought, one would imagine, to have extended no farther, than the persons of the Gibeonites then living, any more than did the sentence of death, in lieu of which that of perpetual bondage is said to have been substituted. The slavery then of their innocent posterity, at least, cannot be said to have been in lieu of death, to which certainly they had never been condemned.

It being therefore evident from the uniform tenour of the Sacred Writings, that neither the reduction of the Gibeonites then living, nor that of their guiltless descendants, yet unborn, to perpetual Slavery, was ever condemned by any mark or intimation whatever of God's displeasure, but manifestly ratified in the sequel by several undoubted assurances of his divine approbation; it is easy to conclude, whether the reducing of the innocent as well as the guilty part of our fellow-creatures to the condition of Slaves, or even to hereditary bondage or Slavery, be in its own nature licit or illicit, criminal or just.

XI. As a mark of the Almighty's undoubted approbation of Joshua's conduct in the transaction just before us, we find in the continuation of this history[55], that He even secured to his

People the possession of these Slaves, and their posterity, by a most signal victory, which he enabled them to obtain over five Kings of the Amorites; who, in consequence of the Gibeonites having made a league and a treaty of peace with Joshua and his People, joined all their forces against them, and made a vigorous attempt to invade this new acquisition of the Children of Israel. The exertions of his divine power for securing to his People this new acquired property of Slaves were so wonderfully great, that he even fought *in Person* against, the invaders; for "The Lord, *says the Sacred Writer*, discomfitted them before Israel, and slew them with a great slaughter at Gibeon, and chased them along the way that goeth up to Bethhoron, and smote them to Azekah, and unto Makkedah. And it came to pass, as they fled from before Israel, and were in the going down to Bethhoron, that the Lord cast down great stones from heaven upon them unto Azekah, and they died: they were more which died with hailstones, than they whom the Children of Israel slew with the sword"[56].

AND, in order to render the victory still more complete, and the part he took in defending the rights of his People over the Gibeonites more visible to the whole world, he even wrought a miracle of the most singular kind; for, *harkning*, as the Sacred Page expresses it, *unto the voice of a Man*, that is, of Joshua, who, in the heat of action, ordered *the Sun to stand still upon Gibeon, and the Moon in the valley of Ajalon,* he stayed them both *about a whole day, until the People had avenged themselves upon their enemies*[57], for attempting to destroy the inhabitants of Gibeon their bond-slaves.

XII. IF these wonderful atchievements of the power of God in favour of his chosen People in the very case of protecting the persons, whom they had so lately reduced to perpetual and hereditary bondage, are not to be considered as so many evident testimonies of his divine approbation of the immediate object of the SLAVE-TRADE, and a positive sanction to the licitness of it, but are still consistent with any intrinsic moral turpitude inherent to the nature of that Trade; the abettors of this opinion must necessarily maintain, that the Supreme Ruler of the Universe, in direct opposition to his own essential attributes and perfections, in manifest contradiction with his own moral laws and commandments, and in vindication of ill-gotten property, displayed to the World the most extraordinary exertions of his Omnipotence, and disturbed the very course of Nature to make it subservient to the vilest of purposes, injustice and oppression.— As the inference is as blasphemous as it is necessary, the very mentioning of it will, I flatter myself, be sufficient to determine the judgement of any religious and candid Reader in favour of the inherent moral licitness of the SLAVE-TRADE.

XIII. I HAVE, I think, sufficiently proved from the Scriptural Passages I have produced in the series of this SECOND PART, that the SLAVE-TRADE has the positive sanction of Divine Authority in its support, and is perfectly consonant to the Principles of the Mosaic Dispensation delineated in the Sacred Writings of the Word of God.

I HAVE, however, this one thing to observe before I proceed to the THIRD PART, in order to preclude every avenue to groundless objections; that there is not a Place in all the Writings of the Word of God, whether of the OLD or of the NEW TESTAMENT, that does so much as insinuate in the most distant manner, that the Slaves bought either within the period of the Law of Nature, that of the Mosaic Dispensation, or that of the Christian Law, were to serve during a certain number of years and no longer, except, the Hebrew Slaves; who, for reasons peculiar only to that People, and not applicable even to Christian Slaves, were to serve no longer than six years in the capacity of Bond-Slaves. In every other case, the words BOND-MAN, BOND-WOMAN, BOND-MAID, BOND-SERVANT, SERVANT UNDER THE YOKE, imply, in the Scripture-language, perpetual and unlimited bondage, bondage for life, both of the male and female reduced to that condition, and even of their posterity or children, if they had any.—Nor is there one instance to be met with in the Sacred Volumes, of the manumission or emancipation of a Slave of either sex, except of the Hebrew race, who ever obtained release from bondage, on account of having served any determinate number of years.

THE dismission of Hagar, bond-woman to Abraham, from her Master's house, is so far from being an instance of this kind, that every circumstance attending her discharge seems to prove the very reverse[58]. She was *sent away* by Abraham, at the earnest solicitation of his wife Sarai, whose counsel the Almighty ordered him to follow: but the reluctance he shewed to turn her out of his house, when it was first proposed to him by Sarai, for *the thing was very grievous in his sight* (or, according to the Original, *The word was very bad in the eyes of Abraham*), and the reason of her dismission, evidently shew that her discharge was not in consequence of any contract whatever, by which she was bound to serve a determinate number of years and no longer, there being not the least intimation given in the Sacred History of any such contract or agreement, but because her son's behaviour to Isaac, the promised and right Heir of the Family, was exceedingly odious and very alarming to Sarai; who, dreading the consequences of Ishmael's *perfection* of young

Isaac, for so the Apostle styles it[59], insisted on his being *cast out* together with his mother Hagar.

XIV. THE Scriptural acceptation and extent of the word BONDAGE, and the relatives to it, being thus fixed and ascertained from the very letter and uniform tenour of Scripture itself, no arguments whatever, grounded on the true and real sense in which that word and its relatives are used in the Sacred Page, will ever evince, that a Slave, within the period of any of the Three Dispensations of true Religion mentioned in the Sacred Annals of the Word of God, not born an Hebrew, was ever bound by contract or otherwise to serve only a limited number of years, at the expiration of which he obtained his freedom, and was left at liberty to chuse for himself.

SECTION III

Scriptural Researches on the licitness of the Slave-Trade, shewing its conformity with the principles of the Christian Dispensation delineated in the Sacred Writings.

I. THE Christian Dispensation, called frequently the Christian Law, the Law of Christ, the Christian Religion, the Law of Grace, the New Law, and the New Covenant or the New Testament, is that most sublime and perfect System of Faith and morality, which the Eternal Wisdom of the Father, Christ Jesus our Lord, both, preached in Person, and sealed with his precious blood. As this New Law and Gospel of salvation is to remain in full force until the consummation of all things, or till time shall be no more, it is not in the power of any creature to ascertain the exact time of its duration and existence from the first promulgation of it; for *Of that day, and that hour knoweth no man, no not the Angels which are in heaven, neither the* SON, *but the* FATHER[60]

II. THE principal transactions relative to this New Law are registered in the several inspired Writings, that compose the Sacred Volume commonly styled THE NEW TESTAMENT. The principles and moral duties of perpetual obligation respecting *Right* and *Wrong, Justice* and *Injustice*, registered in this Sacred Volume, being evidently dictated by the HOLY SPIRIT of God, and God himself, cannot consistently with the essential infallibility of his eternal Wisdom, bear the least opposition to the principles and moral duties of perpetual obligation respecting, in like manner, *Right* and *Wrong, Justice* and *Injustice*, dictated by the same infallible SPIRIT, and registered in the several inspired Writings, that compose the Sacred Volume commonly styled THE OLD TESTAMENT, comprehending such transactions, as relate to both the Natural and the Mosaic Laws. — Were it possible to be otherwise, God would not be consistent with himself, and the Religion of the New Testament, instead of being the perfection and accomplishment, would be the reproach and condemnation of both the former Laws, Natural and Mosaic, on the truth of which its very existence depends.

III. FROM this undeniable position it follows necessarily, that, as the Writings of both the Testaments have the same weight of Authority, essentially incapable of contradicting itself, in support of those principles and decisions, enacted and registered in their respective Records, concerning the intrinsic morality or immorality of human actions, whatever is declared in the One to be intrinsically good or bad, just or unjust, licit or illicit, must inevitably be so according to the principles of the Other. — If therefore, the SLAVE-TRADE appears, as, I trust, it does, from the preceding train of Scriptural arguments, in perfect harmony with the principles and decisions of the Word of God, registered in the Sacred Writings of the Old Testament, respecting the intrinsic nature of that Trade, this, of course, can bear no opposition to, but must necessarily be in equal perfect harmony with, the principles and decisions of the Word of God respecting *Right* and *Justice*, registered in the Sacred Writings of the New.

THIS general but forcible argument, were it even unsupported by any collateral evidences from the Writings of the New Testament, would be fully sufficient to verify my third and last assertion respecting the Licitness of the SLAVE-TRADE, as perfectly conformable to the principles, of the Christian Dispensation.

IV. I HAVE been the more particular in bringing this last part of my Scriptural Researches to this central point of view, as I have more than one reason to apprehend, that several of my Readers will be apt to imagine, that, by the establishment of the Christian Religion, the Law of Moses was wholly abolished and annulled in every part of it, and to every intent and purpose, both typical and moral, of its original institution; and that, of course, the arguments drawn in vindication of the SLAVE-TRADE from the Writings of the Old Testament, can have no weight of conviction or authority with persons, who are subject to no other Laws and Ordinances, but those of a Dispensation, by which that was entirely laid aside.

V. TRUE as this assertion is with respect to the ritual, typical, and ceremonial part of the Mosaic Law, which, in this sense, is now utterly abolished, and no longer obligatory to the Professors of the Gospel, it is not less erroneous and false with respect to those fundamental principles of righteousness enacted in that Law, which relate to the intrinsic morality or immorality, licitness or illicitness of human actions which, from the invariable nature of *Right* and *Wrong*, *Justice* and *Injustice*, must be of perpetual obligation, and as unchangeable as God himself; who never did, nor ever could alter by any Dispensation whatever those eternal principles and laws, which are the very basis and foundation of true Religion, and consequently of the Religion of Christ.

WE have no less an authority in confirmation of this indisputable Doctrine, than the very words of the Son of God, who, in that divine Sermon on the Mount, in which he gave his Disciples a most minute and circumstantial account of the principles and tenets of his Gospel, condemned the above erroneous opinion in the most explicit terms, and forbade them even to think of it: *Think not*, said he, *that I am come to destroy the Law or the Prophets; I am not come to destroy but to fulfil*[61].

IT was on the principle of this Doctrine of the Son of God, and on purpose to guard against every exception to arguments drawn from the Writings of the Old Testament in favour of the SLAVE-TRADE, which some persons would be apt to make in consequence of the above erroneous opinion, that I especially apprized the Reader in the II[d] Number of the last SECTION, that the arguments I meant to enforce in that Section in vindication of that Trade, would be entirely grounded, as they certainly are; on such written and explicit laws and principles of internal moral rectitude, as constituted the true morality of the Mosaic

Dispensation, and not on such Legal observances and practices, as were peculiar to it, and constituted only the ritual, typical, or ceremonial part of its frame.

VI. THE permanent and indefectible authority of the Old Testament, and the necessary conformity of the New with the principles and declarations of the former respecting the intrinsic nature of *Right* and *Wrong, Justice* and *Injustice*, being thus firmly established and ascertained; I shall now proceed, for argument's sake, to substantiate in a more particular manner the merits of the present Controversy with reference to the principles and tenets of the New Testament; which, from the unanswerable, though general, argument just enforced, appears already to give a sanction to the licitness of the SLAVE-TRADE, the intrinsic morality of which is so evidently warranted by those invariable principles and decisions of the Old, with which, as proved before, it must necessarily agree.

VII. THAT there is nothing, in the Writings of the New Testament, that can be produced in justification of the SLAVE-TRADE, has been confidently asserted by many; and from this *supposed silence* of the Inspired Writers, they have as confidently concluded, that the professors of Christianity are not justifiable in prosecuting a Trade, which, not having, in their opinion, the Sanction of the New Testament, must of course be essentially opposite to the principles of true Christianity, which forbids in the most explicit terms, and under the severest punishments, all acts of injustice, unnaturalness, and oppression.

VIII. The stronger this inference, founded indeed on a false supposition, appears to the Advocates for African Liberty against the licitness of the SLAVE-TRADE, the more powerful the following arguments must appear to them; which, from the same negative principle, not of *supposed*, but *real*, silence respecting the pretended illicitness of it, amounting in fact to a positive sanction in our Case, seem manifestly to evince, that the SLAVE-TRADE bears no opposition whatever to the principles of the Christian Law.

1. IF the Writings of the New Testament mention nothing, as it is *falsely supposed*, in vindication of the SLAVE-TRADE neither do they *in reality* and *truth* mention any thing in condemnation of it; if then the *supposed* silence of the Inspired Writers respecting the licitness of that Trade, that is, their not mentioning that Trade at all, as it is *supposed*, can be brought as an argument of its moral inconsistency with the principles of true Christianity; the real silence of the same respecting the pretended illicitness of it, that is, their not condemning the Trade at all, though publickly practiced in their time, and by the very persons whom they were deputed to teach the principles and duties of Christianity, must be a stronger argument by far of the inherent moral conformity of the SLAVE-TRADE with the principles and tenets of the Religion of Christ: for it shews in the strongest light, that the first Teachers of Christianity, who were also the Inspired Writers of the New Testament, never considered the SLAVE-TRADE, or had been taught by their Master to consider it, as an infraction of any of the principles or moral precepts of his Gospel.

2. In effect; this constant and uniform silence of the Sacred Writers of the New Testament in a matter of such public

notoriety; I mean their never disapproving the practice of a Trade, in which the rights of Christian justice and humanity are said to be so materially injured, ought to attract the particular attention of every impartial inquirer into the merits of the present Controversy.

IT is an absolute fact, attested by all Historians, both Sacred and Prophane, that at the very time that Christianity made its appearance in the World, as well as at the time that the Apostles and Disciples of Christ were employed in preaching and propagating throughout the World his holy Gospel and Doctrine, both before and after the same had been committed to writing, that is, before and after the New Testament was written, that the practice of Slavery, or the SLAVE-TRADE, was universally adopted by the very Nations to whom they brought the glad tidings of salvation, and who, through faith, repentance, and obedience to the maxims and doctrine they preached, were received into the Covenant of reconciliation and grace; and yet it is not less certain from the constant tenour of the Sacred Writings of the New Testament, that desisting from the prosecution of the SLAVE-TRADE, or manumitting those who were in actual bondage, was never declared by any of the Apostles or first Teachers of Christianity to be a necessary term of Salvation or acceptance with God, or an indispensable duty of a follower of Christ.

BUT were the Trade so diametrically opposite to the principles of Christianity, as it is asserted, were it a most unjustifiable usurpation of the sacred rights of justice and humanity, would the Apostles have suffered those sacred rights to be thus invaded and trampled upon with impunity, without so much as signifying to those, whom they were commissioned to teach the Gospel of righteousness and peace, of love and charity, that it was in open contradiction with the principles and precepts of that Gospel?

3. INFINE: this manner of reasoning to prove the moral conformity of the SLAVE-TRADE with the principles of the Christian Dispensation, acquires a degree of irresistible force, when applied to the conduct of our Blessed Saviour in his public character of Founder and Teacher of the New Law; for though he embraced every opportunity of reproving in the severest terms such irreligious abuses as were practised by the Jews, and of rectifying such false glosses, traditions, and comments, as had been added by them to the Law of Moses; yet he never once condemned, reproved, or even hinted the least disapprobation of the practice of Slavery, so generally adopted in his time: no, not even in his Divine Sermon on the Mount, in which he spoke on set purpose of the most exalted duties of his Religion, entered into a minute and most circumstantial detail of many reciprocal offices and duties he required of his followers, and rectified some abuses, incomparably less criminal than would be that of enslaving our fellow creatures, were this practice so very criminal and unjust as is represented by some modern advocates for African Liberty[62].

4. THE fact is: that, since neither the SON of God, being himself God, nor his Disciples commissioned to teach his doctrine, could ever alter the intrinsic nature of *Right* and *Wrong;* once the practice of Slavery, or the SLAVE-TRADE,

had been expressly declared by the FATHER essentially just and lawful in the Sacred Writings of the Old Law, which the SON *did not come to destroy, but to fulfil*[63], it was absolutely impossible, that either HE or his Disciples should declare it unlawful and unjust in the Writings of the New, the principles of both the Laws, respecting the intrinsic nature of *Right* and *Wrong, Justice* and *Injustice*, being invariably the same.

IT follows then, that the argument drawn in favour of the SLAVE-TRADE from the constant silence of the Inspired Writers of the New Testament respecting the pretended illicitness of that Trade, that is, from their never mentioning any thing against the licitness of it, which, in the circumstances above related, would have been only a negative inference, though of considerable weight in vindication of it, becomes now, from this last very material circumstance, a most powerful positive argument, shewing in the strongest light, that the nature of the SLAVE-TRADE is perfectly consonant to the principles and tenets of the Christian Law.

IX. THOUGH the argument built on the *supposed silence* of the Inspired Writers of the New Testament respecting the licitness of the SLAVE-TRADE, is very amply confuted by the preceding arguments drawn from the *real silence* of the same Sacred Writers respecting the pretended illicitness of it, which are, indeed, abundantly sufficient to establish beyond the power of cavil or reply this last part of my SCRIPTURAL RESEARCHES; yet, lest any one should still persist in maintaining the opinion so generally received, that there is nothing *positive* in the Writings of the New Testament, that can be produced in justification of the SLAVE-TRADE, I think it expedient to select one or two principal instances out of these Sacred Books, which, I flatter myself, will not only gratify his curiosity, but serve to convince him in the plainest manner, that, however general his opinion may be, it is not so evident as he has been taught to believe.

I. EPISTLE TO TIMOTHY.

X. AMONG the several instructions given in this EPISTLE by St. Paul to his beloved Disciple Timothy for the Government of the Church of Ephesus, of which he was Bishop, there are some concerning the general duties of that part of his Flock, who were under the yoke of bondage or Slavery, that seem to claim our particular attention. The instructions, here alluded to, are in the VIth Chapter of this EPISTLE, and are the following: —

V.1. Let as many servants as are under the yoke, count their own Masters worthy of all honour, that the name of God, and his doctrine, be not blasphemed.

2. And they that have believing Masters, let them not despise them, because they are brethren: but rather do them service, because they are faithful and beloved, partakers of the benefit. These things teach and exhort.

3. If any man teach otherwise, and consent not to wholesome words, even the words of our Lord Jesus Christ, and to the doctrine which is according to godliness,

4. He is proud, knowing nothing, but doting about questions, and strifes of words, whereof cometh envy, strife, railings, evil surmisings, &c.

XI. THE Apostle in these words describes two classes of Christian

Slaves, or Servants under the yoke of bondage: Slaves subject to unbelievers, and Slaves subject to true believers or Christians; and, according to their respective situations, he specifies the general duties belonging to each class.

1. THE former are exhorted to *count their own Masters*, though Infidels, *worthy of all honour:* that is, they are exhorted to shew their Masters, both in words and actions, such unfeigned marks of honour, submission, and respect, as they have a right to claim, for *they are worthy of all honour*, from the superiority of their rank and station in life, and the authority they have acquired over them by the possession of their persons. The reason for enforcing such dutiful deportment is very powerful: you are to exhort them, says the Apostle to Timothy, to behave in this becoming manner, *that the name of God, and his doctrine, be not blasphemed*: that is, left the unbelieving Masters, seeing the contrary deportment in their Christian Slaves, attribute their insolent, disrespectful, and disobedient conduct, to the principles and doctrine of their Religion, and thus bring reproach and infamy upon both.

2. THE latter Class of Christian Slaves, subject to Christian Masters, are earnestly exhorted, not only not to be less respectful and obsequious to the latter for being their brethren in Christ, and joint-members with them of the same Communion and Church, as if they were their equals in every respect, but to show, on this very account, in their readiness and zeal to serve them, a superior degree of submission and obedience to their lawful authority; not considering themselves upon a footing of natural equality with those whose Slaves they are, though entitled at the

same time to all the promises and spiritual franchises of true Believers.

XII. From the tenour of these Apostolic instructions, confirmed by many other similar declarations to the same effect, frequently occurring in the Writings of the New Testament, I am naturally led to deduce the following consequences in support of the licitness of the SLAVE-TRADE.

1. IT is then evident from the Doctrine of St. Paul, that Christians, however entitled by Baptism to the Spiritual freedom of Children of God, and Heirs of heaven, ought yet, when under the yoke of human bondage or slavery, consider themselves under the strictest obligation of reverencing the authority of their Masters, even of unbelieving Masters, *and counting them worthy of all honour.* But were the SLAVE-TRADE, or the keeping of our fellow-creatures in bondage, unnatural and unjust, it could never be said, that Slaves were under the least obligation in conscience to reverence and obey an unjust, an unnatural authority; or that their Masters, who, by reducing them to that abject condition, had trampled on the Sacred rights of justice and humanity, were *worthy of all honour,* or, indeed, of any shadow of honour, but, on the contrary, of all dishonour and reproach.

2. IT is likewise evident from the Apostle's doctrine, that the primitive Christians were not only not forbidden, but expressly allowed by the principles of our Religion the purchasing of Slaves, and keeping their fellow-creatures, nay, even their fellow-Christians, under the yoke of bondage or Slavery; and from the circumstance of their

Slaves being so particularly cautioned not to consider themselves on the footing of natural equality with their Masters, not to despise them and their authority for being their equals in all spiritual attainments and franchises, but to show, on this very account, a greater degree of readiness and alacrity to render them due service, their Masters are evidently declared to have had a just and indisputable claim to that service, as their own lawful property.

XIII. NEITHER can it be said, that this doctrine, perhaps, novel to some of my Readers, which Timothy is directed *to teach and to exhort*, was only the private opinion of St. Paul; for he declares to him in express words, that it is a *doctrine according to godliness*, the very doctrine of Christ himself, and not to be contradicted by any one, without incurring the accumulated guilt of pride and folly with a criminal train of attendants: "If any man, *says he,* teach otherwise, and consent not to wholesome words, even the words of our LORD JESUS CHRIST, and to the doctrine, which is according to godliness, he is proud, knowing nothing, but doting about questions, and strifes of words, whereof cometh envy, strife, railings, evil surmisings, &c.'

XIV. So far then from being true, that there is nothing in the Sacred Writings of the New Testament, that can be produced in vindication of the SLAVE-TRADE, the palpable evidence just produced in justification of that Trade from the authentic words of One of the very principal inspired Authors of those Sacred Writings, must convince every candid inquirer into the merits of the present Controversy, that, if the SLAVE-TRADE, as demonstrated in the two preceding Parts, appears so visibly warranted by the Writings of the Old Testament, the same is not less evidently authorized, but rather more explicitly vindicated from every suspicion of guilt and immorality by the Writings of the New: for, they do not only declare in formal words, that the teaching of the licitness of the SLAVE-TRADE, exemplified in the practice of the Primitive Christians, is a *Doctrine according to Godliness*, and according to *wholesome words, even the words of our* LORD JESUS CHRIST, but they even stigmatize the Teachers of the contrary doctrine with epithets and appellations not of the most pleasing sounds.

EPISTLE TO PHILEMON.

XV. PHILEMON, to whom St. Paul addresses this affectionate Epistle, was a rich Colossian, and a Christian of distinguished merit. The character given of him in the first part of this Epistle, represents him as one of the most zealous and fervent Christians of his time. His assiduity in promoting the interest of Christianity in quality of *Fellow-labourer* with St. Paul[64], his *love and faith towards the Lord Jesus,* and his generous unbounded charity *towards all the saints*, or his fellow-Christians[65], whom he relieved and comforted on all occasions[66], gained him the confidence, esteem, and affection of the Apostle and of the whole Church at large[67].

XVI. THIS Primitive and exemplary Christian had in his service one ONESIMUS, a Slave, who, as it is very strongly intimated by St. Paul, having defrauded his Master of some part of his property, and knowing the influence the Apostle had over him, eloped from his Master's house, went to Rome, where St. Paul was then in prison, was converted by him, and received into the Communion of the Christian Church[68]; and having by his good services and christian conduct, gained the Apostle's favour, he seems to have prevailed on him to write to his Master Philemon in his behalf.

XVII. THE Letter, of which ONESIMUS himself appears to have been the Bearer, is a master-piece of eloquence, and one of the finest Compositions extant in the Epistolary kind. Nothing can be more tender, more pressing, more animated and persuasive: entreaties and authority, praises and recommendations, religious motives and motives of personal gratitude and integrity, are most inimitably well tempered and allayed together. In short; almost every word of this very concise Epistle contains some argument or reason to effect a reconciliation between Philemon and Onesimus, and to obtain from the Master the readmission of his fugitive Slave into his house and service.

XVIII. THE following XIV Verses of this elegant Epistle, which seem to have a more immediate connexion than the rest with the subject of our present inquiry, will afford me sufficient matter for such reflections, as will not only confirm the doctrine enforced in this SECTION respecting the moral conformity of the SLAVE-TRADE with the principles of the Christian Dispensation, but prevent me from proceeding any farther in my SCRIPTURAL RESEARCHES on this interesting subject.

THE following is a literal transcript of the Contents of the Apostle's Letter to Philemon from the VIIIth to the XXII[d] Verse.

8. Wherefore, though I might be much bold in Christ to enjoin thee that which is convenient;

9. Yet, for love's fake, I rather beseech thee, being such a one as Paul the aged, and now also a prisoner of Jesus Christ.

10. I beseech thee for my son Onesimus, whom I have begotten in my bonds.

11. Which in time past was to thee unprofitable; but now profitable to thee and to me:

12. Whom I have sent again: thou therefore receive him, that is mine own bowels.

13. Whom I would have retained with me, that in thy stead he might have ministered unto me in the bonds of the Gospel.

14. But without thy mind would I do nothing, that thy benefit should not be, as it were, of necessity, but willingly.

15. For perhaps he therefore departed for a season, that thou shouldest receive him for ever:

16. Not now as a servant, but above a servant, a brother beloved, especially to me, but how much more unto thee, both in the flesh and in the Lord?

17. If thou count me therefore a partner, receive him as myself.

18. If he hath wronged thee, or oweth thee aught, put that on mine account.

19. I Paul have written it with my own hand, I will repay it: albeit I do not say to thee, how thou owest unto me even thine own self besides:

20. Yea, Brother, let me have joy of thee in the Lord; refresh my bowels in the Lord.

21. Having confidence in thy obedience, I wrote unto thee, knowing that thou wilt also do more than I say.

XIX. THE following obvious remarks, adapted to the subject of our present inquiry respecting the moral licitness of the SLAVE-TRADE, seem naturally to arise from the tenour of this sacred portion of Scripture.

1. The Apostle declares in the first place, that, were he to act in the plenitude of his Apostolic Commission and Authority, without any regard to the dictates of his love and friendship for Philemon, he would not use the style of a suppliant, as he does, but would peremptorily enjoin him to receive his fugitive Slave into his house and service, which he is bound to do in decency and duty: the word *Convenient* in the Original has both these meanings. From which declaration it evidently follows, that the Apostle was so far from thinking, that Philemon had acted wrong or unjustly in keeping Onesimus in bondage, when yet an unbeliever, that he assures him, on the contrary, he would act in opposition to his duty, or unjustly, in not receiving him again, when baptized, into his house and service.

2. This declaration acquires a superior degree of force from the circumstance he subjoins to his request, as a powerful inducement for Philemon to receive him again into his service. This circumstance, alluding to the name of ONESIMUS, which in Greek is the same as PROFITABLE, is both beautiful and interesting. The Apostle owns without disguise, that Onesimus *in time past had certainly been an unprofitable,* or, in Scripture-language, a *bad Servant* [69]: but, as he could now assure Philemon, that he was quite reclaimed, and become *profitable* to both, he earnestly solicits his readmission, in order that he may be enabled to make amends for his past negligence and inattention to

his service by his future diligence and assiduity.—-It was then Onesimus's duty to have been useful and *profitable* to his Master Philemon, whilst under the yoke of servitude; and it was an act of manifest injustice in him to have been *unprofitable* and of no service. Philemon then had a just and undoubted right to the service of Onesimus, as his Slave; or else Onesimus could never have been taxed by the Apostle with acting the part of an *unprofitable* or *bad servant*, or with any personal injustice, for neglecting a service, which Philemon had no right or title to demand.

3. Again: to convince Philemon, how much Onesimus was changed for the better since his elopement, and the great reformation that his conversion to Christianity had wrought in his morals and conduct, he tells him, how much he was inclined himself to keep him in his own service; intimating to him in this delicate and gentle manner, that he could have no objection to receive again into his service a person so well qualified, as Onesimus was then, to be an Apostle's Servant: and he assures him further, that the only reason that has prevented him from indulging his inclination to detain him, has been his not having had his leave and consent for so doing; *without which*, says he, he would never attempt to deprive him of his Slave.—From this declaration it appears in the strongest light, how very sacred and inviolable the acquired rights of Masters over their Slaves, even of Christian Masters and Slaves, were held by St. Paul, who would not by any means deprive Philemon of Onesimus, however useful the latter was to him at that time, and whatever ascendency he had over his Master, without having first obtained his express

approbation and consent: he would then, says he, receive Onesimus, as a *benefit* perfectly gratuitous, as a free and voluntary gift made to him by Philemon of so valuable a part of his property.

4. Till he obtains this consent, he sends Onesimus back to his lawful Master, entreating him in the most pressing and affectionate manner, to use him with all possible tenderness and regard: to consider him now as a member of the Communion of the true believers, and consequently not in the character of a common menial Slave, but as his own brother in Christ, though still his property *according to the flesh*, which to him particularly ought to be dearer than ever, as being now consecrated to God. — And lest Philemon should insist on Onesimus making due satisfaction for having defrauded him of his time, or other property, and should, on that account, use him with severity, the Apostle engages to make him full reparation, and becomes himself responsible for the whole: which is a manifest acknowledgement of Philemon's right, as the lawful Master of Onesimus, to inflict due punishment on his SLAVE.

XX. FROM these observations, so naturally flowing from the Contents of the Apostle's letter to Philemon, these two necessary consequences seem as naturally to follow.

1. Had St. Paul, who had been instructed in the principles of the Christian Religion, not by men, but immediately by Christ himself[70], *whose chosen vessel he was to bear his name before the Gentiles, and Kings and the children of Israel*[71], been taught by his Divine Master, that the SLAVE-TRADE, or the purchasing of Slaves, or keeping those already purchased

in servitude or bondage, was an unnatural, iniquitous pursuit, contrary to the Spirit of his Religion, he would have certainly addressed himself to Philemon in a very different style from that of his present Letter; and, instead of acting the part of a Suppliant, the part of an intercessor and Mediator, as he does, in soliciting of him the re-admission of a fugitive Slave, he would have assumed the style and tone of a Master; would have severely condemned the unjustifiable conduct of Philemon in detaining him in criminal bondage, contrary to the Laws of his holy Religion, would have commended the spirited conduct of Onesimus in shaking off the heavy yoke of servitude, would not have suffered him to return to his unnatural Master Philemon, especially after he had converted him to Christianity, and entitled him by Baptism to the glorious franchises and liberty of the Children of God, and would not have stood on complimentary ceremonies, finding him useful in his actual state of confinement, to retain him in his ministry, without asking his pretended Master's leave, or without his consent.

THIS, I am confident, would have been the language and conduct of the Apostle, had he been taught by his Divine Master, that the principles and doctrine of the Gospel, he was commissioned to preach, were in direct opposition to the practice of the SLAVE-TRADE, to the practice of purchasing Slaves, or keeping those already purchased in bondage or slavery.

2. But, since the Apostle, conformably to the instructions he had received from his Lord and Master JESUS CHRIST, respecting every part of a Christian's duty, expresses

himself in this Epistle, as well as in every other, where he speaks on this much misrepresented subject, in terms and language diametrically opposite to the sentiments just mentioned; we are forced to conclude, that, since Philemon, as well as many other Primitive Christians, cotemporary with the Apostles of Christ and first Teachers of Christianity, kept Slaves, even Christian Slaves, in their service, in the very face of the whole Church, and with the approbation and knowledge of the primitive Apostles and Disciples of Christ, as has been demonstrated from some of the clearest testimonies of the New Testament, the nature of the SLAVE-TRADE, being so visibly authorized by the positive sanction of those Sacred Writings, must be essentially just and lawful in its principles, and perfectly consonant to those of the Christian Law.

XXI. EVIDENT as this conclusion appears from the Scriptural arguments enforced in the course of this SECTION, I cannot close the Subject of these RESEARCHES without taking some notice of what, I apprehend, will be objected against it from the Words of our Blessed Saviour in his divine Sermon on the Mount, which in the VIIIth Number of this Section I declared with particular Stress to contain nothing against the licitness of the SLAVE-TRADE.— The Words, here alluded to, will, I presume, be thus retorted against it.

All things whatsoever, says our Blessed Saviour, *ye would that men should do to you, do ye even so to them; for this is the Law and the Prophets*[72]: whatsoever things therefore we would not, that men should do to us, we are not even so to do to them; but no person whatever would certainly wish, that a fellow-creature should reduce him to the condition of a Slave; therefore no person whatever is to reduce a fellow-creature to that condition.

XXII. HERE again I must observe, that no one can justly tax me with any partiality to the Cause I have espoused: I have, I think, worded the argument against it in terms as forcible, as the most zealous advocate for African Liberty, could use. But unanswerable as the same may appear to them, it is but a plausible argument at the best.

IT is an Axiom in LOGIC, that *An argument that proves too much, proves nothing*: the above is just such a one: for, by the same manner of reasoning, one might equally conclude, contrary to the Law and the Prophets, and the doctrine of the Christian Religion, that not only Slavery, but every other kind of subordination of one man to another, ought not to be suffered to continue in the World. — The argument, if conclusive in the former case, must be equally so in the latter: I enforce it thus:—

All things whatsoever, says our Blessed Saviour, *ye would that men should do to you, do ye even so to them; for this is the Law and the Prophets*: whatsoever things therefore we would not that men should do to us, we are not even so to do to them; but every person would naturally wish not to be controlled by a fellow-creature, not to be under any subjection to him, but to be absolute master of his own actions; no person therefore ought to keep a fellow-creature under any control or subjection whatever.

XXIII. SUCH is the consequence of wresting the natural and obvious meaning of the maxims of Scripture, and applying them to purposes inconsistent with Scripture itself. The GOLDEN MAXIM of our Divine Master, comprehending in two words the whole perfection of a Christian, was certainly intended by him for all stations in life, for of such was his Church to consist to the end of time: from the Throne to the Cottage, in every walk of life, in bondage or at liberty, every Christian is taught and directed To DO UNTO OTHERS, AS HE WOULD BE DONE UNTO; and, by a necessary consequence NOT TO DO UNTO OTHERS, AS HE WOULD NOT BE DONE UNTO: that is, every Christian is commanded to behave to his neighbour, in whatever situation or circumstances in life Providence may have placed them both, just as he would wish his neighbour would behave to him in his situation, were his neighbour's situation and circumstances his own: so that, to apply the MAXIM to a particular Case (even the Case in question), no Christian Master can be said *to do unto others as he would be done unto*, unless he behaves to his Slave with the same tenderness, justice, and humanity, as he would wish his Slave would behave to him, were the Slave his Master, and himself the Slave; and, upon the same principle, no Slave can be said *to do unto others as he would be done unto*, unless he serves his Master with the same fidelity, submission, and respect, which he would expect from his Master, were the latter his Slave, and himself the Master.

XXIV. THE GOLDEN MAXIM then, of DOING UNTO OTHERS, AS WE WOULD BE DONE UNTO, is so far from condemning in the most distant manner the prosecution of the SLAVE-TRADE, that, when applied to the Case of Christian Masters and their Slaves, it serves, on the contrary, to enforce their reciprocal duties in their different spheres of life. Neither could it be otherwise, seeing, that the same Divine Authority, on which the truth of the above MAXIM is founded, has so frequently given his sanction in the Writings of both the Testaments to the licitness of the SLAVE-TRADE.

XXV. I HAVE now, I think, verified in its full extent the Assertion I engaged to prove in the Title-page; that these SCRIPTURAL RESEARCHES on the licitness of the SLAVE-TRADE, would shew the moral conformity of that Trade with the Principles of Natural and Revealed Religion delineated in the Sacred Writings of the WORD of GOD: and as I prefixed to the Whole certain Positions or DATA, on the truth of which the undeniable religious certainty of that moral conformity is entirely founded, so I shall now annex to the whole a few COROLLARIES or Consequences, which, from their necessary dependance on the former DATA, must convince every religious and candid Reader of the necessity of acquiescing in the Scriptural Doctrine enforced in these RESEARCHES.

COROLLARIES.

I. SINCE the Sacred Writings of the HOLY BIBLE contain the unerring Decisions of the WORD of GOD, the Authority of which in both the Testaments is founded on the essential veracity of God, who is TRUTH itself; it follows necessarily, that, as there can be no prescription against that Authority, which, in the several Scriptural passages quoted in the series of the foregoing RESEARCHES, has positively declared, that the SLAVE-TRADE is intrinsically good and licit, this, by a necessary consequence, must be essentially so in its own nature, however contrary such declaration may be to the received opinion of some men for any length of time.

II. SINCE the Supreme Legislator of the World is infinitely just and wise in all his Decisions respecting *Right* and *Wrong*, and is no ways accountable to his Creatures for the reasons of his conduct in the government of the World; so it must be a degree of presumption highly criminal in any creature to refuse assent to those particular Decisions, by which he has so positively declared the intrinsic licitness of the SLAVE-TRADE, only because he cannot account for that impartial justice, which characterizes every Decision of God, from those hidden principles of Eternal Justice, incomprehensible to him, which induced the Almighty to establish in the World that subordinate state of absolute subjection of some of his rational Creatures to others.

III. SINCE no person can be supposed to acknowledge in fact, that the HOLY SCRIPTURES are the unerring WORD of GOD, unless he acquiesces without reserve in every Scriptural Decision, however incomprehensible the reasons and motives of those Decisions may be to him, and that on no other account, but because he believes them to be the Declarations of God, who, being TRUTH itself, can neither err himself, nor lead any one into error; it follows necessarily, that whoever does not acquiesce in those Scriptural Decisions, quoted in the series of the foregoing RESEARCHES, declaring in formal Words the licitness of the SLAVE-TRADE, cannot be said to acknowledge in fact, that the HOLY SCRIPTURES are the unerring WORD of GOD.

IV. SINCE not only one, but several Decisions of the Written WORD of GOD, as appears from the foregoing RESEARCHES, give a positive sanction to the licitness of the SLAVE-TRADE; it is not from the principle of private or National advantages attending the prosecution of it, which can never affect the intrinsic nature of any human pursuit, that any one is to believe, that the SLAVE-TRADE is intrinsically just and lawful in the strictest sense of the word, but from the incontrovertible veracity of the Written

Word of God, whose Decisions they are, and who is essentially incompatible with the least degree of injustice.

V. Since no abuses or malepractices whatever, committed in the prosecution of a lawful pursuit, can ever alter the intrinsic licitness of it; there being no other arguments, that can be produced against the Slave-Trade, but such as are built on the strength of such abuses as are said to be perpetrated in the prosecution of it; no arguments whatever will ever evince any intrinsic moral turpitude in its Nature, so explicitly declared just and lawful in the Sacred Writings of the Word of God, notwithstanding the many abuses to which it was formerly subject, and were formerly practised, as well as now.

VI. Since no abuses or malepractices whatever, though of the greatest magnitude, committed in former times in the prosecution of the Slave-Trade[73], ever induced the Almighty to prohibit or abolish that Trade, but only to check by wholesome and coercive Laws the violence of unnatural Masters[74], and to punish the transgressors with the greatest severity[75]; there appears no reason whatever, why the abuses and male-practices said to be perpetrated in our days in the prosecution of the same Trade, evidently subject to the control of the Legislature, should be deemed a powerful inducement to proceed to the abolition of it.

ADVERTISEMENT.

IT was the Author's design, when he first engaged to vindicate the licitness of the SLAVE-TRADE from the Sacred Writings of the WORD of GOD, to have concluded his RESEARCHES with another SECTION, containing some Scriptural Directions for the proper treatment of Slaves, together with some Exemplary Punishments and Comminations registered in the same divine Repository of religious Knowledge, for deterring the Conductors and Proprietors of Slaves from ever infringing by any acts of violence and oppression the sacred bounds of that Authority, with which they are entrusted for a time, and which they can never trespass with absolute impunity: but the shortness of the time, which his other avocations have allowed him for completing the Scriptural Vindication contained in the three Sections of his RESEARCHES, having made it absolutely impossible for him to execute the whole of his Original Design, he is obliged to offer it to the Public in its present state.

END NOTES

1. Genesis, C. I. V, 27.
2. Exodus, C. 29, & c.
3. Gen. 15. 6. Rom. 4. 3. Galat. 3.6 James, 2. 23.
4. Ibid.
5. Gen. 22. V. 1—13.
6. Gen. 18. 23, & C
7. Gen. 21. 22, & C. Gen. 23. 7, & C
8. Gen. 14. 22, 23.
9. Gen. 21. 22. & C.. Gen. 13. 7, & C.
10. Gen. 18. 19.
11. Gen. 12.1, & C. Gen. 15. 1, & C. Gen. 17. 1, & C. Gen. 18.1, & C.
12. Isaiah, 41. 8.
13. Gen. 26. 4, 5.

14. John, 8. 39,
15. Gen. 17. 23, 27.
16. Gen. 22. V.18.
17. Gen. C. 21. V. 12.
18. Acts, C. 10, V. 34, 35.
19. Gen. C . 25. V. 16.

20. Gen. 39. 2—6. Ibid. 21—23. Ibid. C. 41. 37, & C.
21. Gen. 39. 7—12.
22. Gen. 39. 21—23. Gen. 40. 1, & C.
23. Gen. 40. 8—23. Ibid. C. 41. 1, & C. Ibid. C. 45, 4, & C. Pf. 105. 16—24.
24. Gen. C . 37. 23—28. Ibil. 45. 1—11.
25. Gen. 39.23.

26. Pf. 105. 16—24.

27. Gen. C. 40. 43.

28. Gen. 39, 21—23.

29. Gen. 39.23.

30. Gen. C. 41. V. 47, 49, 55, 56.

31. Gen. 50. 26.

32. Gen. 39. 21, 23.

33. Gen. ibid, and C C. 40.41.

34. Gen. 39.23.

35. Pf. 105. V. 16—24.

36. 1. Kings, C.. 15. 3.

37. Gen. 35. 22.

38. Gen. 27. V. 4, 7, 10, 12, 19, & C.

39. Gen. 49, V. 1, &c.

40. Gen. 47. 28.

41. Gen. 34. V. 25, 26.

42. Gen. 49. V. 22—27.

43. Gen. 34. V. 7, 30, 31.

44. Gen. 47. V. 19.

45. Exod. C. 29, & C.

46. Josh. C. 8. V. 31, 32. Ibid. 23.6. I. Kings, 2. 3. II. Kings, 23, 25.

47. Acts, 15, 1, & C.

48 Exod. C. 21. V. 1—4.

49. Gen. C. 17. V. 11.

50. Gen. 17. 14.

51. Leviticus, C. 25. V. 44—46.

52. Exod, C. 23. V. 31—33.

53. Josh. C. 9. V. 1, 2.

54. Exod. 23. 31—33. Deut. 7. 2. & C.

55. Josh. C. 10.

56. Josh. C. 10. V. 10, 11,

57. Josh. C. 10. V. 12, 14.

58. Gen. 21. V. 9—14.

59. Galat. C. 4. V. 29.

60. Mark, C. 13. V. 32.

61. Matt. C. 5. V. 17.

62. Matt. C C. 5. 6. 7.

63. Matt. C. 5. V. 17.

64. Ep. to Phil. V. 1.

65. Ibid. V. 5.

66. Ibid. V. 7.

67. Ibid. V. 7.

68. Ibid. V. 10.

69. Matt. C. 25. V. 30

70. Galat, C. 1. V.1.

71. Acts, C. 9. V. 15.

72. Matt. C. 7. V. 12.

73. Gen. 35. 22. Exod. 21. 8, 16, 20, 26, 27. Levit. 19. 20. Jerem. 34. v. 8—18.

74. Exod. 21. v. 7, 12, 16, 20, 21, 26, 27. Levit. 19. v. 20, 21, 22. Ibid. 25. v. 39—43.

75. Jeremiah, c. 34. v. 17—22.

EXAMINATION

OF

The Rev. Mr. HARRIS's

SCRIPTURAL RESEARCHES

ON

The Licitnefs of the Slave-Trade.

By the Rev. JAMES RAMSAY.

LONDON:

Printed by JAMES PHILLIPS, George-Yard, Lombard-
Street.

M.DCC.LXXXVIII.

ADVERTISEMENT.

THE following Examination was drawn up in the country, from a casual perusal of Mr. Harris's Scriptural Researches, with a view of putting them into the hands of any person, who might be employed in answering that very extraordinary work. But on coming up to town, and understanding that Mr. Harris's reasoning had produced effects on certain people, who had not studied the scriptures, or attended to that spirit of freedom, which runs throughout the Old and New Testament, and who hitherto had suffered themselves to be reluctantly dragged along by the present prevailing enthusiasm in favour of freedom, but now eagerly seized on a pretence for abandoning the cause, it has been judged proper to give it at once to the publick. Mr. Harris affects to proceed mathematically in the treatment of his subject, and therefore establishes certain data. I had thought it sufficient to contradict their particular application, in my examination of the subject; but others thinking it necessary to take more direct notice of them, I have subjoined the following short observations.

Dat. 1, 2. "The scriptures of the Old and New Testament are of equal authority, and contain the unerring decisions of the word of God.'

Observation. Certainly: but it will not be disputed, that there are many things, not indeed deserving the name of decisions, but that pass without censure, and are seemingly allowed there, which we know to be forbidden to us, and which will not apply to the improved state of mankind. Laws must be adapted, not only to the state of society, but to the present state of the improvement of the human mind, which we know has been gradually advancing from the earliest ages.

Dat. 3, 4. "It is criminal to refuse assent to what the scriptures decide to be intrinsically good or bad.'

Obser. Suppose this. Yet may we not inquire if a thing or practice be really so declared, and if it concerns our salvation, to form a decided opinion on it? Are we not liable to mistake practices, arising out of circumstances connected with the first formation of society, and therefore not positively censured, for such decisions of intrinsical goodness? Thus the eating of swines flesh was allowed before the promulgation of the law of Moses; that law strictly forbad it; the Christian law allows it again as at the beginning: or, the Jews were alone restrained from the use of it; while they continued under a particular œconomy, and their transgression of this law was only a crime, because it was enjoined them; not because it was in itself a thing unlawful, as murder, adultery, and the like.

Dat. 5, 6. "Every scriptural decision, however incomprehensible, must be assented to as a declaration of the word of God.' We must consider the circumstances under which that decision is made; how far it is agreeable to our benevolent religion, and how far it is applicable to our conduct, before we imitate it. The drunken incest of Lot is not censured. It was the means of producing two mighty nations; from which, according to the author's manner of reasoning, he ought to conclude it was approved of; yet I suppose he will not recommend the imitation to any person in these days.

Dat. 7. "The slave-trade must be believed to be intrinsically just and lawful, if the scriptures give a sanction to it.' Suppose the slave-trade to have this sanction (which yet is not true) unless the author can shew how it can be carried on without infringing on our Saviour's golden rule, of doing as we would be done by; unless he can instruct us how we can go to the coast of Africa, and by every fraudulent, violent, oppressive method, rob, murder, and enslave innocent people without a crime; then are we to keep our practice, if not our opinion, suspended.

Dat. 8. "No abuse of a lawful pursuit, can make that pursuit criminal.' It is lawful for a man to provide for his family; but not to rob and murder on the highway under such a pretence. Whenever a man's industry is connected with such practices, the actual exertion of it is a crime in him, though to provide for his family in an honest way would be laudable. That there is an unlawful slavery noticed in the scriptures, is clear, from the punishment that Pharaoh brought on himself and Ægypt, for enslaving the Jews. The author should distinguish, and mark the difference between the slavery that (page 41)† is almost commanded, and that which brings down divine judgments on the oppressor, and shew that his patrons of Leverpool practise only the first.

Dat. 9. "No private or publick advantage will ever justify the slave-trade, till it be proved essentially just and lawful in its nature.' Here we are sincerely agreed and according to the distinction proposed for datum 8, he has only to set heartily to work, and prove the Leverpool slave-trade to be that particular sort of slave-trade, "which God hath commanded as being essentially just and lawful in its nature.'

Dat. 10. "No argument drawn from abuse, can prove the intrinsic deformity of the slave-trade, unless it be proved essentially unjust.' These are words without meaning. We are not combating an ideal slavery; but slavery accompanied with robbery, oppression, misery, murder. Wherever we find slavery so attended, it becomes a horrid crime, be it intrinsically never so just.

Dat. 11. "If abuses committed in the prosecution of a lawful pursuit can be prevented, then the advantages arising from it, ought to have a powerful influence against the abolition.' But if these abuses cannot possibly be prevented (for are we to oppress and murder according to law?) then the greatest advantages attending any practice must be abandoned, till a method shall be discovered, of separating them from iniquity and bloodshed.

Dat. 12. "If the slave-trade is to be abolished, because of the abuses committed in it, then every other branch of trade, in which abuses are committed, ought to share the same fate.' Most certainly in turn, in proportion to the atrociousness of each. Let us once get this staring monster subdued, and we will be obliged to the author for pointing out any other iniquitous traffick that deserves to follow immediately in the train of the Leverpool slave-trade. The fallaciousness of this author's reasoning, is exceedingly well exposed, in the Critical Review of April, 1788, to which I refer the reader.

From this view of the author's data, it will appear, that he has totally confounded times and circumstances. The law of Moses was enacted in aid of natural religion, till the perfect religion of Christ should be given to the world. The doctrines of this last, enjoin us to consider and treat all men as our brethren; and its effect was gradually to take away all burthensome ceremonies, all oppressive distinctions. Why are we then sent back to less perfect institutions for the rule of our practice? We are to go on to perfection, refine sentiment, and extend benevolence. What has raised Europe above the rest of the world, but the abolition of domestick slavery? What degrees of opulence and prosperity might it acquire, if the abominable, contracted, branch of trade in the bodies of our fellow creatures of Africa, were changed to a fair, equitable intercourse of productions and manufactures!

J. R.

EXAMINATION, &c.

THIS gentleman professes to treat the subject seriously, and to submit his opinion to the decisions of revealed religion. No man has a right to dispute his sincerity, as far as his own way of thinking is concerned; but few serious people will peruse his extraordinary positions, without having their reverence for their Creator shocked, and their benevolence to their brother affected. The Scriptures, from which he draws his conclusions, we believe to teach, that all men are equally dear to their Creator, and that we owe love and good offices to each other. But if his deductions be fairly made, we must no longer entertain this opinion; for one part of mankind is to be kidnapped, evil intreated, oppressed, murdered, to indulge the avarice of another; and, page 76, Corol. 3d. "He doth not believe the Scriptures, who is not persuaded that this doctrine is taught there.'

But the author stumbles at the very threshold. Our Saviour (John v. 39.) bids the Jews to search the scriptures; "for in them ye think ye have eternal life; for they are they which testify of me,' the Saviour come to free men from the bondage of sin, into the glorious privilege of the sons of God. But it seems something else is meant. We are to search the scriptures (see title page) for a commission to Leverpool captains for fitting out ships, and loading them with powder, shot, and cutlasses, to set the Africans on to assault, kidnap, and enslave each other; to be transferred over to them; to be murdered by bad air, thirst, and famine, in the passage to the West-Indies; where the poor remains are to be set to hard labour, without food, without cloathing, without rest, sufficient to support nature.

It is true (preface, page 5.) he, with all the other advocates for slavery, declares himself "an enemy to injustice and oppression.' But the design of his book is to shew, that the ill-treatment of slaves is not an object of divine animadversion; for (p. 16.) Sarah was permitted without censure, "to use cruel oppressive treatment to Hagar;' and (p. 26.) Joseph is approved of by God for the cruel manner in which he enslaved and exchanged the abodes of the Egyptians. Which of these is to be believed; his general assertion, or his particular application? Or may we conclude, that he reserves to himself the feelings of humanity, and sells tyranny and oppression to his friends of Leverpool.

In the scriptures servants are frequently mentioned; but, in this dissertation, they are transformed into "slave trade'. The places where traffick in slaves is related, are Joseph's brethren (Gen. xxxvii.) selling him to the Ishmaelites, who sell him to Potiphar; the Tyrians (Ezek. xxvii. 13.) who had a market for the persons of men; and Babylon, the mother of abominations, (Rev. xviii. 13.) who exposed to sale, slaves and souls of men. I hope none of these instances are proposed to the imitation of the "ancient and loyal town of Leverpool' for a black mark is set on them to prevent them from being followed.

Now there is some difference between dealing in slaves as a branch of trade, and buying the service of a domestic; even as it is not every man who eats meat, that is or could act the part of a butcher. In the case of the Jews there was something particular. They were obliged to admit their slaves to all the national privileges, to circumcision, the pass-over, and other solemn feasts, and to instruct them in the true religion (Gen. xvii. 13. Exod. xii. 44. Deut. xvi 11. and xxxi. 12. Josh. viii. 35.) In buying them from the Heathen around them, they recovered them from idolatry; they gave them a weekly sabbath. In their treatment they were commanded to remember, that they themselves had been slaves in Egypt. When they are threatened for their sins, the ill treatment of their slaves makes a capital part of the charge against them. But modern masters think that nothing of this sort concerns them.

The Jews were intended to communicate to the world the knowledge of the true religion. He who brings good out of evil made use of the slavery, in practice, to extend this knowledge to persons, whom it could not at that time have otherwise reached. But nothing in the bible countenances a trade in slaves. Even the transferring them in ordinary cases is checked as in that of wives and concubines, (Exod. xxi. 11.) Their ill treatment was guarded against, by that law which gave them freedom if their master had struck out a single tooth.

Indeed, among the Jews, the number of slaves must have been small. They were numerous in a narrow territory, and were in general husbandmen, and used ploughs and other instruments of agriculture, and wrought in the field with their servants. Ziba, who appears to have been steward to the house of Saul, had only twenty servants to assist him and his sons in cultivating the lands belonging to the family. The Jews on their return from captivity had only one servant to six persons, or one in each family. The remnant of the Gibeonites, who served the temple, was then 392. It is not therefore fair to consider every accidental possession of a servant, either as an instance, or as a vindication of the Leverpool "slave trade;' of which no ancient nation could ever form an idea. We may rather conclude, that though the Jews were permitted to buy slaves from the Heathen, they did not traffick in them; and forcibly to enslave their brethren was death. (See Exod. xxi. 16. Deut xxiv. 7.)

Of Mr. Harris's data as general propositions, I shall say little more; the application alone is what the present subject is concerned in. I shall only suggest an additional datum, as necessary to complete his principles of reasoning.

Dat. 13. If the slave trade, though "intrinsically licit,' cannot now be carried on, without breaking through every human and divine law, without cheating, violence, oppression, murder, then must it be laid aside, till we shall have discovered a way of carrying it on, agreeably to the doctrines of the gospel, by which we are enjoined to consider all men as our brethren, and to deal by them as we wish them to deal by us.

Page 16. Speaking of Abraham's possessing of servants, he calls it, "a positive approbation, a sanction of divine authority in favour of the slave-trade.' What a change is put on the Reader! Abraham possessed servants; therefore the Leverpool slave-trade has a divine sanction. For if this be not meant, nothing is meant. His book is published to vindicate this trade; it is dedicated to the corporation, who must so understand it. Now let a man only read Mr. Newton or Mr. Falcon-bridge's or any other eye-witness's account of this trade, and what horrid impiety must of necessity be understood! Is there "a divine sanction' for all the iniquity accompanying this very diabolical business, the kidnapping, chaining, murdering, suffocating of millions of unhappy fellow creatures? Are such things not barely permitted, but (p. 42.) approved, encouraged, and seemingly enjoined?

Abraham was a rich, powerful, prince. As he travelled through various countries, numbers must have been desirous of attaching themselves to his fortune, and have offered themselves for his attendants. His humanity might have induced him to purchase children from unnatural parents, or captives from robbers. But all in his family were in a situation very different from that of West Indian slaves. We learn, that on the supposition of his dying childless, he intended one of them for his heir; that he intrusted a servant to chuse a wife for his son Isaac; that he put arms in his servants hands, and led them out to battle. There is nothing of West Indian slavery in all this.

But a particular stress is laid on the story of Hagar, and Sarah's ill treatment of her. Page 19. "She obtained no favourable sentence from the Divine Tribunal for leaving her mistress, nor was Sarah censured for her severity.' Sarah was not present when the angel appeared unto Hagar, therefore she is neither praised nor condemned. But that Hagar believed she had a favourable sentence, and that her conduct was not condemned, when assured that the Lord had seen her affliction, which is the scripture phrase for deliverance (Gen. xxix. 32, and xxxi. 42. Exod. iii. 7.), and that she should have a son, and that her seed should be multiplied, appears from her acknowledgment of the vision, and returning to her mistress. Nor can we imagine in what more flattering manner her affliction could have been recompensed, or how she could have been afflicted so as to have deserved a recompence, and her mistress not to have been in fault. It was necessary for her to return to her mistress, that her son might partake of the sign of the covenant, and be instructed in the true religion.

Hagar's case (p. 19.) is compared with an African female slave in the West Indies. Nothing can be more opposite. Josephus says, Pharaoh made Abraham a present of money; and the scriptures say, that he intreated Abraham well for Sarah's sake, adding immediately, he had cattle, and men servants, and maid servants, as if Pharaoh had presented them; among whom Hagar might have been one; or, as it appears she was a worshipper of the true God, she might voluntarily have entered into Sarah's service. Certainly she had never been cooped up in a Guinea trader, nor set to plant the sugar-cane; nor was she ordered to return and submit herself for her mistress's profit, but for her own and her son's sake; and when that purpose was answered she was dismissed.

There is therefore no foundation for the author's deduction, p. 20. that "a divine voice declares her to be her master's indisputable property, and the original bargain to be just and lawful in its nature; and that the (Leverpool) slave-trade, even attended with circumstances not conformable to the feelings of humanity, is essentially consistent with the rights of justice, and has the positive sanction of God for its support, however displeasing these circumstances may be to his fatherly providence.' Let any man make sense of this who can. I understand only the extreme boldness of the expression. Here is a right to enslave and an approbation, and also a censure of the exercise of this right. Here our natural notions of benevolence are set in opposition to revelation, p. 42. Revelation commands us to enslave our brethren, even against the suggestions of the feelings of humanity. Surely the writer should shew the high purposes answered by slavery, to gain which it is an act of piety to violate our benevolent feelings.

We come now to the story of Joseph, which, p. 23, "ascertains the inherent lawfulness of the' (Leverpool) "slave-trade.' The first thing that strikes us in his account is, his illustrating his doctrine by Joseph's political arrangements of the kingdom of Egypt, rather than by Joseph's own story; which, except in the horrid circumstances of the middle passage, agrees, entirely with the Leverpool slave-trade. Joseph is found at a distance from protection. His enemies kidnap him and sell him to slave-brokers, who carry him into Egypt, and dispose of him as an article of commerce to Potiphar. His kidnappers saw, and like Guinea captains disregarded, the anguish of his soul. It is true, afterwards, when they believed themselves in danger of being enslaved in turn, they upbraid each other with their unfeeling cruelty, and charge their distress to its account. But this was only because Scriptural Researches had not then been published: for they, p. 20, would have proved, that "though the action was not altogether conformable to the feelings of humanity, and was even displeasing to his Fatherly Providence; and though doubtless God would see, and of consequence recompense, Joseph for his affliction as he had Hagar; yet this stroke in the slave-trade is essentially consistent with the unalienable rights of justice; has the positive sanction of God in its support, nay, his approbation, p. 16, and p. 42, even his command.'

But let us examine Joseph's management of the Egyptians, not as this author, but as the scriptures represent it. In the years of plenty Joseph stored the extraordinary produce of each district in the neighbouring cities. One tenth part belonged of right to the king; the rest he purchased at a low price with the king's treasures. In the years of famine he sold the corn out to the inhabitants of the districts nearest to his respective storehouses at an advanced price, and accumulated the money, cattle, and moveables of the whole kingdom, and at last made a bargain for their lands and persons. It is not to be supposed that any property, except money, was taken out of the original possessors hands; for this would have answered no purpose, but to distress the people and embarrass government. Indeed, where could the whole cattle and moveables of the kingdom have been stored? When the seven years of famine were ended, Pharaoh was the sole proprietor. Joseph then gives the inhabitants a charter, restores them their lands and cattle, on condition of paying to Pharaoh a second tenth of the produce of the land, which made their contributions to the revenue a fifth part of their crops. It appears no other badge or burden of slavery was imposed, except this rent, which was a tenth part more than they had formerly paid.

The common rent of the bare land in England is estimated at one-third of the produce, and the farmer must supply himself with stock, except perhaps buildings, and also contribute largely in a variety of ways to the publick revenues: but by Joseph's regulation the Egyptian farmer paid only a fifth part for the use of his stock and land, and for the support of government. After having transferred themselves and property to Pharaoh, they could not have been freed on easier terms: and as we often see, that he who hires a farm, grows rich on a possession on which the owner had been ruined, probably the Egyptians became as happy under their new tenure as they had been under their old. In the most unfavourable light, it may be compared with the change that took place at the conquest, when free tenures became feudal charged with certain services.

Our translation, Gen. xlvii. 20, 21. says, "So, the land became

Pharaoh's; and as for the people, he removed them to cities from one end of the borders of Egypt, even to the other end thereof.' In the Septuagint it is, "and the land became Pharaoh's, and he subjected the people to be servants to him from one end of Egypt to the other.' It is to the same purport in the Samaritan copy. This reads better, and is more probable, than that Joseph should have made the whole nation, as Mr. Harris affirms, change settlements in such a manner as if the people of Kent were sent to the Orkneys, and those of the Orkneys were brought to Kent. This would be such a trifling with peoples lives and feelings, such a waste of property, such a perversion of all experience, and particular knowledge of the agriculture proper in each district, as is only applicable to the Leverpool slave-trade; but cannot, on such slight grounds as this general expression is, be imagined in a man of Joseph's character, with a pretended view to prevent rebellion Or the expression in our translation may bear, that the people were distributed so as to be near the respective store-houses, on which their maintenance was assigned.

Therefore "the change made, p. 25, 26, in the happy condition of the Ægyptians, the transportation of 7 or 8 millions of every age, sex, condition, rank; infants, children, decrepit, infirm, delicate through the scorching sands of a parched up country,' is the mere fiction of imagination, to palliate the still more shocking conduct of the writer's patrons of Leverpool. The Ægyptians offered themselves for servants, to save themselves from starving. His patrons force the Africans to be slaves, not as he says, from "a state of absolute indigence,' but reduced from plenty and ease to famine, nakedness, and want, by stripes, setters, cruelty and oppression.

Page 28. It is said, "Joseph, when able to relieve them, took advantage of the extreme indigence of the Ægyptians, to reduce them into the condition of slaves, and in this acted by the immediate direction of God, who made this work to prosper.' Supposing all this true, yet there is nothing common between this transaction and the Leverpool African commerce; but the author's having given them one common name, "slave-trade.' The Ægyptians, after a fair transfer of themselves and goods, are left in full possession of their lands and property, on paying such a rent as would act as a spur to industry, while it checked that luxury which the author describes, p. 25, as prevailing in Ægypt. The Leverpool slaves are reduced from freedom to a base, helpless, unprofitable, wretched state.

When this writer, p. 27, considers the four-fifths of the produce left with the Ægyptian farmer, as only equivalent to the keep of a West-Indian slave, he must raise a blush on the sugar planter's cheek; who willingly would leave but one fifth, (the rum) both to support his plantation stock, and maintain his slaves.

But let Joseph's conduct be what the writer pleases to describe it. He was not the legislator of Ægypt, but the minister of Pharaoh, and obliged to govern himself by the prevailing customs of the kingdom. It appears, he extended only the king's revenues, and gave him such a command over the property of the people, as might enable him to arrange the management of it to the best general advantage. This might be peculiarly proper in Ægypt, though not necessary to be imitated here. Its fertility depended on the equal distribution of the waters of the Nile. It was necessary for the general benefit, that there should be an indisputed power to direct the course of the various canals, which communicated the water to each district. While the king had an equal interest in all, no particular part would be neglected. Joseph gives four-fifths of the produce, "for seed of the field, and for your food, and for them of your housholds, and for food for your little ones.' This confines the peoples share to their own maintenance, and the supply of seed. We are left to conclude, that every expense attending the distribution of the river, except perhaps manual labour, was paid out of the king's fifth part: and as in all good governments, the interest of the king and the people is one, Joseph, by his nominal purchase of the people and their lands, might probably have in view such an accession of power, as might enable him to direct the whole to general advantage. After the charter was confirmed, no ill use could be made of the power, and an English farmer would gladly pay one-fifth of his produce to him who should stock his farm, and pay his rent, and all his publick and parish taxes.

Page 38. "The Jews are not restrained from purchasing their own brethren.' The Jews were commanded to treat their brethren, when reduced to a six years servitude, with lenity, as hired or free servants, and to send them out in the sabbatical year free, and not let them go away empty. The only cases in which we can suppose Jews could be made to serve, are their being sold for debt, or their preferring the service of a master to labour on their own account. In these cases, the laws of Moses take care of them, that they be not oppressed, and, besides the original purchase-money of their services, to have a recompence when the period is finished.

It is in this case of an Hebrew servant, that we are to look for the genuine Mosaic principles of slavery. Even here the law expresses a jealousy of the master's conduct, and guards against the abuse of his authority, restricting it to six years, and prescribing the manner of exercising it. Therefore when the Jews are allowed to make perpetual slaves of the Heathen, we are to consider it as a particular dispensation respecting their situation among idolaters, by which, in every slave, they made a proselyte to the true religion; or like divorces, an indulgence to their hardness of heart, which was not then capable of the purity and benevolence of the gospel, by which, marriage was made perpetual, and all men were to be treated as brethren. We can infer the doctrine of perpetual slavery as little from its permission to the Jews, as we can the keeping of concubines from the practice of Abraham, or David. Divorces are permitted to the Jews in similar expressions with the permission to hold slaves; yet our Saviour tells us, it was not so from the beginning. Moses (Deut. xvii. 14.) gives directions for the choice and duty of a king, yet Samuel tells the Jews, they had offended God in asking for a king. And though God condescended to give them a king in a manner which more unequivocally shewed his assent, than that approbation, sanction and command, which the author incautiously affirms to be given to the "slave-trade;' yet Samuel concludes them to be not the less guilty, for persevering in the request. We should be more careful than this author shews himself, how we apply our ignorant conjectures to the divine conduct; as p. 16, "Without allowing the licitness of the slave-trade, it is impossible to reconcile the justice of God with his own scriptural decisions concerning its nature;' that (p. 32) "God, without a glaring opposition to the rights of his justice, could not have approved the conduct of Joseph in enslaving the Ægyptians, and inflicted a lasting punishment on Reuben for his incest, if his enslaving of the Ægyptians had been a crime.' These expressions would be shocking from an infidel; in what an horrid cause doth a clergyman use them?

The minds of the Jews had been broken and debased by the Egyptian bondage; the law was given them as a school-matter to train them up for the perfect religion of the gospel. Their conduct in the wilderness, their frequent rebellions amidst miracles, and in the immediate presence of their Divine Deliverer, can only be imagined by those who have had opportunities of seeing how man is shorn of his worth by slavery. Only two men of all who were grown up when they came out of Egypt, were thought deserving to enter into Canaan. That whole generation must be worn out in the wilderness; and their children must be trained for 40 years before they are permitted to take possession. Their laws therefore respected the hardness of their hearts, though founded on principles which led insensibly to perfection. Thus while the perpetuity of the servitude of the Heathens condescended to the hardness of their hearts, the easy temporary service of their brethren looked forward to the gospel times, not differing, but in being for a fixed period, from modern servitude for wages in free states.

Therefore when this writer, p. 39. calls this latter service, "A Slave Trade;' the meaning of the terms is perverted. Or let him reduce his Leverpool slave trade to the circumstances of a Jew serving his brother for six years, and we shall have few objections to bring against it. What he calls there "selling him again,' was transferring his service to another brother (not an Heathen) for the remainder of the term, as an apprentice is turned over to a second master.

Page 40. "If a Hebrew servant had married a wife with consent of his master, she and her child became her master's property for ever.' This seems not to be candidly expressed. This wife must have been an Heathen slave, for Hebrew women had the privilege of the Sabbatical year; but if he chose to continue with his wife, he had only to renew his contract with his master. Indeed the regulation appears to have been intended as a check to the connection with slaves in the poor reduced Hebrews.

Page 41, 42. When he speaks of the (Leverpool) "slave trade having the sanction of being encouraged, almost commanded, and even enjoined, to be prosecuted by the Supreme Legislator,' he puts opposition to silence. But when, p. 43. he talks of "the Almighty's forgetting himself, when he encouraged the slave trade, if it be a crime,' I am happy for his sake to recollect, that the author tells us, till he was 27 years old, he knew not the value of an English expression.

Page 43. The slavery of the Gibeonites.

The land of Canaan was allotted to the Jews for an inheritance. The former inhabitants, for their sins, were to be extirpated, or expelled. The Gibeonites preferred slavery to this. Their services were allotted first to the tabernacle, then to the temple. It appears from David's application to them, on account of the famine brought on the land for Saul's massacre of them, that they were kept distinct as a people. We may suppose that they continued to occupy part of their ancient possessions (for we find in David's time that even Araunah a Jebusite was a proprietor of land) and that they were in their turn draughted off for the service of religion; those who occupied the lands maintaining those who served. There is not one common circumstance between the manner of their becoming servants, and the present Leverpool slave trade, and hardly any more in their treatment.

Page 50. On the supposition of the iniquity of the (Liverpool) "slave trade,' he speaks of the Almighty disturbing the course of nature, when the sun stood still at Joshua's command, to make it subservient to injustice and oppression, in vindication of ill-gotten property. Here he may be assured the horror of the expression will secure him from contradiction.

Page 54. "The slave trade,' (still Leverpool slave trade) is in perfect harmony with the principles of the word of God respecting justice.' P. 58. "The inspired writers of the New Testament did not consider it as an infraction of the principles of the gospel.' Nor did these declare their own persecution for righteousness sake, to be an infraction of the principles of the gospel. The keeping of slaves, which the author constantly calls "the slave trade,' was a custom then generally prevalent over the world. Neither were masters or slaves prepared for a general manumission. The spirit of Christianity was suffered gradually to undermine this mass of oppression, and wherever the gospel has prevailed, it has in fact abolished it.

We have a similar instance of this management, in the abolition of the ceremonial law of Moses. The first disciples, and even the apostles, conformed to it, though they had declared it to be an unnecessary yoke, and they suffered it to wear out gradually. That slavery was an evil, and therefore a sin in all those who inflicted it on others, in such a degree as to become an evil, is plainly declared in the gospel. Our Savior tells the believing Jews, If ye continue in my word, ye shall know the truth, and the truth shall make you free; or shall confer new privileges on you. If freedom be a privilege or an advantage, slavery is a degradation and a disadvantage. But is a man be degraded or injured for the caprice or profit of another, that other, under whom he suffers such injury, is guilty of a sin.

Again, St. Paul, 1 Cor. viii. 21, says, "Art thou called being a servant, care not for it; but if thou mayest be made free, use it rather.' Here is plainly a direction to the disciples to submit to their situation, but to prefer freedom when fairly offered; which in this case was its being purchased for them by the Christian congregation. This is explained, ver. 23. "Ye are bought with a price, be not (Greek become not) ye the servants of men.' Avoid a situation which must debase your mind. In the Revelations, xviii. 13. slaves and souls of men are said to be articles of traffick in Babylon, the Mother of Abominations. This supposeth nothing very excellent in slavery, to make it be approved of, and commanded to be prosecuted by God.

We may now account for the manner in which St. Paul applies to Philemon in behalf of his servant Onesimus. He desires him to receive him back into his family, not now as a servant, but above a servant; a profitable inmate, a brother beloved. He would not take advantage of the privilege of an apostle, to withhold Onefimus from his service, or consider his conversion as a bar to it, and therefore endeavours to effect a reconciliation between them. But from the manner in which the apostle solicits this favour, it is clear the situation of Onesimus in the family was desirable; for he requests it as a favour to Onesimus, and considers not his interposition, as the conferring of an obligation on Philemon. All this is very opposite to that West-Indian slavery with which this of Onesimus, p. 65. is compared. For the master only is considered here; neither the feelings nor profit of the slave is taken into account.

Page 72, 73. I shall not dispute his exposition of doing as we wish to be done by, as far as it goes, of "a slave's serving his master, as he if a master would wish to be served.' But I would carry it a step farther. As I, a free man, settled with my family and friends about me in my native country, would not wish to be kidnapped, or to have my family enslaved, separated, and carried bound neck and heel, and stifled in the foul air of a ship's hold, all to be sold in a distant country, to toil incessantly for a man we never knew, without food or raiment, except such scraps as we may procure by breaking the sabbath; under the lash of any unfeeling boy, who may be set over us with a whip in his hand; so would not I be concerned in any such cruel oppressive inhuman treatment of others. When this author publishes his Second Part, it is to be hoped, this will be pressed home on his Leverpool patrons.

It is curious to remark, that in these researches, in which the wisdom and goodness of God is so freely applied to the Leverpool slave trade, there is not even a distant hint given of the purpose which is to be served by slavery, to shew it to be worthy "of this divine approbation, the almost divine commands.' When God commands us to love our neighbour, our heart goes along with the precept. But if, as this author incautiously affirms, we be commanded to exercise the slave trade, bow down our brother's body in bondage, and treat him ill, as Sarah did Hagar with impunity, we have no clue to trace out the agreement of the doctrine with divine goodness. If commanded or enjoined to use the slave trade as it is now carried on, we are commanded, (horrid even in the supposition) to commit murder, to starve, oppress, suffocate, and lead into exile, our brother, who never offended us. Suppose slavery approved of in revelation, yet surely robbery, murder, and oppression, are not approved there: and yet no man is originally reduced into a state of slavery but by such methods:—at least, when the advocates for slavery plead for a divine sanction to it, they should be able to lay down a method of making slaves of others, which shall be innocent, and may deserve that sanction.

The Jews, for their sins, were given up to captivity. Their cities were to be destroyed, their princes murdered, and their people carried to Babylon. The prophets invited the surrounding nations to come to the slaughter, and to the spoil. Here is a divine command in stronger terms than can be shewn for the Leverpool slave trade, or any other slave trade or holding of slaves. Yet what follows. These very nations thus invited, and even commanded to execute the divine judgments on the Jews, are destined to destruction, are made to cease as nations, for having obeyed the call to vengeance. Edom was amongst the first in this field of blood, and slavery, and plunder. Hear the prophet Obadiah address him:—"Thou shouldest not have laid hands on their substance in the day of their calamity: thou shouldest not have stood in the cross-way to cut off those of his that did escape: thou shouldest not have delivered up those of his that did remain in the day of distress. For the day of the Lord is near on all the heathen; — as thou haft done, it shall be done unto thee.'

The reason is plain, though instruments in God's hands to punish a wicked people; yet in the execution of his justice, they only satiated their own hatred, cruelty, and avarice. Let therefore the Leverpool slave trade be not only approved of, but even, as he says, commanded by God; yet if the corporation, in prosecuting the infernal business, be actuated by avarice, or any other unworthy motive, and use cruelty, oppression, and inhumanity in the course of it, (and let those who use the trade lay their hands on their hearts, and let them, if they dare, deny the charge), then, sooner or later, divine vengeance will find them out, and plunge them into ruin with all those who encourage or abet them in it.

Page 75. Corol. 1st. "The Scriptures declare the slave trade to be intrinsically good and licit.' Not in any other manner than Jewish arbitrary divorces, plurality of wives, or their original desire of a king; all of which we know to have been wrong from the beginning.

Corol. 2d. "He is highly criminal who refuses assent to the intrinsick licitness of the slave trade, declared in the Scriptures.' I hope not, if he cannot find it there, and resolves not to meddle with it, till he has discovered it.

Corol. 3d. "He who acquiesces not in the licitness of the slave trade, disbelieves the Scriptures.' Answered in Corol. 2.

Corol. 6th. "The abuses of the slave trade not an inducement to the Legislature to abolish it.' If the slave trade be, as it certainly is, inseparably connected with murder, oppression, and every iniquity that has from time to time drawn down divine vengeance on guilty nations; and if the Legislature be instructed in the nature of it, and be called on to put a stop to this murder and oppression, and cannot possibly do it but by the abolition of the slave trade, (were the slave trade even commanded in the clearest terms, which is not the case, but the contrary) then is the Legislature obliged, and called on by every motive of religion and prudence, to put an immediate stop to it, that it may not bring ruin on the state.

†Editor's note: This and subsequent page references are to the original edition and not to this reprint.

THE
ABOLITION
OF THE
SLAVE TRADE
CONSIDERED IN A

RELIGIOUS POINT OF VIEW.

A SERMON

PREACHED BEFORE THE CORPORATION

OF THE

CITY OF OXFORD,

AT St. MARTIN's CHURCH,

On Sunday, February 3, 1788.

By WILLIAM AGUTTER, M. A.

Of St. Mary Magdalen College.

LONDON:

Printed for J. F. and C. RIVINGTON, St. Paul's
Church-yard; and G. PHILIPS, George-yard,
Lombard-street. MDCCLXXXVIII.

To GRANVILLE SHARP, ESQ.
CHAIRMAN

Of the Committee of the Society instituted for the Purpose of abolishing the African Slave Trade; A Gentleman eminently distinguished for his publick, his private, and his Christian Virtues; Who has been conspicuous in supporting the Cause of Humanity for many Years, at great Expence, and with unremitting Zeal; This Discourse is humbly dedicated, by his most obliged, most obedient humble Servant, The AUTHOR.

ACTS xvii. 26.

God hath made of one blood all the nations of men, to dwell on all the Face of the Earth.

THERE is no truth more obvious to the simple conceptions of man, than that the human race have natural rights, and common relations to each other; yet, there is no truth which may be more easily overlooked, or sooner perverted, when the principles of ambition, avarice, and cruelty, have blinded the understanding, and hardened the heart. Men's judgements are easily bribed by a vicious inclination; and they will soon persuade themselves to believe that to be true which they are unwilling to discover to be false.

This observation is strictly applicable to the case of Slavery; a case, which now promises to undergo a thorough discussion: not, it is hoped, merely to please the speculations of the curious, or to interest the feelings of the humane; but to vindicate the wrongs of thousands; to restrain the hand of cruelty; and to let the oppressed go free [1].

The subject of Slavery has been examined in a moral, a historical, a political, and a commercial point of view, by authors of distinguished eminence; whose clearness of comprehension and powers of reasoning have honoured and advanced the cause of humanity in which they have warmly engaged.

It is my intention in this discourse to consider the subject in a religious point of view.

Slavery, or servitude, was indeed connived at by the Jewish Laws; but then it was restrained by wise and merciful regulations: and we know that GOD winked at the times of that ignorance, when men could not receive a purer law, or be influenced by better motives than those temporary rewards and punishments which were the sanctions of that dispensation.

But. "GOD hath made of one blood all the "natives of the earth.' Creation is a comprehensive system of goodness; and the various parts thereof are so admirably connected together, that, if "one member suffer, all the "members suffer with it.' This goodness, discoverable in creation, is a communicative principle, flowing from the Author of all life and blessedness, and imparting itself to all his creatures; and his creatures are so far blessed, and rendered capable of superior enjoyments, as they are influenced by this communicative goodness; and, in consequence thereof, become instrumental in promoting each other's happiness.

All the relations of humanity, all the ties of kindred, are established for this benevolent purpose; that we may feel, reason, and act as members one of another. For "have we not all one Father? hath not One GOD created us? Why do we deal treacherously every man against his brother, by profaning the covenant of our fathers?' [Mal. xi. 10.] "The LORD He is the God; it is he who hath made us, and not we ourselves. We are his people, and the sheep of his pasture.' [Ps. c. 3.] "O LORD, thou art *our Father*, we are the clay, and thou art the potter; and we are all the work of thy hand.' "[Isaiah lxiv. 8.] "Doubtless thou art our Father; thou, O LORD, art our Father, our Redeemer; thy name is from everlasting.' [Isaiah lxiii. 16.]

If then GOD be our Father, surely we are all brethren; and this sacred relationship, "this covenant of Brother,' is not to be set aside by any distance of place, or by any accidental difference of appearances, or peculiarity of advantages. Wherever we see the human form, we see an image of GOD, and a brother according to the Flesh. Justly then might we call out to the African Trader, and the Indian Planter, if they had but hearts to hear, "Sirs, ye are brethren, why do you wrong one to another?' [Acts, vii. 26.] If this relationship be established by *Creation*, how much more important, more extensive, and more sacred, must it appear, when considered with a view to *Redemption*. "GOD was manifest in the flesh to reconcile a world of sinful creatures to himself, and to unite them in the bonds of eternal amity and love.' He came to destroy the kingdom of darkness, evil, and misery; and to establish his everlasting kingdom of light and truth; of goodness and righteousness.

The extent of this great plan of mercy is as wide as the misery of sin, as universal as the empire of death. "Christ tasted death for *every man;* there is one Mediator between GOD and *man,* the man Christ Jesus, who gave himself a ransom for *all,* to be testified in due time (or rather χαιροις ιδιοις, in proper seasons). [1 Tim. ii. 6.] "We have an advocate with the Father, Jesus Christ the Righteous; and He is the propitiation for our sins; and not for ours only, but also for the sins of *the whole world.*' [I John ii. 2.] "For as in Adam *all* die, even so in Christ shall *all* be made alive.' [I Cor. xv. 22.]

All men, then, are heirs of the heavenly inheritance, and are capable of being translated from the kingdom of Satan into the kingdom of Christ. Gentiles and Jews, Heathens and Christians, on their belief of the Gospel, are fellow heirs together in a glorious immortality; for they are now the adopted children of one common parent, the purchased property of the same Saviour; and the same new and living way into the true holy of holies, even into Heaven itself, is open to all, through Jesus Christ our Lord.

The great and comprehensive mercy of the Gospel has united men more closely in the bonds of mutual charity. The endearing term of *brother*, as pointing out a special relationship between man and man, is there introduced. If I stand without excuse for injuring my brother after the flesh, how much more inexcusable am I, if, to increase my wealth, to flatter my vanity, and to exercise a wanton cruelty, I injure and degrade my brother after the Spirit, for whom Christ died?

The mild and benevolent spirit of Christianity, in proportion as it prevailed among the nations which became converted to the Gospel, abolished the servile condition, and taught mankind that the lowest as well as the highest, the ignorant as well as the wise, had rights which were sacred, and prospects which were eternal.

The happy revival of literature and religious knowledge at the time of the Reformation abolished all the remains of domestic slavery in our own country; but, about the same period [2], a more systematic and more horrid species of slavery was introduced; I mean, that of working the Western Islands, which the Spaniards had almost depopulated by their cruelties, by means of slaves imported from Africa. This evil is the more dreadful, because it is far removed from the observation of the wise and the good;

it is practised by the avaricious and the cruel, who are interested either to conceal their outrages by falsehood, or to defend them by sophistry. It is practised in all the horrid luxuriance of iniquity by the English, a nation who boast that they are free, and profess that they are Christians. It is to this practice in particular that I wish to confine your present attention.

The evil consequences of the unnatural and degrading relation of Master and Slave are thus described by an able advocate. "It corrupts the morals of the master, by freeing him from those restraints with respect to his slave, so necessary for the controul of the human passions, so beneficial in promoting the practice and confirming the habit of virtue.—It is dangerous to the master, because his oppression excites implacable resentment and hatred in the slave; and the extreme misery of his condition continually prompts him to risque the gratification of them; and his situation daily furnishes the opportunity.——To the slave it communicates all the afflictions of life, without leaving for him scarce any of its pleasures; and it depresses the excellency of his nature, by denying the ordinary means and motives of improvement. It is dangerous to the State, by its corruption of those citizens on whom its safety depends; and by admitting within it a multitude of persons who, being excluded from the common benefits of the constitution, are interested in scheming its destruction"³.

But how are these evils aggravated, when considered in a religious point of view—as affecting the slave and the master—the interests of the Gospel, and the welfare of the nation which tolerates such conduct!

In the extensive kingdoms of Africa, the most horrid wars, rapine, and desolation, have been encouraged for more than 200 years, to promote this trade in human blood. Some are entrapped by deceit, but the generality are seized by violence. Their fields are desolated; their houses are burnt with fire. The mild and peaceable Negro is driven from his comfortable home; torn from all the tender connections of social life; branded with a hot iron; confined on shipboard amidst chains and nakedness, filth and pestilence. There they are crowded in such numbers, and treated with such cruelty, that death brings a happy release unto thousands, who only experience "the beginning of sorrows.'

For those who escape the dangers of the sea, and endure the hardships of the voyage, new calamities are reserved in store when they arrive at the place of their destination.

Here the complicated evils of slavery properly begin: here they are exposed like cattle in a market; sent to the distant plantations; roused before the rising sun; and employed in the hardest labour; trembling under the tyranny of a master, who is exercised in scenes of blood, and knows scarce any restraint from the fear of unrighteous laws.[4]

Here the sad remains of a wretched existence are dragged out; harrassed by exhausting labour, surrounded with the view of the miseries of their countrymen; supported by the scanty pittance of the worst food; deprived of all the comforts of this life; and uninstructed in any hope of a better. Their lives are not esteemed by their owners of so much value as the life of a beast; though even the life of his beast a merciful man will regard. Their misery is often so extreme that they seek for refuge in the arms of death. Some lay violent hands on themselves; and others refuse all sustenance, that they may find that rest in the grave which is denied them by men, by Englishmen, by Christians.

In the British Plantations it is no uncommon thing to behold the insolence of power and the wantonness of cruelty; to hear the groans of despair, and the cries of deserted infants. "The plowers plough upon their backs, and make long furrows.' The fruits of the earth are produced amidst tears of blood, and groans of anguish. The prospect to them is hopeless: no industry can regain their freedom, no time can restore them to their native country. No distinction is made; no respect is paid to age or sex; but all are crowded together like a herd of brute beasts: and here we behold the wretched effects of this traffick in human blood; to degrade, to corrupt, to brutalize mankind.[5]

Thus does our brother, for whom Christ died, become vile in our eyes.

Yet this most horrid traffick has continued for ages; in which; to speak within compass, not less than an hundred millions of the human race have most wretchedly perished, in hunger and in cold, in pestilence and in desolation, without a protector, without a comforter; without an avenger.

Yet the condition of the *Slaves,* though thus humiliating and severe, is infinitely preferable to that of their tyrants and oppressors, it being always better to suffer wrong than to inflict it.

But here I am happy to make some exceptions, though I fear they are but few; some Planters there are who treat their Slaves with mildness and compassion. These, although they have not an outward law to claim this, yet "they are a law unto themselves;' and they do not, in the actions of every day, "deny the LORD who bought them.'

It will easily appear how much more deplorable is the state of the cruel Master than that of his suffering Slaves, if we consider his conduct here, as preparatory to an awful and eternal state hereafter.

There are but two Beings whom men worship and obey—these are GOD, who is Love; the Father of mercies and the GOD of all consolation, the Saviour of mankind: and the Devil or Satan, who was a murderer from the beginning, who is the destroyer, who delights in beholding acts of cruelty and bloodshed. The unrighteous Merchant, and the tyrannical Planter, "are of their Father the Devil, and the lusts of their Father they do.' In his works of darkness they zealously engage, and "they shall in no wise lose their reward.'

Of the peace and happiness resulting from benevolence, gentleness, meekness, and forbearance, they have no knowledge or experience: but, by the indulgence of every contrary temper, as cruelty, violence, and revenge; they exclude the Kingdom of Heaven from their souls; they fill up the measure of their iniquities; they lead a life of misery upon earth, which riches cannot console, nor intemperance enliven; and at death they pass into the eternal world, to meet their GOD and their Judge; to receive the fruit of their own doings; and to reap a full recompence of reward.

These infamous Traders, who have heaped up their riches, "the price of blood,' and hardened themselves against their own flesh, will then lift up their eyes in torment, while they see Jesus afar off, and many of their once insulted, degraded, maimed, and murdered Slaves now happy in his bosom. Then perhaps they may beg that one of these may be sent with a drop of water to cool their tongues, because they are "tormented in that flame;' but even this request will then be denied by the Father of Mercies, for "as they shewed no mercy nor compassion on their poor slaves and dependents, so neither shall their Lord have pity on them.'

But this unrighteous traffick in human blood is not more

destructive to those concerned in it, than disgraceful to the religion they profess, and to the nation which tolerates their crimes. By their means the holy name of Jesus is blasphemed, and an invincible obstacle thrown in the way, to hinder the glorious Gospel of Christ from being received by these Heathens. Darkness is not more opposite to light than the principles of this traffick to the spirit of Christianity.[6] That commands us "to preach good tidings unto the meek;' but these men deliberately withhold from their Slaves all rational instruction, and all religious improvement. The Prince of Peace sends us "to bind up the broken-hearted;' but these men bow down their fellow-creatures by oppression, and "regard not the cry of the poor destitute.' The spirit of the Gospel "proclaims liberty to the captive, and the opening of the prison to them that are bound:' but these men rivet the chains of slavery; "the iron enters into the Negro's soul,' while his mind is left in all the darkness of ignorance, without one ray of those comforts which Christianity affords, to strengthen with patience, and to animate with hope, them that endure affliction, suffering wrongfully.

But these dreadful crimes are not only the crimes of individuals, but also of nations, which are conscious of these enormities, and do not interpose to restrain the fury of the tyrant, and to set the oppressed free. England is deeply stained with this guilt;[7] she must answer for the blood of millions, for she knows, and yet she tolerates, this inhuman traffick. It was one of the sins of Tyre, that she "traded in the persons of men,' [Ez. xxvii. 13.]. And if we as a nation resemble her in our sins, we have reason to fear that we shall resemble her in our punishment. "Wherefore, O Nation greatly beloved, let my counsel be acceptable to thee, and break off thy sins by righteousness, and thine iniquities by shewing mercy to the poor [especially to captive Negros], if it may be a lengthening of thy tranquillity.' [Dan. iv. 27.]

May not the LORD of Heaven and Earth say unto this nation, as he did unto the Israelites of old, "Your hands are defiled with blood, and your fingers with iniquity. None calleth for justice, nor any pleadeth for truth. Go to now, therefore, ye rich men; weep and howl for your miseries that shall come upon you; your heart goeth after your covetousness, and your land is defiled with blood. Behold the prayer of the needy, and the voice of the innocent blood which is shed, crieth and entereth the ears of the LORD of Sabbaoth, for a witness against us.—-Shall I not visit for these things, saith the LORD, shall not my soul be avenged of such a nation as this? Behold, the LORD cometh out of his place, to punish the inhabitants of the earth for their iniquity; the earth also shall disclose her blood, and shall no more cover her slain. Vengeance is mine; I will repay, saith the LORD.'

The Western Empire is gone from us, never to return; it is given to another more righteous than we; who consecrated the sword of resistance by declaring for the universal abolition of slavery.[8] The West India islands have been visited with most tremendous hurricanes and earthquakes; by these, the cruel traders have been deprived of all their unrighteous gain, or have been involved with it in one common grave. "Verily, there is a reward for the righteous and for the wicked: doubtless there is a GOD who judgeth the earth.'

As then the English have been most forward in promoting this abominable trade, "as the blood of the souls of the poor innocents is found in their skirts;' so let the English now stand forward to suppress this disgrace to their country.

Next in guilt to those who perpetrate these abominations

are those who, knowing these enormities, do not interfere to prevent them. Every one may do something; he may declare his testimony against violence and wrong; he may appear on the side of humanity, equity, and religion.

Let every man then do what he is able against it, lest the guilt of innocent blood should lie at his door. As we value liberty ourselves, let us glory to make others free; as we have obtained mercy ourselves, so let us never rest, till this mercy be extended to others, and all tears be wiped from off all faces.

Then by all the glorious attributes of our GOD and Saviour, which are insulted by this inhuman traffick—be all the laws of divine love, which he has established; by all the glories of heaven which are displayed to the eye of Faith: —by the common blood which flows in all our veins; and by the blood of Christ which was shed for the sins of the whole world—by that freedom which is the common birth-right of all, and the distinguishing privilege of Englishmen—by the right-aiming thunderbolts of the Almighty, prepared to execute vengeance on nations which deal in oppression—by the tender ties of domestic connections; by all the comforts we enjoy here; and, by all the happiness we expect hereafter;—let us unite with all our powers to vindicate the English name, to honour the Gospel of Peace, and to avert the judgements of Heaven, by the abolition of the Slave Trade, by "restraining the fury of the oppressor,' and by the "letting the captive go free.' The poor and afflicted slaves can never know their friends and benefactors; "they indeed cannot recompense us; but we shall be recompensed at the resurrection of the just.'

Notes

1. To the honour of the illustrious Bishop Warburton, let it be recorded, that he was the first who openly stood forth and condemned this conduct in England. The consistency and the perseverance of the Quakers in this great cause of humanity must highly recommend them to every friend of religion and liberty.

2. In the year 1563 the English commenced this most horrid traffick. The Portuguese set the example to the rest of Europe.

3. Hargrave's Argument in the Case of J. Somerset, and Edit. p. r6.

4. The fine for the wilful murder of a Negro is less than twenty shillings.

5. See Montesquieu's Spirit of the Laws, p. 348.

6. "Whereas Thou hast given us great honour in the presence of nations around us, and power over remote people which sit in darkness;

   "We have not profited them by the preaching of thy word, or the example of righteousness; but have oppressed them and been a snare unto them.

   "And we have even caused them to abhor thy word because of our iniquities and unrighteous dealings, and have given occasion to the blasphemers to blaspheme.'

   King's Hymns to the Supreme Being, p. 136.

7. The Spaniard, the French, and the Portuguese, endeavour to instruct, to improve, and to convert their slaves: but the Protestants the English do not; nay, it is a notorious fact, that they oppose any endeavours towards this Work of Mercy, this Labour of Love. The reason is obvious, that, having little or no regard for their own souls, they have no concern for those of others.

8. See the Declaration of the Congress in 1774.

AN APPEAL

TO

Candour and Common Sense,

RESPECTFULLY ADDRESSED,

TO THE MEMBERS

OF

Both Houses of PARLIAMENT,

AND THE

COMMUNITY AT LARGE.

━━◈━━ ◈━━

By an Individual of *LITTLE NOTE.*

━━◈━━ ◈━━

MDCCLXXXIX.

An Appeal, &c.

WHEN the Minds of Men are artfully misled, when they are deceived by Misrepresentations, and deluded by false Assertions, it behoves every Man of Integrity and Honor, to step forward in the Cause of Truth, to endeavour to check the Torrent of popular Phrenzy, lest, by acquiring Strength from Delay, it should at last become irresistible, and overwhelm us all in one general Ruin.

I am aware of the tender Ground on which I tread; but I will nevertheless fulfil the Duty of a good Citizen, and boldly reprobate those Measures, which, if pursued, must shortly effect the Destruction of this once powerful Empire.

Mr. WILBERFORCE open'd the Business of the Slave Trade, in the House of Commons, with such a powerful Appeal to the Passions, that he extorted Approbation both from the Minister and the great Leader of Opposition:—Nay! even from him[1] who was never known to approve before. Let us examine how far he was entitled to such flattering and general Praise. Whilst we give him Credit for good Language and much Ingenuity, we must censure him for many glaring and positive Contradictions; for a partial Selection of Evidence from the Reports; for Arguments founded on mistated Facts, and for the consequent unwarrantable Conclusions. He tells you, "That he comes not forward to accuse the West India Planter; he comes not forward to accuse the Liverpool Merchant; he comes forward to accuse no one; He comes forward to confess himself guilty, &c. &c.' and then, in a few Seconds, he says, "The Gentlemen who defended this Trade were warped and blinded by their Interests, and WOULD not be convinced of the Miseries they were daily heaping on their Fellow-Creatures.' Is not this an Accusation of the most serious Nature, against a large and very respectable Body of Men, as well Members of the House of Commons, as others? and most strangely does it contradict his Declaration, *"That he accused no one.'* That the Selection of Evidence, from the Reports, on which Mr. WILBERFORCE chose to ground his Arguments, was partial and unfair, must be obvious to every one: Or why is the Story of CALABAR dwelt upon, with such Emphasis, and no mention made of Mr. NORRIS? and why are the Testimonies of the two Swedes courted and admitted of, whilst those of Admirals BARRINGTON and EDWARDS are rejected? The two first sail'd from France, and, both by their Evidence and from their Connexions, may be very reasonably supposed to favor the Interests of that Country; but it cannot be imagined that the two worthy Admirals who have fought the Battles of this, and bled in its Cause, could be guided by any other Motives than the Love of Truth, and a hearty Wish to promote the Interests of Great Britain—These Gentlemen, as well as that illustrious Youth, the Glory of the British Navy, whose long Services in America and the West-Indies, entitle him to our warmest Gratitude and Regard, will rescue the Planters from every Imputation of Cruelty, so ungenerously laid to their Charge; and vouch for the Situation of our Negroes being infinitely preferable to that of the Poor of this Country, according to the present existing State of our Poor-Laws.

Mr. WILBERFORCE next quotes Mr. LONG, but mistakes the Business entirely. That Gentleman certainly did make an Experiment with the Plough in Jamaica: it fail'd however of Success, and was in a short Time totally laid aside. Yet, mark the wonderous Consistency of Mr. W's Argument. After having pourtray'd the English Planters under the most hideous Form, and in the darkest Colours, he contends, they are either so blind, or so indifferent to their own Interest, as not to prefer the Plough to the Labour of One Hundred Negroes, whom they must purchase at a great Expence, maintain them in Health and Sickness, and whose Value is daily decreasing, as Old Age advances, and its natural Infirmities increase.

He then tells you, "that it is not likely the French should carry on the African Trade if we abolish it.' From whence does he draw this Conclusion? Is it from the Premium of eight Pounds per Head which the French pay on the Importation of Negroes into their Colonies?—Is it from the great Encouragement which they give to the fitting out of Ships for the Slave Trade from Havre; where Mr.___a Bankrupt from Liverpool is absolutely establish'd under the immediate Protection of Government for the purpose of forwarding the Trade to Africa? Or is it from Mr. Necker's own Letter, wherein that able Minister "admires the Motives of Humanity which urge the English to abolish the Slave Trade, and laments that his Country is not in a Situation to do the same?" Is it from this Letter, I ask, that Mr. Wilberforce concludes Mr. Necker will follow our Example? Strange Infatuation! But, even, had Mr. Necker made a positive Declaration that his Court would imitate us, he would still be subject to Suspicion.—The Perfidy of France has ever been proverbial in this Country, and every Page of History justifies the Idea. Sound Policy should ever teach us to mistrust our natural Enemies.

—— et dona ferentes.

We should never loose Sight of that great Truth which the

French most certainly ever have in View, that they can only rise by our Fall, and that our Ruin must be the Foundation on which alone they can establish their Greatness.___But observe another very ingenious Argument held by Mr. Wilberforce "that, if the French took up the African Trade, it must be of Use to us, for that Money was the Sinew of war, and if they spent their Capital in little Service to themselves, it would be of Service to us.' Have the Liverpool Merchants spent *their* Capitals in little Use to us? Has not the African Trade made their City one of the most thriving, and most opulent in the world? In Peace, are not Riches daily flowing into their Port from every Quarter of the Globe? And, in War, are not their Privateers the Terror and Destruction of the Trade of our Enemies? Yet, all this real Wealth, this real Greatness is to be given up, and we are told, that ample Amends are to be made to the Public by substituting some wild, imaginary Branch of Trade, which the visionary Schemes of Mr. Wilberforce's enthusiastic Constituents have suggested. Thus, whilst he reprobates the African Trade, as the Grave of our Seamen, he proposes,—for their Preservation no doubt—the adopting ONE in lieu of it, to the SAME Country and Climate. But the Public only, are taught to expect an Adequate:—As to Individuals, I learn from the Minister, they are to hope for no Compensation whatever. Mr. Wilberforce very aptly, quotes from Holy Writ: May I not do the same, and say "Thou shall not steal.' And ask the Minister, —if private Property is invaded, and what was once held inviolate under the Sanction of Parliment, is now to be sacrificed to popular Phrenzy, or private Views;—is not that great Commandment broken? Does Mr. Wilberforce recollect the Effect which the Revocation of the Edict of *Nantes* in favour of the Protestants, had in France?

that it drove Thousands of good Subjects, with their Fortunes, Families, and their Manufactories from that Country, to enrich their natural Enemies? If this strange Project is persisted in, will not *Havre* and *Rouen* soon become what *Liverpool* is now? But the Bugbear HUMANITY is to be held out to gull the ignorant and unwary. Let us then fully investigate that Subject. Mr. Wilberforce mentions the Traffic of Human Flesh being carried on in England, not many Years ago, and quotes the Inhabitants of Bristol, in the Reign of Henry 7th, who used to sell their Children to the Irish. Was it necessary to refer to so remote a Period of History to establish the Fact? could not the glorious Reign of George the Third have furnished an Example more repugnant to *every* Feeling of Humanity than the African Trade? Have we already forgot the Purchase of Men we made last War? when Sir. Wm. Fawcett was the Broker, and absolutely tranfer'd to the British Government, from the Landgrave of Hesse, and Margrave of Anspach, many Thousands of Germans, who were hurried from all they held dear, —to a Country they had never heard of,—to fight for—they knew not what. I will not dwell on the Manner in which they were convey'd to America, the wretched Transports appointed to carry them, or the ignorant, and unskilful Captains to whose Care they were committed.—I will not enumerate the Numbers which consequently perish'd before they arrived at the Place of their Destination; but, Pity prompts me to shed a Tear over those, who, having survived the Loss of Limbs, are now to be seen in the Towns, and Villages of Germany, sinking under a most complicated Load of Misery, begging their daily Pittance from Door to Door, the woeful Monuments of BRITISH HUMANITY. Should the present Minister plead State Necessity, or excuse himself, by tell-

ing me he had no Hand in such Transactions, I will remind
him of the *late* inhuman Tragedy of *Sierra Leona*, and the Fate
of two Hundred Negroes, mostly Slaves, who, having eloped
from their Masters in Virginia, and the Carolinas, during the
American Contest, had enter'd on board our Ships of war, and
were paid off, at the Peace, at our different Sea Ports; who, taken
up, together with threescore Prostitutes with whom they had
connected themselves, were put on board a Ship bound to the
Coast of Africa, and suffer'd to remain at the Mother Bank, 'till
a putrid Fever appear'd among them, and carried off many: That
the Contagion encreased when they reached the hot Latitudes
may be easily conceived; but the Fact will scarcely be credited,—that when the Ships of war which convoy'd them out, left
them on their destined Spot,—THAT SPOT, *now* represented as
so capable of *Fertility* and *Civilization*,—there remained alive,
only FOURTEEN NEGROES and ONE WOMAN. In this Instance,
I presume, neither the Plea or the Excuse will be admitted of;
for, it is evident, that two Hundred poor Wretches were sacrificed, at a vast Expence to Government, who, had they been
embodied, divided into Companies, and attach'd to the different
Regiments on foreign Duty, for the Purpose of wooding, and
watering, might have been now alive, of Service to the State,
and the saving of many Europeans.

As the two Instances I have mentioned might perhaps be
deemed *perishable Records*, and that the Fame of British Humanity
may be founded in the most remote Quarters of the Globe;
have we not most *humanely* invaded the peaceful Inhabitants
of New-Holland? Have we not sent them such a select, and
admirable Colony, under the Command of Commodore
PHILIP, as will introduce to them every Vice, every Wickedness,

and every Disorder that were ever bred in the Purlieus of St. Giles, and brought to systematic Perfection within the Walls of Newgate? still, should they be blind to the Advantages of this British Method of Civilization, their friendly Visitors will adopt the proper Means to convince them of their Error.

> "On the New Island clap King George's Seal,
> A sharp Impression too of hardest Steel,
> Whilst Witness Pistol, and his Brother Gun,
> Look with a pointed Approbation on.
> A decent Method of Appropriation,
> And adding Glory to the British Nation.'

But the Subject is serious—and, all this is done under the Sanction of Laws enacted by the Promoters of Freedom, and the Advocates for Humanity. But, let me ask those worthy Gentlemen! should they succeed, and obtain their grand Object, under the Cloud of Error that now prevails, will they accomplish the Ends they profess to have in View? will they prevent *France, Spain, Portugal, Holland, Denmark*, the States of *Barbary*, and all *India* from purchasing African Slaves? will they thereby obviate future Wars between the petty Princes of Africa, the Kidnapping of Children hereafter, or any unjust Sentences in *their* Courts of Judicature? Let them recollect that every Discovery made by Captain Cook, and other Circumnavigators, most incontestibly, prove, that every Nation in a savage State, is in a constant State of Warfare; and that the inevitable Fate of their Prisoners is Death. This Truth is illustrated even by the humane, and gentle Inhabitants of *Pelew*; and that this was the State of Africa, long before it was visited by Europeans, is evinced by the Testimony of LEO AFRICANUS, the best Historian of that Country we know of. And the Accounts of every modern Traveller worthy of

Belief, tend to corroborate this Fact, "That Wars are not made in Africa for the Sake of obtaining Prisoners for Sale, but, if they did not find a Method of disposing of them, they would not be suffered to exist.' And, it appears, besides, that the greatest Number of those who are sold, are Convicts for various Crimes, but particularly for Witchcraft, which, among that superstitious, unenlightened People, involves the whole Family of the guilty Person in one general Sentence.[2]

But to continue. The welfare of our Islands, tho' inseperably connected with the great commercial Interests of this Kingdom, seems at present to be totally unworthy of Attention. Ministers appear to have forgot, that the Tie between the Mother Country and her Colonies is mutual, the Obligation reciprocal; and that the *one*, no longer owe Duty, Affection, and Obedience, than the *other* shelters them under her protecting Arm, and affords them all that parental Assistance, to which their worth entitles them. Instead of that, let us view their present Situation. The Trade of the islands was formerly divided into three distinct Classes, viz. To America, to Africa, and to Europe. The first is totally annihilated by excessive Restrictions: The second is about to be abolished: and the third is so fetter'd with Duties, and so loaded with Taxes, as scarcely to retain any Power of Motion. The Hour is perhaps not far distant, when France, recovered from her intestine Commotions, may offer that Protection, and Assistance, which is now claim'd in vain from England. She will find the Planters (notwithstanding the Threats of the Minister) ready to accept the Boon, and will wrest from this country those valuable Possessions which have ever contributed to render this Kingdom the Glory, and Envy of the World. No Reliance is now to be placed on the Testimonies of the West India Merchants, and Planters, or Deference to their commercial Weight; but, the immaculate Mr. Ramsay is to be credited on *every* Occasion, and *his* Revenge for private Quarrels is to be satiated by the Extension of public Oppression on his Opponents. —I will not so libel the character of Sir Wm. Dolben as to suppose him acquainted with *that* of Mr. Ramsay, but I will appeal to every Negroe in St Kitts, if the Name of Ramsay is not, proverbially, used, throughout that Island, as a Threat, which conveys with it the Horror of the severest Chastisement. Yet, this Man, after having left in the West Indies the most odious Recollection of him, that ever disgraced the Character of any European, dares, boldly, to venture forward, and preach the Cause of Humanity, patronised by some who are misled by his Plausibility, and Deceit; and by others, who, thro' his means, at the Eve of a general Election, with to pave their way to a future Seat in Parliament. But, let these Men reflect, e'er 'tis too late, that tho' they may now "lead the Rabble after them as Monsters make a Shew,' when they shall have carried a fatal Blow to the commercial Interests of this Kingdom, they will be execrated by every reflecting Patriot, nor will they meet with the Consolation, they expect, from the Prayers, and Benedictions of the swarthy Sons of Africa.

The Author of the foregoing Pages, however, hopes not to be mistaken. Tho' he has the Good of his Country at Heart, and feels all the consequence of the African Trade; yet, he is sensible of the Value of Liberty, and lays in as strong a Claim to Humanity, as even Mr. WILBERFORCE himself. He, therefore, presumes to suggest some Regulations which he conceives will, much, contribute to the Health, Preservation, and Comfort of the Slaves, in their Passage from Africa to our Colonies: He wishes only, that they may serve as Hints, and that some more able Pen will improve and meliorate them. And he concludes, with hoping that the mention of many worthy Names which has, unavoidably, been made thro' this little Work, will not be construed into Personal Disrespect. He well knows how to value Merit, even in those who differ with him in Opinion, to court Instruction even from his Opponents, and, like our able Minister, to be ever open to *Conviction*, when founded on JUSTICE, SENSE, and REASON.

Regulations proposed for the African Trade.

I. The Number of Slaves to be in Proportion to the Tonnage of the Vessel, and the Height between Decks to be likewise ascertain'd.

II. That no Insurance whatever shall take Place on the Lives of Slaves.

III. That every African Trader give One Month's Notice of his Sailing, to the Navy Board, who shall furnish him (according to the Size of the Vessel) with one or more Surgeon's Mates, who have passed their Examination for first Mate of a first Rate.

IV. That the Surgeons should be paid by the Owners of the Ship, Five Pounds per Month Wages, and shall be entitled to Two-pence per Month for every Sailor and Slave during the Time they are on board the Ship, to be paid also by the Owners; and shall further receive from them, the Sum of Five Shillings as a Premium for every Negroe landed and sold.

V. At those Ports where there is an Agent Victualler, the Surgeon on his Arrival at the Ship shall apply to him, and they shall jointly make a Survey of the Provisions, &c. The Drugs shall be furnish'd from Apothecary's Hall, according to the Usage of the Navy: And they shall immediately make their joint Report to the Navy-Board, who shall immediately give the proper Orders to the Collector of the Customs to grant or withold the Clearance.

VI. The Surgeon to keep a daily Journal with the Names and Numbers of the Ship's Company during the whole Voyage. He shall likewise keep a Journal of the Negroes, and shall be very particular in specifying their Complaints, his Mode of Treatment, &c. as in the 10th Article of Naval Instructions for Surgeons: and such Journal shall be delivered upon Oath within fifteen Days after his Arrival to the Physicians in the Commission of sick and wounded.

VII. That, in each Ship, a sick Birth as airy and commodious as possible, be fitted up for the Slaves, so that no sick Slave should remain with the healthy.

VIII. The Surgeon shall take every Opportunity of airing, fumigating, and washing the Ship with Vinegar between Decks; for which Purpose every Ship shall be furnish'd with a sufficient Quantity of that Article, likewise two Ventilators and proper Windsails.

VIII. That no Sailor, shall, on any Account, be discharged from any African Trading Vessel, either on the Coast, or to any Place to which they may Trade, 'till he has absolutely found an Opportunity of reshipping himself for England: nor shall he then quit the Ship 'till he has received his full Wages to the Day of his Discharge, and one Month's extra Pay from the Captain or Master, in Presence of the Surgeon: and all such Wages and Pay shall be paid in Dollars or the current Coin of the Country, and not by any Means in Bills. —Any Sailor aggrieved by the Non-performance of this Article, by making his Complaint to the Naval Commander on that Station, and entering on board one of his Majesty's Ships, the same shall be transmitted to the Admiralty, and their Solicitor order'd to prosecute.

Notes.

1. Mr.Burke.
2. See the Reports.

THE

TRUE STATE OF THE QUESTION,

ADDRESSED TO THE

PETITIONERS

FOR THE

ABOLITION

OF THE

SLAVE TRADE.

BY A PLAIN MAN,

WHO SIGNED THE PETITION AT DERBY.

———————

LONDON.

PRINTED FOR J. BELL, BRITISH LIBRARY, STRAND.

MDCCXCII.

[*Price Sixpence.*]

THE
TRUE STATE OF THE QUESTION.
Friends, and Fellow Countrymen,

WHEN an honest man has been led into error, it is his duty not only to recant himself, but being fairly convinced, to warn others in the same situation, and save them as much as possible from fruitless repentance and regret.

I am a plain well-meaning man, who thought I was doing my duty to my God and my Country, in signing the Petition from this Town. The Squire is a rich man, and they say printed a Book of Verses some years ago, so I thought he must be a wise man ; moreover, he is my Landlord, and he said, "*Thomas*, it is your duty to sign against this unchristian wickedness,' and so I signed. Many, thousands set their names to these Petitions in the same manner, for we in the country know nothing of what is doing in India, and Africa, and those parts, but what we are told; the more infamous those who deceive us with falsehoods, and get us to sign Petitions, which if Parliament attends to, I now plainly see, must reduce thousands of families to beggary, put the Blacks in a much worse state than they are, and end in Old England paying about two millions of additional Taxes, a sum now paid by the Planters on goods imported from the West Indies, which it is impossible to produce without the labour of the Blacks.

This information I owe to a Parson who was on a visit at Nottingham, and who had been Chaplain to a Regiment in Jamaica. He said he wished our labouring poor were half as well off as the Negroes: they have each a little snug house and garden, and plenty of pigs and poultry: that exclusive of every

Sunday, and half every Saturday, their Masters allow them one day in fourteen for themselves. Those who are industrious are much at their ease; and the Parson says it is a common thing to see at their feasts, fine fowls, very good beef, English bottled porter, and wine. Who has ever seen such fare in a Labourer's house in England? Who can expect to see it even in a Farmer's, when we shall have those taxes laid upon us, now paid by the West Indians, which must be the case if our Petitions succeed. Were a poor man here to give one such dinner as the Negroes, the savings of his whole life would not suffice; for small indeed will be the savings of a Labourer, who must clothe his wife, clothe his children, nourish his family, pay the doctor when they are sick, pay his rent, and purchase even the tools with which he earns his scanty and precarious subsistence. He is the slave of the most inexorable master—Necessity—and even the Game that ravages the little corn, or small garden, he possibly may have, and which might occasionally procure him a wholesome hearty meal, he dares not touch. As the Parson properly observed, we should in the first instance restore freedom to, and relieve the wants of our own poor.—Remove the beam from our own eye, before we meddle with the mote in our brother's.

He proceeded to give me an account of the Negroes on the Plantations where he had been.

They have a house and garden for nothing, clothes found them, food found them, both good and sufficient, the best doctors in the Country to attend them when sick, their wives and children provided for, and all without any expence. The Parson, who lived there three years, says this is the general state of the Negroes on all the Plantations he saw; and that in a great many parts they catch, by the means of springes or snares, abundance of wild pidgeons and Guinea-hens.

He acknowledges some of them are at times whipped ; but generally for crimes for which in England they would be hanged, or (in our great mercy) sent to starve to death in Botany Bay. He concluded by saying, that in Africa they are in a wretched situation, and in a much more abject state of slavery than in our Islands; that we had mistaken the matter grossly; that to abolish the Trade, would not be to make the Blacks free, but to leave them a prey to every misery that savage Tyranny can inflict. To prove this, he sent me next day the following paper, which I recommend to your serious perusal: it clearly shews, that the Africans are brought from the most barbarous state, where no comfort or enjoyment is known, to one of great comparative happiness, and not subject to so much labour as any working man in England.

The above I have written from a thorough conviction of my error, and I am really sincerely sorry, that my name appeared to any Petition against a Trade, productive of such partial evil and general advantage.

I am, Friends and Fellow Petitioners, Your Well-wisher, A CONVERT to the TRUTH.

A TRUE *and* ACCURATE ACCOUNT *of the* Condition *of the,* NEGROES *in* their own Country; *taken from the* EVIDENCE *given before the* LORDS *of the* COMMITTEE *of the* COUNCIL, *appointed for the Consideration of all Matters relating to Trade and Foreign Plantations.*

SIR GEORGE YONGE, Was four times on the Coast, which is chiefly divided into petty States; the Sovereigns have power of life and death, regard their subjects as slaves, and treat them accordingly.

Mr. ALEXANDER FALCONBRIDGE, Surgeon, Who had made five voyages, "spoke of the Fantyn Nation as more civilized than most others, but even there the confidential Servant, male and female, of every person of distinction, are actually put to death, and interred with them; and that tradition says, formerly a much more considerable number were put to death with their Lords.'

It is a fair inference, that the opportunities they now have of selling their Slaves to Europeans, has so much diminished this barbarous practice.

RICHARD MILES, Esq. LATE GOVERNOR OF CAPE COAST CASTLE, Resided on the Coast of Africa eighteen years, and asserts, "that he had ocular demonstration of human sacrifices still being made to their idols, which are Reptiles, Rivers, Rocks, and other material objects!'

JEROME BERNARD WEAVES, Esq. GOVERNOR OF ANNAMABOE, Resided in Africa fourteen years. He has seen the human victims parading about, and dressed out, who were to be sacrificed at the death of persons of distinction. This horrid custom Europeans have endeavoured to prevent, but without effect.

ARCHIBALD DALZELL, Esq. FOUR YEARS GOVERNOR OF WHYDAH, Speaking of the Kingdom of Dahomy, which is the largest bordering on the Gold Coast, declares, that in the whole Kingdom there is no individual Freeman, except the King, who is absolutely master of the lives and properties of his Subjects, and he sports with their lives in the most wanton and cruel manner.

ROBERT NORRIS, Esq. A CAROLINA MERCHANT, Has seen, at the Gates of the King's Palace, two piles of human heads,

THE TRUE STATE OF THE QUESTION

like shot in an Arsenal. When an audience is given, the heads of persons newly put to death are strewed in the passage that leads to the Royal Apartment, in order to inspire the person to be admitted with awe. The roof of the Palace is decorated with human heads. Parents have no sort of property in their children; they all belong to the King, and are taken by his order from their Mother at an early age, and distributed in Villages remote from the place of their nativity, where there is little chance of their being ever recognized by their Parents. When the King waters the graves of his Ancestors, (a phrase for deluging them with human blood) which is an annual custom, very many are put to death, particularly such as Europeans may have refused to purchase.

Another proof, that the Slave Trade tends to preserve the lives of the Blacks.

Mr. NORRIS adds, "that if the King is in want of European Goods, a small number of Slaves are executed; but the number increases as his wants are fewer.'

Suppress the Slave Trade, and it is evident human sacrifices would be endless.

Mr. NORRIS, not willing such horrid, and to English ears, incredible instances of cruelty should rest on his simple assertion, called on

WILLIAM DEVAYNES, Esq. Who was Governor in Africa twelve years, to corroborate his evidence.—Mr. DEVAYNES confirms Mr. NORRIS's accounts of the annual sacrifice of about sixty men and women to the manes of the King's Ancestors; and adds, that if a man falls down in the space before the King's Palace, which is of four or five hundred yards, he is immediately put to death, it being presumed he had some disloyal thoughts in his head to make him fall on level ground. —When the Queen's Mother died, he was present at one of the Chief Officers' being taken to be put to death, merely as a mark of respect. While he was there, he does not recollect one of the King's Officers dying a natural death.

GOVERNOR DALZELL Declares, that in Whydah, on the death of a Man, his Wife and Property all go to the King, but he *sometimes* restores it to those families whom he finds meritorious.

Mr. DALZELL, at an Annual Feast where the King regales the people, saw a Man tied, an Alligator tied, a pair *of* Pidgeons also tied, flung from a stage, *all* of which, as he was informed, were put to death by the people below.

During this Feast, which continues some days, Mr. DALZELL always found, upon going to the King's house, heads that appeared to have been newly cut off; and he has seen about twenty of those victims at a time. Previous to their execution, they were tied to stakes, and exhibited for a day or two before their execution, which he presumes was done in the night; he has been desired to go and see it, but never would.

These victims, he understood, were sent to attend the King's Ancestors in the other world.

Mr. PENNY, Saw human sacrifices made to the manes of a deceased King of Bonny. This Country, Mr. PENNY declares to be like the rest; the lives and properties of the People being at the disposal of the Prince.

Now follows the Evidence of Mr. FULLER, Mr. LONG, and other Gentlemen, respecting the state of the Negroes in the West Indies, given before the Lords of the Committee.

Their State in the Islands.

A Slave cannot lose his life, nor be imprisoned for life, but on being found guilty of certain crimes, by Nine Freeholders, no ways interested in the case, before Three Justices of the Peace, all sworn to do justice.

The life of a Slave is held as sacred as that of a white person, and any Master occasioning the death of a Slave, is guilty of Felony, without Benefit of Clergy.

Such is the commerce that the industrious Slaves carry on in pork and poultry, and corn and vegetables, that they are in actual possession of nine-tenths of the smaller silver currency of the Island; nor has any example been found in the memory of man, that the Owners of such Negroes have deprived them of any part of their acquisitions, which by long practice and usage, are universally considered as their own property; which they may keep, dispose of, or devise at their own pleasure; and many could purchase their Freedom, were they of opinion it would render their condition more comfortable and happy than it is at present.

The Law obliges Planters to furnish sufficient clothing to the Negroes, and they are generally well clothed ; besides, there are few Sugar Estates where the Negroes do not from their own private earnings provide themselves with extra clothes for Sundays and Holidays.

The established Negroes live in houses perfectly convenient to themselves, and adapted to the climate; when they want repairing, time, materials, and assistance are allowed them for those purposes. Upon the whole, we believe them to be far better clothed, lodged and fed in Jamaica, than the Peasantry of Europe in general.

The Negroes have on an average fifteen hours in every twenty-four, for the purposes of repose and refreshment.

EXTRACTS *from the* LAWS i*n force in* JAMAICA.
When punished for crimes by whipping, the Laws allow at most thirty-nine lashes for the same offence.

Are the Armies in Europe under such restrictions?
It is now enacted by a positive Law, which before was only custom, that the Negroes have one day, exclusive of Sundays, in every fourteen, over and above the usual holidays, for the cultivation of their own grounds and gardens.

Lord RODNEY, Sir PETER PARKER, Admiral BARRINGTON, Sir JOSHUA ROWLEY, Admiral HOTHAM, and others,

All declared before the Committee, that during their residence in the West Indies, they observed the Slaves were treated with great humanity; that they were satisfied with their condition; that they were not over-worked ; that they were well clothed, well lodged, well fed ; in a word, they generally declared, they thought them better off than the labouring Poor in this Country.

I suppose, now, my good Friend, you have read the accounts drawn from Evidence given before the Lords of the Committee, you will there perceive, without any comment of mine, what was the situation of the Black in Africa, and what it actually is in our Islands ; you will see, that he is brought from a Country where Laws are yet unknown; where he has no property even in his life; where all that man holds dear is at the disposal of a Despot, at whose nod Children are torn from the breast of the Mother ; where the Parents are offered in sacrifice to the vanity of the Tyrant; where the miserable Slave creeps to his pallet, surrounded but by horrors, and awakes only to new scenes of bloodshed and of oppression ; where murder is magnificence, and acts of cruelty alone proclaim the Power of the Prince. From this abject, this disgraceful condition, which makes the mind thrill with horror to contemplate, and the hand tremble in the description, he is brought to us in a state of Slavery it is true; but how mitigated, how different from the tyranny and scenes of carnage he has left! With us his life is inviolate, his property is protected, and by a late Act, the slightest punishment cannot be inflicted, but as regulated by Law; he lives amongst his children, who share his labour in the vigour of his life, and are his comfort and solace in his age ; he dies surrounded by his friends and relatives, to whom he bequeaths in confidence and security the earnings of an industrious life. And shall we close the asylum to him for ever? The interests of humanity more even than the interests of the State, forbids it.

If we are to solicit the interference of Parliament, let it be to enforce the regulations already made for his instruction in our Holy Religion, so that the finishing feature may be put to this faithful picture of his condition; so that this Trade, which interest has belied, ignorance reprobated, and credulity endeavoured to destroy, shall not only be the means of rescuing thousands of our fellow-creatures from tyranny and death, but bring them from the grossest idolatry to a knowledge of the True God, make their lives comfortable here, and insure their everlasting happiness.

I am, my dear Friend, Your Well-wisher,
Late a CHAPLAIN *in the* ARMY.

P. S. In one or two places in the Evidence respecting the state of the Blacks in Africa, you will see a line or two *scored under* ; those lines are my Observations, and not part of the Evidence.— In speaking of the state of the Blacks in our Islands, I have confined myself chiefly to the Evidence respecting Jamaica, being the Island I am best acquainted with, and the condition of the Negroes being much the same in all the Island.

AN

ADDRESS

TO THE

Inhabitants of Glasgow, Paisley, and the Neighbourhood,

CONCERNING THE

AFRICAN SLAVE TRADE,

BY

A SOCIETY IN GLASGOW.

GLASGOW:

PRINTED BY ALEX. ADAM,

MDCCXCI.

GLASGOW, 18th Jan. 1791.

AT a Meeting of the Society in Glasgow, for co-operating with the other Societies in Britain, in effecting the abolition of the Slave-trade: DAVID DALE, Esq; in the Chair.

THERE was read over to the Meeting, a paper on the Slave-trade, intended to be addressed to the Inhabitants of Glasgow, Paisley, and the neighbourhood, which being considered, is approved of, and ordered to be printed at the expence of the Society, and a Copy of the Section of the Slave-ship, published by the Society in London, to be annexed to every Copy of the address.

(Signed) DAVID DALE.

N. B. Papers for obtaining Subscriptions, are appointed to be lodged in *the Royal Bank-office; and the Tontine Coffee-room, Glasgow.*

ADDRESS CONCERNING THE SLAVE TRADE.

THE question now in dependence before the British House of Commons, relative to the abolition of the African Slave Trade, must be highly interesting to every feeling mind. It respects the essential rights of human nature, and millions of rational beings are involved in its determination.

If it be true, as has been insinuated, that the people of Great Britain, are in any measure unconcerned about the issue, this must be owing to the want of proper information upon the subject. It cannot otherwise be believed that a generous nation, would remain indifferent to a discussion, which is to determine the happiness or misery of so great a proportion of their fellow creatures.

A variety of recent events have conspired to direct the attention of enlightened men to subjects formerly neglected. The situation of the wretched Africans in particular, has been inquired into: And our conduct towards them has been demonstrated to be inhuman and unjust in the extreme.

The circumstances attending the African slave trade, must fill with horror, every person of common humanity. It would be endless, to enumerate all the facts, by which the iniquity of that barbarous traffic, has been proved in the fullest manner. It cannot be denied, that on the coast of Guinea, the miserable natives are in great numbers seized by violence, or carried off by fraud and perfidy—that wars are kindled and dreadful devastations produced, for the sole purpose of enslaving the inhabitants of towns and villages[1]. There is likewise but too much reason to believe, that those Europeans employed in the trade, not only give encouragement to those shocking measures, but sometimes take an active part in the execution of them. The following well authenticated narrative, is perhaps, the best illustration of what has just been mentioned.

"In the year 1767, the ships Indian Queen, Duke of York, Nancy and Concord, of Bristol, the Edgar of Liverpool, and the Canterbury of London, lay in Old Calabar river.

It happened at this time, that a quarrel subsisted between the principal inhabitants of Old Town, and those of New Town, Old Calabar; which had originated in a jealousy respecting slaves. The Captains of the vessels now mentioned, united in sending several letters to the inhabitants of Old Town, but particularly to Ephraim Robin John, who was at that time a Grandee, and a principal inhabitant of the place. The universal tenor of these letters was, that they were sorry that any jealousy should subsist between the two parties; and that if the inhabitans of Old Town, would come on board, they would afford them security and protection, adding at the same time, that their intention in inviting them, was, that they might become mediators and heal their disputes.

The inhabitants of Old Town, happy to find, that their differences were likely to be reconciled, joyfully accepted the invitation. The three brothers of the Grandee just mentioned, the eldest of whom was Amboe Robin John, first entered their canoe, attended by twenty-seven others, and being followed by nine canoes, directed their course to the Indian Queen. They were dispatched from thence the next morning to the Edgar, and afterwards to the Duke of York, on board of which they went leaving their canoe and attendants by the side of the same vessel. In the mean time the people on board the other canoes, were either distributed on board, or lying close to the other ships.

This being the situation of the three brothers and of the principal inhabitants of the place, the treachery now began to appear. The crew of the Duke of York, aided by the captain and the mates, and armed with pistols and cutlasses, rushed into the cabin with an intent to seize the persons of their three innocent and unsuspicious guests. The unhappy men, alarmed at this flagrant violation of the rights of hospitality, and struck with astonishment at the behaviour of their supposed friends, attempted to escape through the cabin windows, but being wounded, were obliged to desist, and to submit to be put in irons.

In the same moment in which this atrocious attempt had been made, an order had been given to fire upon the canoe, that was then lying by the side of the Duke of York. The canoe soon filled and sunk, and the wretched attendants were either seized, killed or drowned. Most of the other ships immediately followed the example. Great numbers were additionally killed or drowned on the occasion, and others were swimming to the shore.

At this juncture the inhabitants of New Town, who had concealed themselves in the bushes by the water side, and between whom and the commanders of the vessels the plan had been previously concerted, came out from their hiding places, and embarking in their canoes, made for such as were swimming from the fire of the ships. The ships boats also were instantly manned, and joined in the pursuit. They butchered the greatest part of those whom they caught. Many dead bodies were soon seen upon the sands, and others were floating during the whole of the day upon the water; and including those that were seized and carried off, and those that were drowned and killed, either by the firing of the ships, or the people of New Town, *three hundred*, were lost to the inhabitants of Old Town on that day.

The carnage, which I have been now describing, was scarcely over, when a canoe full of the principal people of New Town, who had been the promoters of the scheme, dropped along side of the Duke of York. They demanded the person of Amboe Robin John, the brother of the Grandee of Old Town, and the eldest of the three on board. The unfortunate man put the palms of his hands together, and beseeched the commander of the vessel, that he would not violate the rights of hospitality, nor give up an unoffending stranger to his enemies. No intreaties could avail with the hardened Christian. He received from them a slave of the name of Econg, in his stead, and then forced him into the canoe, where his head was immediately struck off, in the sight of the crew, and of his afflicted and disconsolate brothers. As for them, they escaped his fate, but they were carried off with their attendants to the European colonies, and sold for slaves[2].

This, (says Mr. Clarkson) is a specific instance, and an instance neither to be denied, controverted, nor palliated, of the behaviour of the Europeans to the innocent and unguarded natives of Africa.

When I was at Goree, (says Mr. Wadstrom) in the year 1787, accounts came down by some French merchantmen from Gambia, of the following particulars.

The captain of an English ship, had enticed several of the natives on board, and finding a favourable opportunity sailed away with them. His vessel however was, by the direction of Providence driven back to the coast, whence it had set sail, and was obliged to cast anchor on the very spot where this act of treachery had been committed. At this time two other English vessels were lying in the same river. The natives determined to retaliate, boarded all the three vessels and killed most of the crews; the few that escaped to tell the tale, took refuge in a neighbouring French factory[3]."

It is not disputed, that, in time of peace, British vessels alone annually carry off about 38,000 Africans from their native shore. The most extravagant credulity cannot believe that such immense numbers are got by fair means, or that the conductors of this trade are ignorant of the enormities by which this multitude of slaves is procured. Mr. Clarkson, who, for several years, has devoted himself wholly to the investigation of the facts in question, has specified such a multiplicity of particular instances, as cannot fail to produce the fullest conviction[4].

Of the situation of the negroes, aboard the British vessels, it is painful to give a particular account. The annexed plan presents it to the eye, more powerfully than words can express it. We may easily conceive the tortures endured by such a multitude lying in close vessels, and in a warm climate for sixteen hours together, the men chained in clusters, in a space not exceeding six feet in length, and sixteen inches in width, for each man, the women and children confined in a still smaller compass, and in most cases with so little room above their heads, that persons of ordinary size cannot raise themselves up; with such rigorous oeconomy, at the same time, that no place capable of holding a single person, from one end of the vessel to the other, is left unoccupied. It is believed there are not many, who can behold such a scene without horror and indignation; or if there should be any person, who can so far divest himself of humanity, as not to be strongly affected by it, it is not likely that he would be much moved by any description that can be given.

The reader may be assured, that what is here delineated, is the real and simple state of the fact. The patrons of slavery, at one time, insinuated that this representation is exaggerated. But a particular investigation of the circumstances tended to confirm all that had been asserted. Government sent a competent judge to measure the Liverpool vessels, and to report. Captain Parry accordingly stated the facts. It appeared undeniable that the men were confined, by the platform above their heads, to the space of two feet seven inches in height. This was the average of nine vessels, and in others the space was still less.

In such a state of confinement, during the passage to the West Indies, putrid fevers and dysenteries must often happen. Instances are accordingly produced in evidence, in which, vessels have lost a third, a half, and even two thirds of their whole number, upon the passage[5]. Even in ordinary cases, the mortality is great. Mr. Beaufoy has shown, from the evidence produced by the friends of the slave-trade, that, during the space of six weeks, five persons, at an average, in each hundred actually perish, that is, forty three for every hundred in the year; which is seventeen times the usual rate of mortality, "a destruction, which, if general but for *ten years*, would depopulate the world, blast the purposes of its creation, and extinguish the human race[6].' This statement refers to the trade in favourable circumstances. From the more distant parts of Africa the greatest proportion of slaves is brought, and among them the mortality is more than double. Besides all this, there are instances of cruelty, with regard to the treatment of the slaves aboard the vessels, so horrible that they almost exceed belief. One shall now be mentioned, which happened in September of the year 1781.

"The captain of a ship, then on the middle passage, had lost a considerable number of his slaves by death. The mortality was still spreading, and so rapidly, that it was impossible to say either where, or when it would end. Thus circumstanced, and uneasy at the thought of the loss, which was likely to accrue to his owners, he began to rack his ingenuity to repair it. He came at length to the diabolical resolution of selecting those that were the most sickly, and of throwing them into the sea: conceiving, that, if he could plead a necessity for the deed, the loss would devolve from the owners to the underwriters of the vessel.

The plea, which he proposed to set up, was a want of water, though neither the seamen, nor the slaves had been put upon short allowance.

Thus armed, as he imagined, with an invincible excuse, he began to execute his design. He selected accordingly *One hundred* and *thirty two* of the most sickly of the slaves. *Fifty-four* of these were immediately thrown into the sea, and *forty two* were made to be partakers of their fate on the succeeding day.

But here, as if Providence expressly disapproved of the design, and had determined to cut off his excuse, for sacrificing the rest, and exhibit a proof against him, a shower of rain immediately succeeded the transaction, and lasted for three days.

Notwithstanding this, the remaining *twenty-six* were brought upon deck to complete the number of victims, which avarice had at first determined to sacrifice to her shrine. The first *sixteen* submitted to be thrown into the sea; but the rest with a noble resolution, would not suffer the contaminated RECEIVERS to touch them, but leaped after their companions, and shared their fate[7].

Thus was perpetrated a deed, unparalleled in the memory of man, or in the history of former times, and of so black, and complicated a nature, that, were it to be perpetuated to future generations, and to rest on the testimony of an individual, it could not possibly be believed.

When the reader is informed, that such a fact as this came before a court[8] of justice in this very country[9]; that it is incontrovertibly true, that hundreds can come, and say they heard the melancholy evidence with tears; what bounds is he to place to his belief? The great God, who looks down upon all his creatures with the same impartial eye, seems to have infatuated the parties concerned, that they might bring the horrid circumstance to light, and that it might be recorded in the annals of a public court, as an authentic specimen of the treatment which the unfortunate Africans undergo, and at the same time as an argument to shew, that there is no species of cruelty, that is recorded to have been exercised upon those wretched people, so enormous that it may not *readily be believed*[10].'

Those, who survive the hardships of the voyage, are exposed to sale in the West Indies, in whatever way is best suited to the market. They are disposed of to different owners, and in different islands, without regard to the ties of blood, or of friendship. Husbands are separated from their wives, and children are torn from their parents for ever.

We wish not to enter into particulars concerning the treatment of the negroes in the West Indies; yet the truth cannot be altogether concealed. It is allowed that there are feeling masters, and even compassionate overseers. But whether this be their general character is very different matter; certain it is, that the miserable slaves have no legal protection even for their lives. The late amendments proposed, and enactments made by the assembly of Jamaica, however insufficient[11] for the end proposed, are an acknowledgment of the former situation of the negroes. There is reason at the same time to believe, that they have been suggested merely from the parliamentary investigation, and that, when this is over, unless a more effectual remedy be applied, they will no longer be heard of.

But whatever may be said, with regard to the injustice and cruelty of the slave-trade, *dire necessity* is urged for its continuance. We have been told with confidence, that the abolition thereof would *hurt our revenue*, and *ruin our West India settlements*.

To this argument it might be sufficient to reply, in the spirited language of a great commoner, that, if the trade be founded in iniquity, it ought to be abandoned, whatever may be the consequences. But it has been shown with convincing evidence, that the trade is as impolitic, as it is unjust; and that any inconveniencies, attending the abolition, would be inconsiderable and of a temporary nature; that this measure, so essential to justice, in process of time, would even be of great advantage[12].

If the importation of slaves was prohibited, the stock already in the islands would be treated with greater tenderness. The great annual decrease of negroes in the West Indies, must be chiefly imputed to their excessive labour, and scanty subsistence. The Author of Nature has formed every species of beings so, as to keep up their numbers under ordinary treatment, and even to increase. It cannot be imagined that the hardy race of negroes, who multiply in Africa so prodigiously, as to spare 100,000 annually (which is the number computed to be exported thence by the Europeans) would, if properly treated in the West Indies, by no means a worse climate, diminish so rapidly as to require an immense annual supply. From the experiments made by individuals, and from the opinion of persons in the West Indies, who are well acquainted with the trade, it appears incontestable, that, under proper management, the stock of negroes in that country would not only maintain itself, but even produce a gradual augmentation.

But the fact seems to be, that slaves have hitherto been frequently treated like post horses. It is thought by many, however injudiciously, that it is more profitable to work them hard, and to supply their place by fresh stock, than to labour them moderately, and to be careful about rearing their children. This is a system so contrary to every sentiment of humanity and religion, that it must be rejected with abhorrence.

The absence of the proprietors is believed to be a frequent cause of this inhuman and pernicious system. Owners, who live at a great distance, from different considerations, are induced very often to change the persons, whom they intrust with the management of their estates in the West Indies; and as every new overseer is eager to recommend himself to his master, by procuring to him an immediate increase of produce, he is tempted for that purpose to over-work his negroes. The fatal consequences of this conduct are not felt till afterwards; and, when a report of the decrease of the slaves is made, it is ascribed to other causes The cruel treatment they received is carefully concealed. And thus, the maxims of severity, so agreeable to the domineering spirit of mankind, having become general, are propagated by the force of example; and it requires more than common discernment and boldness, to discover their hurtful tendency, and to try the effects of more gentleness and moderation.

The attempt now making to put a stop to the slave-trade, if successful, must induce the slave-owners to be more careful about rearing the offspring of their negroes. Marriage, so important for that end, will be encouraged among them. All the parental and filial relations will be strengthened; and even under few advantages, the West India slaves may undergo a considerable degree of culture, both intellectual and moral.

Those, who have not attended sufficiently to the subject, are apt to suppose that the design of the present interposition of parliament is entirely to abolish slavery in the West Indies. Could the emancipation of such a number of rational creatures be brought about with safety, it would be a glorious work. But this does not enter into the view of the friends of the abolition of the trade. They are sensible that the present rude and uncultivated state of the slaves does not admit the thought. Men must be formed for enjoying freedom, before they can with propriety be made partakers of it; and the state of the society must be such that no danger to freemen is likely to ensue.

All that is just now in contemplation is to put an end to the importation of fresh slaves into the British West Indies. And consequently to promote attention to those already in the islands; to their health, their subsistence, and the rearing of their children. For these purposes many salutary regulations might be introduced among them. There will be favourable to sobriety, temperance, and virtuous conduct in general. We indulge the pleasing hope, that, along with other advantages, by enjoying the means of religious instruction, they will gradually rise in the scale of being; till in process of time, having become attached to the islands as their native soil, they shall be found qualified to enjoy a higher degree of liberty. A state of well regulated vassalage would be an important step in the progress; this at length might give way to the enjoyment of the full rights of *freemen*. Should that day ever arrive, there is every reason to believe that the prosperity of those islands, the happiness of their inhabitants, would go hand in hand.

In order to give effect to the necessary and laudable measures now carrying on, in behalf of the much injured natives of Africa, great exertion is requisite, on account of the powerful opposition arising from the contracted views and prejudices of interested persons. In this line of conduct, the society of London for effecting the abolition of the slave-trade, to their immortal honour, have set the example. Neither their time, nor their money has been spared. Amidst many difficulties and discouragements, they have persevered for years in the generous undertaking. Their labour has not been in vain. Conviction has been carried home to the minds of many. Senators of distinguished name have come forward, and, in the most unequivocal terms, have testified their abhorrence of the traffic in human flesh. It is pleasing to contemplate the force of truth. Amidst the contentions of party, we behold the most illustrious characters, forgetting their private differences, combining together in support of a measure which recommends itself to every dispassionate inquirer, and which nothing but the groundless terror of innovation, and the panic arising from a great imaginary interest, could induce any person to oppose.

Let us not however be too secure. Let us not think it sufficient to commend others. If we approve of the design, it is unquestionably our duty to assist those who are immediately engaged in it. The flourishing towns of Leeds and Manchester, and other parts of Britain, have already joined in co-operating with the society of London, not only by declaring publicly their sentiments in favour of the present measure, but also by contributions to defray the expence, with which it must necessarily be attended. The inhabitants of Glasgow, Paisley, and the neighbourhood, whose manufactures and trade are, by the blessing of God, in so thriving a condition, will surely not be averse to join the general voice of the disinterested part of the nation, and to add their mite in supporting the cause of justice and humanity. It is hoped that even those individuals, who are concerned in the trade of the West Indies, will not be intimidated from doing their duty by a mere shadow of pecuniary interest; and still more, that those who are but remotely connected, by friendship and acquaintance with such traders, will not be deterred by such a paltry consideration, from avowing their opinions, and obeying the clear and strong dictates of morality and religion. We are unwilling to believe that in this enlightened age, a narrow selfishness, and a sordid attention to mere profit and loss, has taken such hold of mankind, as to deaden their feelings of right and wrong, and to render them indifferent to the sufferings of their fellow-creatures.

Notes

1. See Clarkson, on the slavery and commerce of the human species.
2. Essay on the slavery and commerce of the human species, Pag. 33, 34, 35.
3. Wadstrom's Observations during a voyage to the coast of Guinea, in 1787, and 1788.
4. Essay on the slavery and commerce of the human species, particularly the African.
5. See Clarkson on the comparative efficiency of regulation and abolition, page 29, 30, 31.
6. Beaufoy's speech in the house of commons, 17th June, 1778, page 6, 7, 8.
7. Essay on the slavery and commerce of the human species, page 98, 99.
8. The action was brought by the owners against the underwriters, to recover the value of the *murdered slaves*. It was tried at Guildhall.
9. i.e. of England.
10. Essay on the slavery, &c. p. 114, 115.
11. See *notes* on the two reports from the committee of the honourable *house of assembly of Jamaica*, relative to the slave-trade, &c. by a *Jamaica Planter*.—In this small tract several astonishing facts on this head are specified.
12. Clarkson on the impolicy of the African slave-trade. This tract deserves to be read throughout.

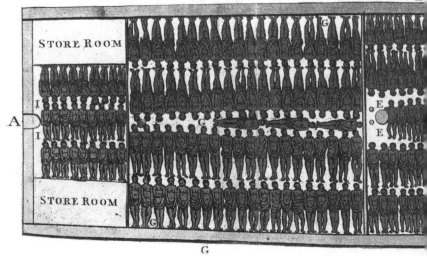

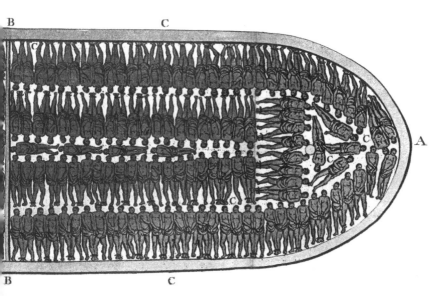

Diagram of the Liverpool slave ship 'Brookes'. This emotive image appeared in many anti-slavery publications, including the 'Address to the inhabitants of Glasgow, Paisley and the neighbourhood concerning the slave trade', in which it was printed on a folded sheet at the end of the pamphlet. Only part of the image is shown here.

SUBSTANCE

OF

THE SPEECH

OF HIS ROYAL HIGHNESS

THE DUKE OF CLARENCE,

IN THE

HOUSE OF LORDS,

ON THE MOTION FOR

THE RECOMMITMENT OF THE SLAVE TRADE LIMITATION BILL,

ON THE FIFTH DAY OF JULY, 1799.

𝔉𝔬𝔲𝔯𝔱𝔥 𝔈𝔡𝔦𝔱𝔦𝔬𝔫.

[*Published at the Request of the West India Merchants and Planters, and the Mercantile Interest of Liverpool.*]

LONDON:

PRINTED BY C. WHITTINGHAM, DEAN STREET, FETTER LANE;
AND SOLD BY F. AND C. RIVINGTON, ST. PAUL's CHURCH YARD.

[PRICE TWO SHILLINGS.]

TO THE PUBLIC,

THE WEST INDIA MERCHANTS and PLANTERS, *together with the* MERCANTILE INTEREST *of* LIVERPOOL, *acknowledging, with the most lively sensibility, the very eminent services of His Royal Highness the* DUKE OF CLARENCE, *were eagerly solicitous to publish his Sentiments on the last Discussion of the* SLAVE TRADE. *Their application meeting with the desired effect, they now offer the* SUBSTANCE *of* HIS ROYAL HIGHNESS'S SPEECH, *in the present form, not only as a testimony of their greatest esteem, but as the best means of combating, in a rational and argumentative way, the erroneous and dangerous doctrines of their adversaries.—For similar reasons, they have also requested the publication of the very able* SPEECH *of the Earl of* WESTMORELAND, *whose permission has also been obtained.*

SUBSTANCE OF THE SPEECH, &c. &c.

MY LORDS, WHEN contemplating the vast importance of the present question, I feel concerned and perplexed that it should fall to my lot to open a discussion of such magnitude. It would have been fortunate indeed for those materially interested, had some of your Lordships undertaken the arduous task—Some of your Lordships who are much older than myself, consequently from years, knowledge, and experience, much abler and better calculated to form a correct judgment of the subject.

The Noble Secretary of State (*Lord Grenville*) has frequently thrown out the idea, that the delay originated with those Peers who had taken a decided part against the Bill. If professional knowledge and local experience have extended the examination at the Bar to a length that may, in the opinion of some Noble Lords, have been much more than what was satisfactory, I, for one, plead guilty. It was my wish, by the most minute research, to produce such a body of evidence as would convince your Lordships of the rectitude and policy of those with whom I have the happiness to act. We have not been the cause of unnecessary delay. The delay has, in fact, originated with the Noble Secretary himself; for on the day appointed for the second reading of this Bill—upon which I had intended to have submitted a motion to your Lordships—he presented a petition from the Sierra Leone Company in favour of it. I beg, therefore, that the delay may be attributed to those who have actually produced it.

Having, on every occasion, when the subject of the Slave Trade has been mentioned in this House, declared, that I never would act but in the most open, honourable, and candid manner; and it being the intention of those Noble Lords with whom I have the honour to agree, to persevere firmly in their resistance of any plan of Abolition, I did not, although fully empowered, object to the Petitioners being heard by counsel at the bar. It is not my most distant intention to throw any censure upon the Noble Secretary of State, whose general conduct, during the present critical situation of Europe, has been such as to prove his affection to the King and country. To him I impute no blame upon the subject of the Petition in favour of the Bill; but far differently do I think of those Gentlemen who drew it.—When the Bill was first brought up to this House, my Lords, I own I did not conceive it possible for its supporters to defend the measure, but upon the general grounds of Abolition; and indeed, thanks to *Mr. Plomer*, he took care to defend it upon the principle of total and complete Abolition. I may, therefore, be permitted to enter with the same firmness into the general principles of the whole question.

To persons so well acquainted with the history of this country as your Lordships, it would be too great presumption on my part to engage your attention, by a detailed account of the African Trade carried on by the European nations; suffice it to say, that in the year 1442, the Portuguese began it. In 1471, the Portuguese built the first forts on the Gold Coast, and had thirty-seven vessels in the trade. In 1502, the Spaniards commenced the same trade; and in 1517, *Charles* V. allowed the Portuguese to furnish Hispaniola, Cuba, Jamaica, and Porto Rico, with 4000 slaves annually.

That able navigator, *Hawkins*, in 1562, first sailed to Sierra Leone; and at that time the African Trade was considered of such importance in this country, that *Queen Elizabeth*, the ensuing year, sent *Hawkins* to trade there. He gives an account of their barbarity, and states, that the people were at that time mere slaves. He also mentions, that he found the French trading in that quarter of the world; so that your Lordships may perceive, that even so early as the latter part of the sixteenth century, the different nations of Europe that had possessions in the West Indies, considered the Slave Trade as absolutely necessary for the existence of these colonies. It is said, that *Queen Elizabeth* gave the first charter, and I believe the fact, as it comes from a very respectable channel. In 1618, *James* I. granted a charter to *Sir Robert Rich* and others. In 1631, *Charles* I. granted another; but the troubles opened the trade till 1660.

The dreadful events of the Civil War, during the latter part of the reign of the unfortunate *Charles*, and the capture of the Island of Jamaica, during the Protectorate of *Cromwell*, are historical facts well known to your Lordships. But even these calamities did not annihilate the trade. Upon the capture of Jamaica, *Cromwell* promised to send a supply of Africans; and highly requisite indeed it was, for the British settlers would not undertake to cultivate the lands in Jamaica, unless encouraged and protected by this promise of the Usurper. To confirm the settlers in their opinion of that necessity, those of Barbadoes had, by fatal experience, ascertained the impossibility of carrying on labour in tropical climates by Whites. In 1662, *Charles* II. granted a new charter to the African Company; his brother, the *Duke of York*, was at the head of it. In 1665, the Company's factors settled at Jamaica. In 1672 another African Company was formed, the King himself, the *Duke of York*, *Prince Rupert*, with others, appeared as the patrons, and many of high rank, amongst whom was the celebrated *Mr. Locke*.

In 1688, the Revolution put an end to the Company, because all monopolies were contrary to its spirit and principles. In 1698, the first Assiento Contract was entered into with the Spaniards, and encouraged by *King William*. In the same year the famous Act was passed by *King William*, entitled, "An Act for the Protection of that Trade, and for the Advantage of England, and the Preservation of its Colonies.' This Act is considered by the West Indians as their birth-right. Now, my Lords, who were the men that passed this famous Act? They were those great and illustrious characters, who, under the blessings of Divine Providence, secured to this country the happiness of the constitution under which we now live, and many of whose descendants I have the honour of addressing.

During the latter part of *King William*, and the whole of the reign of *Queen Anne*, the Parliament was engaged in the African trade. In the proceedings of Parliament from 1707 to 1713, are records to support the trade. Your Lordships may recollect the long, the great, and glorious war, the war of succession, carried on in the reign of *Queen Anne*, and your Lordships may also have impressed on your minds, that the treaty of Utrecht was the consequence of that war. The Commissioners appointed by her Majesty for the peace, were the *Earl of Strafford* and the *Bishop of Winchester*. In their instructions, the Assiento Contract was one of the articles of peace; and I cannot suppose that a Right Reverend and Learned Prelate would have undertaken to go as a Commissioner with such an article in his instructions, had he considered the Slave Trade as contrary to the benign dictates of the Christian religion. *Queen Anne*, in her most gracious speech of June 6th, 1712, from the throne of the very House in which I have now the honour of addressing your Lordships, mentions this essential advantage in favour of Great Britain.

Now, my Lords, I have ever understood the speech of the Sovereign to be the speech of the Minister; I am therefore to suppose that the then Ministry considered the Assiento Contract, as a matter of the highest advantage to the Queen and her subjects, and an article to be insisted upon, in consequence of the glorious termination of the war. But a reference to the speech itself may serve to dissipate any doubts which may arise in your Lordships minds. In one passage Queen *Anne* says— "The apprehension that Spain and the *West Indies* might be united to *France*, was the chief inducement to begin this war; and the effectual preventing of such an union was the principle I laid down at the commencement of this treaty.'

Again, "The division of the Island of St. Christopher between us and the French, having been the cause of great inconveniency and damage to my subjects, I have demanded to have an absolute cession made to us of that whole island; and France agrees to this demand.'

And lastly, which is by far the most essential passage of the speech, her Majesty most emphatically states: "But the part which we have borne in prosecuting this war entitling us to some distinction in the terms of peace, I have INSISTED and OBTAINED, That the ASSIENTO or CONTRACT FOR FURNISHING THE SPANISH WEST INDIES WITH NEGROES, shall be made with us for the term of thirty years, in the same manner as it has been enjoyed by the French for these ten years past.'

After these pertinent quotations, I need scarcely farther impress on the minds of my auditors the vast importance of the *West India* Settlements. Here I might make my stand, were it not that the spirit of perversion and falshood, ever hostile to the rights of the Liverpool Merchant and West India Planter, demanded my most serious and active interference.

The Treaty to supply the Spaniards with 4800 Negroes annually, lasted till 1750. Upon the Peace of 1763, the Assiento Contract was not renewed; and, my Lords, a Right Honourable and eloquent Author, now no more (*Mr. Burke*) wrote in the strongest manner possible against the impolicy of the peace of 1763, because this country not only neglected to supply the Spaniards, but even the French, with Negroes; and in 1765, upon the change of Administration, the Right Honourable Gentleman brought in his first Free-Port Act, and which has continued to be adopted by the Government down to the present moment. It may, my Lords, be thought singular, that in the latter part of *Mr. Burke's* life, he should have voted for an Abolition of the Slave Trade; but in his character, like that of many other great men, there are several shades irreconcileable with the prominent features. I perfectly well remember, my Lords, that when I thought it my duty as a Member of Parliament to take a decided part in this important business, I had occasion to mention to the Right Honourable Gentleman his change of sentiments. He acknowledged that my observation was just, as referring to his former conduct; and emphatically concluded—"My own words must rise up in judgment against me.' I recur to this great and enlightened authority for the rectitude of my position; and if in the vale of life he chose to deviate from his previous principles, sanctioned by years and fortified by experience, I have yet to learn the cause of his conversion.

But we shall, my Lords, take a more minute survey.—At the very moment in which I address your Lordships, the state of the African Trade is thus: One hundred and eighty-three vessels, measuring 49,065 tons, navigated by 6276 seamen.

Having given this account of the African Trade, and brought it down to the present moment, I beg leave to call your Lordships attention to the Sierra Leone Company, who are the Petitioners in favour of this Bill. *Mr. Stevens* has informed us, that the object of the Company was not so much that of commerce, as a total and complete Abolition. I approve of his confession, and admire his candour: but while I bestow encomiums on the power of his talents, and the honesty of his avowal, I implore your particular attention, my Lords, to the interest of the West-India Merchants and Planters, who adventure in Colonial Commerce, on the solemn pledge and honour of the British Government.

From what I have submitted to your Lordships, relative to the History of the Trade, it is evident that the traffick in Slaves is congenial with and suitable to the manners, laws, and customs of Africa. No wonder, therefore, that the chiefs, princes, and the different native powers of that country, should set their faces against the New Settlers at Sierra Leone.

Mr. Dawes and *Mr. Macaulay*, the only two evidences produced at the Bar in favour of the Bill, are men, it must be confessed, of the most accommodating memories. It is difficult to follow them through all their various digressions. When it is convenient, they appear to possess the most tenacious and perfect recollection; and when it suits their purpose, their memories, with remarkable facility, totally fail them. *Mr. Dawes*, a marine officer, who had the honour of serving the King the whole of the last war, and the greater part of it in America, does not recollect what both these gentlemen chose to call the Nova Scotia Blacks! These Blacks were Slaves in the American Colonies, and promised their freedom by Royal Proclamation, upon condition of serving the whole war with the army; in which situation they acted as guides and pioneers, and in every menial capacity that an army requires. On the Peace of 1783, these Negroes were carried to the remaining part of the British settlements in North America, where the government of this country, with great liberality, gave them tools and utensils for the erection of houses and the cultivation of their lands; in addition to these cherishing acts, they were also supplied the first year with twelve months provisions; the second year with a sufficiency for six months; and the third year with what would answer for three months consumption. But in this instance, the fostering hand of government was stretched out in vain; these Negroes, after the irregular and wanton consumption of the provisions so humanely bestowed upon them, sold their utensils of husbandry, relapsed into a state of idleness and dissipation, and by various stratagems arrived in this country, where they were taken up by the Sierra Leone Company, to be transplanted as a Colony on their part of the African shore.

Can your Lordships be surprised, that with all the ingenious and logical arguments of *Mr. Stevens*, the learned counsel should be obliged to admit, that the Imports from the establishment of the Colony of Africa is 4000*l.* per annum, while their expence is 10,000*l.* Your Lordships will observe, that the Sierra Leone Company set out with a capital of 250,000*l.*; that *Mr. Stevens* has laboured to prove, that at present they are worth 50,000*l.* though I have the strongest reason to believe that they are not worth more than 30,000*l.* By *Mr. Stevens's* own account, there is an annual deficit of 6000*l.* a year; so that these great and flourishing colonists, as they wish to be thought, must shortly dissolve partnership, or continue trade at an immense loss, and consequently increase their capital, or become bankrupts.

Considering, my Lords, the manner in which this investigation has been carried on by those Noble Peers who support the Bill, I am confident, that if *Mr. Mungo Park* had been favourable to the Abolition of this Trade, he would have been brought to your Lordships Bar. I am, therefore, not a little surprised to hear *Mr. Stevens* quote certain pages in *Mr. Park's* very excellent work. And, my Lords, nothing could so completely refute *Mr. Stevens's* different quotations, as the simple but elegant and forcible passage, quoted from the same author, by my valuable and learned friend, *Mr. Law.* The interior of Africa, my Lords, is at best but very little known to Europeans; nor indeed can it be a matter of astonishment, when, with one exception, or two, the only occasions on which that coast has been visited by

Europeans, were for the purposes of traffic; and it is well known, that on such adventures, the whole time of the Merchants and Masters of Vessels is occupied by objects of commerce. But, my Lords, it is to me highly gratifying, that the plain, undigested, and simple account, presented at your Lordships Bar, both on the present investigation, and on the general inquiry made some years ago by the African Merchants, agrees with the statement of *Mr. Mungo Park*, relative to the intended prohibited district. It is therefore but fair to presume, that had *Mr. Mungo Park*, or any other unprejudiced and impartial traveller, visited the other parts of the Slave Coasts, the evidence produced upon the general investigation, at your Lordships Bar, by the African Merchants, would have proved equally true and correct. For the sake of humanity, therefore, my Lords—and I repeat it—for the sake of humanity—this Trade ought to continue; for how many thousands, how many millions of lives have been saved in the Kingdom of Dahomy! and how much bloodshed has been spared amongst the wretched and miserable victims in that quarter of the globe, thus rescued from the knife.

Mr. Macaulay, that very accommodating Witness, who sometimes inadvertently glances at the truth, has entered into the different causes of Slavery in Africa, and has given a very minute account on the subject of kidnapping, in which, my Lords, he does not dare to insinuate that the British Trader is indirectly concerned. As for war's being the cause of Slavery, it is proved by *Mr. Park*, that whether upon the Coast or the Interior, so far from that being favourable to the Slave Trade, that in either situation the Trade for the time is utterly suspended: therefore it is not the interest of the British Trader to encourage wars amongst the natives. But I beg pardon of the Commercial

World.—I have too great a respect for the character of a British Trader, to suppose that he would be guilty of such infamy. His conduct is distinguished by plain dealing and honest meaning; and he has too much pride of character to deviate from the paths of honour.

In all climates, where food is easily obtained, cultivation is little attended to. *Mr. Park* bears strong testimony to that fact. For having been in the East Indies, on mentioning to the inhabitants of the interior of Africa the advantageous uses to which the Elephant and Bullock are applied on that continent, the natives laughed at him, and observed, that the only beast of burden was the ass. Whenever a famine arises in any country where cultivation is little known, the consequences must indeed be fatal; and during dearths, *Mr. Park* mentions several instances of the natives selling themselves for food.

As for crimes being the cause of Slavery in Africa, it is, my Lords, even no more than the law of this country; for what are the Convicts that are annually transported to Botany Bay but Slaves? The last cause of Slavery in Africa, and which *Mr. Stevens* has, with his usual candour and close argument, dwelt largely upon, is the crime of Witchcraft. Now, my Lords, though this country has been for many centuries under the benign influence of Christianity, it is a fact well ascertained, that at the close of the last century, people were tried and convicted of Witchcraft. Can your Lordships, therefore, be atonished, that the wild, ferocious, and ignorant African, unenlightened by the Christian Religion, should frequently consider persons conversant with, and consequently guilty of a communication with evil spirits? Indeed, my Lords, though the civilization of Africa was professed to be, together with the Abolition of the

Slave Trade, the principal object of the Sierra Leone Company, it does not appear that any great benefit can soon arise from the propagation of Christianity under the influence of this Colony; for even *Mr. Macuulay* has acknowledged, that for the last three years no Clergyman of the Church of England has been within the Settlement; and indeed, notwithstanding that the salary of Chaplains was 140*l*. per annum, no clergyman, after earnest solicitation, could be procured to venture to this pernicious climate.

I have heard that the staple commodity of Africa is Slaves. Every other article of Commerce, even including ivory, is very small; and many of these articles, it has been satisfactorily proved at your Lordships Bar, have lain upon the hands of the merchants of this country at a considerable loss. It has been stated by *Mr. Macaulay*, and likewise by *Mr. Dawes*, that the Grumattes, or domestic Slaves, who attend the caravans of Slaves down to the coast, must be in great numbers, in order to carry back the different British Manufactures bartered for a ton of ivory. It is a very specious, though a very fallacious argument, in support of the idea intended to be impressed upon your Lordships minds by the friends of the Bill, that the Slave Trade is not so materially an object with the natives, as that of other productions in Africa. *Mr. Macaulay* and *Mr. Dawes* are obliged to admit, that the ivory brought down to the markets is suspended upon the backs of the Slaves for sale, and, consequently, that it cannot be brought down from the interior in any other manner: From my own experience, my Lords, amongst the Indians in North America, the use of any beast to carry burthens is equally as unknown as in Africa. The reason, my Lords, I take to be the same with the Indians as with the Africans; namely, that the conveyance is water-carriage; and that the Africans, as well as the North American Indians, have only a few carrying places between their great water communication: Therefore, my Lords, it is evident, that these goods, bartered in lieu of ivory, are only carried short distances by men, and transported chiefly by water. Far be it from me, my Lords, to draw any insidious inference from the evidence of *Mr. Macaulay* or *Mr. Dawes*, relative to Grumattes, or Domestic Slaves, employed by the Colony, notwithstanding that the charter does not permit such a conduct, directly or indirectly; but Slavery is so congenial to the laws, habits, and customs of Africa, that even *Mr. Park*, with his extensive knowledge of that territory, was not able to distinguish the Freeman from the Slave.

I do not wish to make any wrong impression on the minds of your Lordships; but a man less suspicious than myself might have good grounds for insinuating, that some Members of the Sierra Leone Company view, with an envious eye, the advantageous traffic now carried on between the African and British Trader. If the grand object of the Sierra Leone Company, like every other Commercial Association, be gain rather than loss, I have a right to think that some of the Members lament their exclusion from the Slave Trade. If there be no cause for this suspicion, why molest and annoy the British Trader in the exercise of that traffic sanctioned for such a long series of years by custom and by Parliament? Surveying the subject in this view, I have a right to maintain, that the British Legislature, on the passing of the Act for Incorporating and Establishing the Sierra Leone Company, renewed and confirmed all their former Acts in favour of the Slave Trade. So tender was the Parliament of that period, namely, that of 1790, about the acknowledged right of the British Trader to Africa, that fearful of affecting the interest of the West India Merchants and Planters, by the monopoly or prohibition of the Slave Trade, they cautiously introduced in the Bill, for the Establishment of the Sierra Leone Company, the following protecting Clause:

"Provided also, and be it further enacted, That it shall not be lawful for the said Company, either directly or indirectly, by itself or themselves, or by the Agents or Servants of the said Company, or otherwise howsoever, to deal or traffic in the buying or selling of Slaves, or in any manner whatsoever to have, hold, appropriate, or employ any person or persons, in a state of slavery, in the service of the said Company.'

And here, my Lords, I have additional proof to offer concerning the protecting wisdom of the Parliament in favour of the British Trader to Africa. In another part of the same law is a Clause, expressly "securing the British Merchants to Africa from the operations of the Act.' What am I, my Lords, to conclude from this protecting Clause, but that the wisdom of Parliament, penetrating into futurity, had resolved that all the former Acts of the Legislature should be respected and confirmed beyond the possibility of a doubt? If I am wrong in my conclusion, then why pass such a Clause in an Act of such vast importance to the interest of the Sierra Leone Company? Why attempt to fix a stigma upon their future conduct, by supposing that they would infringe upon the rights of the British Trader in the Slave Trade? Why introduce such a protecting Clause? If found requisite to check and control future avarice and ambition, my argument is fortified in an impregnable manner. If useless and of no avail, this part of the act is an exposure of the folly and absurdity of Parliament. It is a mere piece of waste paper, and serves to commemorate the weakness of the legislature. But, my Lords, I have too great respect for the proceedings of a British Parliament to entertain for a moment such an opinion. In acts framed and passed by the collective wisdom of the British empire, by whom every consequence is fully weighed, it would be a libel on Parliament to suppose that it could pass a Clause without some specific object in view. The object, my Lords, was certainly the protection of the right of the trader, acknowledged and established for time immemorial. I confess, my Lords, my astonishment at the presumption of the men calling themselves the Sierra Leone Company. They audaciously appear at your Lordships Bar, and arrogantly insinuate, that you are incapable of deciding on the merits or demerits of an important case of legislation. On the ill-founded plea of humanity, they desire you to relinquish your colonial wealth, the sinews of our commercial existence, and sink into insignificance and contempt in the eyes of Europe and the world, by the adoption of their new system of philosophy and humanity! They call upon you to disfranchise the West India Merchants and Planters—to depopulate Liverpool —and to deprive some thousands of industrious and respectable men of their birth-right as British subjects. These are incontrovertible facts; but your Lordships penetration will easily discover the true aim of the petitioners, who labour so anxiously to destroy your former acts of Parliament. From principles of honour and justice to the West India Planters, I appeal to the protecting Clause alluded to. But do not, my Lords, take my ipse dixit—let the Clause speak for itself:

"Provided always, and be it enacted, That nothing in this act contained shall extend, or be construed to extend, to affect the rights of any other British subjects trading to Africa, so as to prevent, or in any manner to obstruct the ships or vessels belonging to British subjects from anchoring in Sierra Leone or Camaranca Rivers, or in any of the creeks, bays, or harbours within the limits specified in this act, for the purpose of refitting and repairing as heretofore, with full liberty to the same to erect temporary tents, huts, or sheds, on the shores of the said peninsula, for the security of the stores and accommodation of the persons employed upon such occasions.'

It has been falsely asserted, and an attempt has thence been made to mislead the public mind, that European nations only carry on the Slave Trade with Africa. Even *Mr. Stevens* allows, that Blacks are carried into Turkey for the purposes of state, of luxury, and even for the seraglios of Mahometans. As to the fact, I will admit that gentleman to be right; but he is erroneous as to numbers; for, my Lords, the numbers annually transported by the Eastern channels to Turkey, to Egypt, to Russia, and to the East Indies, are immense. I will not shock your Lordships minds by the horrid cruelties and barbarities which the miserable and devoted wretches experience from the gratification of their Mahomedan and Eastern masters. And here, my Lords, I have a right to draw a contrast between the humanity of the West India Traders, and the atrocity of those now described. In one case, we find the milk of human kindness; in the other, acts of turpitude and violence which outrage the sensibilities of nature, and mortify and disgrace mankind.

The Portuguese transport 40,000 annually to the Brazils. The French, previous to the revolution, during the last peace, supplied their own islands with Negroes, from the eastward of the Cape of Good Hope. I beg leave, my Lords, to impress upon your memories a few stubborn facts. The Portuguese and native merchants in India, carry on at this time the Slave Trade through Bombay. Since that period, a tax has been laid upon the importation of Negroes into that place by British merchants. I am the last man in the world, my Lords, to detract from the merits of those concerned in the management of this business; and I dare say, the Court of Directors of the East India Company were actuated by the most laudable and humane motives, when they imposed a duty upon the importation of Negroes in British bottoms.

But with all deference to that high and respectable Association, I think it a matter of great national importance, seriously to consider, how far it is prudent to encourage not only the Portuguese, but even the native powers, in efforts for the improvement of navigation, and the consequent increase of seamen, in seas so remote from our home possessions. And here, my Lords, I wish to remark, that this observation arises from pure motives of patriotism, as I am fearful of impolicy and danger from such rival powers, when usurping and armed with the authority of the moment.

Permit me, my Lords, to illustrate these observations by some additional truths. It is a fact, perhaps well known to every British Officer of the army and navy who has been at Gibraltar, that the Emperor of Morocco has a very large black army within his dominions, the number of which he regularly maintains by sending down armed Moors to bring away, by force, the negroes from their wives and families, without the advantage of barter, and without the most distant respect to the customs and manners of the Africans.

I have said thus much, my Lords, upon the subject of Africa, upon its trade, and upon the state of the petitioners in favour of the Bill, namely, the Sierra Leone Company. I shall therefore conclude my remarks on Africa with the strong and memorable words of Mr. *Park:* —

"Such are the general outlines of that system of slavery which prevails in Africa; and it is evident from its nature and extent, that it is a system of no modern date. It probably had its origin with remote ages of antiquity, before the Mahomedans explored a path across the desert. How far it is maintained and supported by the Slave Traffic, which, for two hundred years, the natives of Europe have carried on with the natives of the coast, it is neither within my province, nor in my power to explain. If my sentiments should be required concerning the effect which a discontinuance of that commerce would produce on the manners of the natives, I should have no hesitation in observing, that in the present unenlightened state of their minds, my opinion is, the effect would neither be so extensive nor beneficial, as many wise and worthy persons fondly expect.'

Having, in what I have already had the honour of submitting to your Lordships, stated, that I should discuss this business upon the general question of Abolition, and being indeed supported by the arguments used both by Mr. *Plomer* and Mr. *Stevens*, I naturally come, having left the African Coast, to the Middle Passage. This subject having lately been much debated before your Lordships, I shall not labour under the unpleasant necessity of taking up a great deal of your time. I have declared, and I always shall declare, that I have been, that I am, and that I always shall be, a sincere friend to wise and humane regulations in transporting the Negroes from Africa to the West Indies.

The noble Earl, my friend, *(Liverpool)* who so advantageously for the King and Country, and so honourably for himself, presides at the head of the trade of this kingdom, in the year 1788, brought in the first Carrying Bill—a very wise and useful measure: For, my Lords, should the British merchants, under any false principle of gain, crowd the slave ships to that degree so as to produce pestilence and disease among the Negroes on board, it is humane, it is wise and praiseworthy, of this Great Commercial Nation, to prevent diseased and infected Negroes from being imported into the British West India Plantations. Let foreign nations, my Lords, if they choose it, make no regulations for their own vessels, and let them import into their own islands, disease and discontent amongst the slaves brought from the coast of Africa; but we, thank God, are actuated by other considerations than mere gain. We are actuated by principles of humanity. To prove to your Lordships the wisdom and the efficacy of my noble friend's arrangement upon the subject of the Middle Passage, I will beg leave to call your Lordships attention to the following statement and calculation:—

MIDDLE PASSAGE.

By an account delivered in by Mr. *Cock*, the very able and intelligent Commercial Agent for Liverpool, in a paper already much commented upon, it appears, that out of 15,508 Negroes, shipped in the year 1796, 559 died, being about 3½ *per Cent*.

That according to the New Carrying Bill, the above 15,508 Negroes will be reduced to 10,352, which is a reduction of one third; besides that a great many ships will be altogether excluded from the trade, wherein the slaves have been carried in most health, as will be seen from a calculation made on a number of ships which traded in the

YEARS 1794, 1795, AND 1796.

vessels wherein the space per slave was	received on board	Died.	
Under 26 feet ...	5,602	142	Average 2½ *per cent*
Above 30 feet ...	19,284	739	Av above 3¼ *per cent*

vessel s betw s. een deck	received on board	Died.	
Under 4 feet 1 inch	4,912	96	Average 2 *per cent*
Above 4 feet 1 inch	30,734	1,268	Av 3¼ *per cent*

Several of these vessels were altered to their present heights, at a very great expence, in consequence of an Act passed in the year 1797, for regulating the height between decks, which will not bear further elevation.

Your Lordships will therefore perceive, that every attention has not only been paid to the health of the slaves, but by the experience of eleven years, and by the documents I have already shewn, that that object has been completely and fully established.

Much having been said in a former debate upon the subject of the height between decks, and a vessel named the Plumper, particularly alluded to by the Noble Secretary of State, I have to observe, that the Plumper being only two feet seven inches between decks, as stated by the Secretary of State, shipped 140 slaves, out of whom only two died.

Great stress has been laid upon the evidence of Captain *Schank*; and, my Lords, to prove that my words and my actions shall always be the same, and that upon this grand and important question I shall always act with liberality and candour, I did not propose to Captain *Schank* certain questions relative to the height between decks of vessels, though I was possessed of his sentiments, that the height between decks, by his experience, was a matter of no moment to the health of men on board of the ship. Being myself an advocate for height between decks, I had at all times, where the vessel would admit, wished it as high as possible. But, my Lords, I always shall oppose any proposition brought forward for the mere purpose of harassing and distressing the British Slave Trader, after every wise and good regulation has been established for the health and comfort of the Negroes by the Bill of 1788. In short, my Lords, the Carrying Bill just passed, is merely for the purpose of harassing and distressing the British Merchant; and it is not more conducive to the health of comfort of the Negro. Even the Bounty Clause, as an inducement for the Master and Surgeon to take care of the health of the Negro, is omitted. We are, my Lords, and it is with pleasure I affirm it, the ablest sea-faring nation on the globe; and it is therefore to be presumed, that the health of the Negro Slave, whilst on board British ships, is as much attended to as on board the ships of any other nation, and *Mr. Park* corroborates my opinion in the following words: —

"The mode of confining and securing Negroes in American Slave ships (owing chiefly to the weakness of their crews) is abundantly more rigid than in British Vessels.'

Having now brought your Lordships to the West Indies, I trust I may be allowed for a moment to pause, and consider a little who are the West India Proprietors: They are our fellow-subjects—they are English-men —they are, if not born, at least educated in this country. From local knowledge, and personal experience, I must bear testimony to the affection and to the loyalty they entertain for their KING and the Mother Country. It has been frequently, my Lords, mentioned, whenever this question has been agitated in this House—the riches and flourishing state of the West Indies. I admit it, and rejoice at the fact; and may therefore fairly assert, that in a free country, where, thank God, every thing is to be attained by individuals, it cannot be supposed that a West India proprietor pays less attention to the education of his child than any other British subject; and indeed, your Lordships know, that the great schools of Eton, Westminster, Harrow, and Winchester, are full of the sons of the West Indians. It would be a reflection indeed, which the Right Reverend and Learned Prelates I am sure would contradict, to say, that young men quitting these great public schools, to complete their educations at the seminaries of Oxford and Cambridge, and the universities of Scotland and Ireland, should turn out disgraceful to human nature, and destitute of heart and common feeling. It is not to your Lordships that I address this observation, because it is with real pleasure I observe, that all the idea of inhuman treatment from the British planter to the slave was done away in the opinion of your Lordships, shortly after the investigation first took place, by the examinations at the Bar of this House. I mention this, my Lords, that as an eye witness and a resident for some years amongst those West India planters, I may bear witness to their good conduct, to their humanity, and to the care and attention of their Slaves.

Facts, my Lords, speak for themselves:— Since the year 1792, and since the commencement of the French War, three events have arisen in the British West India islands. The first, the Maroon War, in the island of Jamaica. A tribe of Coromantine Negroes (part of the Maroons) in amity with the British Nation, unjustly made war upon the inhabitants of Jamaica. From the British officers employed in that war, I understand these Maroons, notwithstanding constant intercourse of more than a century with christians, to be totally void of all religion whatsoever; to be completely savage and barbarous, and to go entirely naked, with the exception of short trowsers. Neither have they, though surrounded by the British plantations, shewn any degree of cultivation excepting by the provisions which they grow for their own use. During this Maroon War, my Lords, the slaves on the island of Jamaica remained quiet, peaceable, loyal, and affectionate. The war was soon concluded, and the slaves had the warmest approbation of their masters.

In the Island of St. Vincent the second event took place, namely, the Carib War. The Caribs are the *Aborigines* of the country, and were permitted to remain in quiet possession upon the mountains of that island. It was not till the peace of 1763 that St. Vincent was entirely ceded to the King of Great Britain; and the Caribs, previous to this cession to England, having had communication with the French, maintained it during the whole of the peace. The island was consequently captured last war with the assistance of the Caribs; and this war, at the instigation of the French, the Caribs began a new rupture with the British inhabitants of St. Vincent's. Hostilities were fortunately concluded, and the Caribs, since that time, have been removed off the island. During this war, the slaves upon the different estates have remained steady and quiet, and still continue loyal and dutiful to their masters.

The third and last event was, I confess, an insurrection of slaves in the Island of Grenada; but, my Lords, it was an insurrection of French slaves belonging to French masters, tainted with French principles; for even at that time, the slaves belonging to the British never joined in the revolt, but remained quiet upon the plantations of their owners. I trust, my Lords, that these three material circumstances will bear me out in my assertion respecting the general good treatment of the British Planters to their slaves in the West Indies. I may also with truth, my Lords, affirm, that the treatment of the Negro slaves in the British Islands, is far superior to that of all foreign nations.

In the year 1788, I was in the island of Jamaica, when the first consolidated Slave Act was passing; and an honourable Gentleman, a member of the Assembly of Jamaica, who had just then arrived from England, bit by the rage of the day for the Abolition of the Slave Trade, was desirous of introducing additional clauses whilst in the committee. I was at Spanish Town on the morning of the day on which the Bill was to be committed; and was told by this Gentleman of his intention to add clauses; and that he was going to Kingston to attend the debate, after having sold a particularly fine able-bodied Negro to a French gentleman, to carry to the island of St. Domingo; because, as this slave was an ill-behaved man, whom he would not punish upon his own estate, he meant to part with him. This gentleman, upon his return from Kingston, came up to me—having myself had frequent conversations with him upon the folly of the Abolition, and the absurdity of going against the common usage in the British islands as to the treatment of the Negroes—and said, that the slave was returned to his estate, and should be punished in the usual manner; for, upon his offering him to sale to the French gentleman, the latter asked him if he was mad; and upon the Honourable Gentleman mentioning that his reason for selling this slave was to avoid punishing him, the French gentleman made this answer: "*Si nous avions cet Negre chez nous, nous assemblierons les Negres de quartier, et nous le ferrions mourir a coups de fouet.*' The Englishman, consequently, instead of proposing his amendments, voted for the Bill as it stood.

In the session of 1797, the House of Commons presented an Address to his Majesty, and a Circular Letter was sent out to the different Governors in the British West Indies, to recommend colonial regulations, and to pass different acts of the Legislature for the amelioration of slaves. It is, my Lords, with real pleasure I can observe, that the British Planters in the different islands have, with that proper deference which is due to their King and the Mother Country, given the most satisfactory answers upon that subject. All the islands indeed have taken some steps, except the island of Dominica, where the Assembly happened to be dissolved. However, my Lords, it is but justice due to the Proprietors of the British West India islands to observe, that all that has been gained upon the subject of the amelioration of the state of the Negro is, that that is now made law which before was an universal and established custom. In confirmation of my remark, I must refer your Lordships to *Mr. President Thompson* of St. Kitt's, who, in his Letter to the *Duke of Portland*, says—

"I have the satisfaction to observe to your Grace, that one sentiment seemed to pervade the whole of the Members who composed the General Council and Assembly, which was a sincere desire to adopt such measures as they thought would tend to make the Negroes happy and contented, and thereby promote the desired object of increasing their numbers by propagation.'

I must bear my public testimony to the character of *Mr. Thompson*, who is an active, popular, and intelligent servant of the Crown. I trust, therefore, my Lords, that I have said enough to prove the superior good treatment of the British Planter to his slaves, when compared with that of foreign nations.

To prove to your Lordships how very little can be effected by men who are unacquainted with the prejudices and customs of those who bear the relationship of master and slave, I am to inform your Lordships, from the most undoubted and respectable authority, that the East India Directors have lately sent out, certainly from the best and most laudable motives, a new code of laws to be observed on the Island of St. Helena, relative to the treatment of Slaves. So far, my Lords, from producing any good effect, that the Slaves themselves are rendered unhappy by it; and if a remonstrance has not already arrived in England from the inhabitants, a very serious one may shortly be expected.

A few more words, my Lords, on the subject of Abolition. In the year 1787, the Island of Jamaica was in extreme distress for provisions, and the Assembly presented an Address to the then Governor, to induce him to allow supplies to be imported in American vessels. They therein state, that between 1780 and 1787, from the dreadful effects of hurricanes, and their disagreeable consequence, such as famine and disease, that notwithstanding the annual importation of Negroes from the coast of Africa into Jamaica, at the time of presenting the Address, the Negro population was 15,000 short of what it was in 1780. It is true, that upon some estates, the Negro population may and does increase; and it is equally clear, that upon many others it rapidly diminishes: consequently the planters are obliged to purchase Slaves annually. In the Island of Jamaica, a particular friend of mine has two adjoining estates, both in Montego Bay. On the one the Negroes increase; and on the other, though adjacent, they are obliged, by the decrease of population, to make annual purchases. Some estates in St. Vincent's increase, whilst in Tobago there is little probability of an increase; and as the latter, in most cases, diminish, there is consequently a very great inconvenience. In case the Abolition should unfortunately take place, the English Planter, more active and more fertile at expedients of commerce than any other, would inevitably, upon those estates that increase in Negro population, turn Slave-breeder, and then supply different states and different islands. The consequences that have been so often drawn,—the tearing of the Slave from his country and family, would indeed, in this case, take effect, for the civilized and domiciliated Slave would be torn from his family and connections, to supply the deficiencies on those estates and islands where the Negro population does not increase.

To give, my Lords, the sentiments of foreigners, even upon the subject of Abolition, and to prove that they are congenial with those of the British Planter, I beg leave to quote a memorial presented to the States General by the Dutch inhabitants of Essequibo and Demarara, upon being precluded from the importation of Negroes by foreign ships. The words are:

"It is impossible to inform your High Mightinesses of the real annual diminution of our Slaves, but it is generally calculated at FIVE in the HUNDRED, or a TWENTIETH PART. This is little felt the FIRST year: nineteen Negroes hardly perceive that they do the work which the preceding year employed TWENTY; but the second year, the same work falls to EIGHTEEN; and if another year passes without any augmentation by purchase, SEVENTEEN must do the work FIRST allotted to twenty. This must give rise to DISCONTENT, DESERTION, and REVOLT; or if the Negroes put up patiently with this surcharge of labour, ILLNESS, and AN EARLIER DEATH, must be the consequence; or lastly, if the Planters seek to avoid these inconveniencies, they must gradually contract the

357

limits of their plantations, and of course diminish their produce.'

Whenever, my Lords, I have the honour of addressing your Lordships, God forbid that I should say any thing that could do the smallest injury to any single individual, or to society collectively considered; but it is necessary, on a subject of such importance, to make a fair and candid statement of the various circumstances requisite for the illustration of the subject. It is not for me, my Lords, to dwell upon what may be the conduct or the disposition of the British West India Islands, should the Abolition of the Slave Trade take place. I cannot, however, help calling to your Lordships attention the Address to the King from the Assembly of Jamaica—

"We can with truth assure your Majesty, that no opportunity, no circumstance, which may enable the Assembly of Jamaica to make further provisions to secure to every person in this island the certain, immediate, and active protection of the law, in proportion to their improvement in morality and religion, shall be neglected; but we must at the same time declare, that we are actuated by motives of humanity only, and not with any view to the termination of the Slave Trade.

The RIGHT of obtaining LABOURERS from Africa is secured to Your Majesty's faithful subjects in this colony BY SEVERAL BRITISH ACTS OF PARLIAMENT, and by SEVERAL PROCLAMA-TIONS of Your Majesty's Royal Ancestors. They, or their pred-ecessors, have emigrated and settled in Jamaica, under the MOST SOLEMN PROMISES of this (absolutely necessary) assistance, and they can never give up or do any act that may render doubtful their essential right.

We have the utmost reliance on Your Majesty's paternal goodness, that this right shall remain inviolate, as long as they shall remain faithful to Your Majesty, and true to the allegiance they owe to the Imperial crown of Great Britain.'

Much more, my Lords, might be said upon that subject; but I shall avoid all unnecessary illustration, either by facts or arguments. All European nations are anxious to wrest this valuable trade out of our hands. I shall not, like some advocates for the measure, advance as an argument that the French have abolished the trade, because they have at this time no settlements in the West Indies. That is a specious but a weak position. I have every reason to believe, that the motive for the removal of VICTOR HUGUES from the Island of Guadaloupe, by the French Directory, was for the express purpose of re-establishing the Slave Trade in that island, which, since the passing of the Abolition, had been found very beneficial in a state point of view. The new opinions adopted in France, engendered in the madness of the moment, and productive of the anarchy and confusion observable by every wise man, were certainly consonant to the sudden impulse for the Abolition. By the circumstances stated, respecting the Island of Guadaloupe, it is evident, that there is a considerable change of opinion on this subject in France; and that opinion, report mentions, has been strongly corroborated by a reference to the policy of the Portuguese, who carry on that trade with great advantage and profit.

Much stress has been laid upon the Abolition of the Trade by the Danes. But, my Lords, I beg leave to state that I now hold in my hand a Bill received this day, drawn upon the Danish Consul in this country, in payment for Slaves bought so late as the 12th of February 1799; and it is equally well ascertained, that the Danish Factors have, within these last twelve months, returned to the Coast of Africa. In these instances, my Lords, which I have as great a right to impress upon your Lordships minds as the supporters of the Abolition have to statements of a contrary nature, I am warranted by the evident acknowledgment of error on the part of the two countries mentioned.

Some enthusiasts for Abolition have endeavoured to maintain, that America has abandoned the Slave Trade; but it is a fact upon record, that the Americans are now carrying it on for the Spaniards; and it is a truth as well known, that notwithstanding an Act of Abolition has passed the Congress, the government of that country is not sufficiently strong to enforce its own laws on this particular subject. This spirit of resistance to the American Legislature is not a little heightened and inflamed by the many advantages obtained under the sanction of the Spanish Government. So far back as the 24th of January 1793, the Court of Madrid issued the following Declaration in favour of foreigners who may chuse to supply the Spanish Settlements with Negroes:

AN EDICT
TRANSLATED FROM THE SPANISH.

"His Excellency Don Diego de Guardoli has communicated to this Consulate, under date of the 24th of January last past, the following Royal Order:

The Spanish nation, being one of those which most frequented the Coast of Africa to obtain Negroes, before the first contract was made with the English, and his Majesty knowing the advantages that may arise to the State from our Merchants recommencing this traffic direct, has been pleased to grant, in order to promote so important an object, the following indulgences:

That all Spaniards may undertake these expeditions from any

of the Ports of Spain or America:

That the Crews of the Negro Vessels may be half foreigners, provided the other half—and the Captain in particular—are Spaniards:

That every thing shipped for this trade, direct, shall be free of duties:

That the vessels of foreign build, that shall be purchased expressly for the African Commerce, shall be exempted from paying the foreign and every other duty: —All which I communicate to you for your information, and that of the Commercial World.'

These are the sentiments of the Court of Spain in favour of the Slave Trade; and by another Edict of a more recent date, from the same high authority, still greater encouragement is given to adventurers in that trade. It has been proved at the Bar of this House, that even the Spanish frigates carry on this trade; and that at present there are cargoes of Slaves now waiting on the coast of Africa to be conveyed to the Spanish part of America.

Having said thus much upon the West Indies, and upon the subject of Abolition, I beg leave to conclude this part with the words of an able writer:

"You have invited and persuaded us to purchase and occupy Crown lands in the islands; you have undertaken and promised to furnish us with labourers sufficient for the cultivation of those lands; you have encouraged us to invest our fortunes in these plantations; you have encouraged not only your merchants, but foreigners, to advance their money in loans, to a vast amount, for the improvement and extension of this culture. If you now put a stop to the cultivation, we and our creditors have a right, upon every principle of justice, to demand from you a full indemnification."

I come, now, my Lords, to the last, though not the least, part of the subject, namely, the importance of the West Indies. However much I may regret the difference of opinion with any noble Lord upon this great and important question, I am confident that the documents which I shall have the honour of submitting to the House respecting the present flourishing state of our West India Settlements, must be a picture highly gratifying to every well-wisher of this country. It is highly gratifying, indeed, that I can attract your Lordships attention with this agreeable object, after we have for seven years experienced all the difficulties and dangers of a widely-extended and expensive war—a war, my Lords, in which our naval and military prowess has rivalled, if not surpassed, the most brilliant periods of antiquity.

I shall proceed, my Lords, to the statements which I promised, with assurances that they all are extracted from the best and most incontrovertible authorities:

IMPORTANCE OF THE WEST INDIES.
1788.

450,000 Negroes, at 50*l.* per head	£.22,500,000
Utensils, mules, and crop on the ground, double the value of the Negroes	..45,000,000
Value of houses in towns, trading and coasting vessels, and their crews	.. 2,500,000
	—————
Capital	70,000,000

Employing 689 vessels, 148,176 tons,
equal to the whole trade of the country
at the end of the last century,
navigated by 14,000 seamen, exclusive
of African, American, and
Newfoundland Colonies, and the
American States.

The gross duties to the British Empire ..　　..　　.. 1,800,000

Permit me, my Lords, to make some few additional remarks. Since the year 1788, at which period I trust I have proved that the British West India capital amounted to 70,000,000*l.* sterling, great political events have happened. Early in the year 1793, war took place between this country and France; and by the characteristic bravery and active exertions of our army and navy, the islands of Martinique, St. Lucia, and Tobago, have been conquered from the French; the island of Trinidad from the Spaniards; and the settlements of Demarara and Essequibo from the Dutch. Hence our additional wealth and splendour in the West Indies; and hence that unbounded influence which commands the peace of our settlements, and protects them from the introduction of that political phrenzy that has outraged and convulsed the civilized society of Europe.

I cannot give your Lordships a more clear or demonstrative proof, than that the trade in 1796 required 350,230, tons, navigated by 24,000 seamen.

1798.

Gross duties to Great Britain	.£. 3,000,000
Value of Imports to the Ports of Great Britain	.. 45,000,000
Of which West India Imports only	.. 11,000,000
Tonnage of the Port of London.	.. .400,000
Of which West India Duty	.. 96,000

After describing our national happiness and prosperity in the West Indies, resulting from the united efforts of our commercial and military enterprize, it may not be amiss, by way of contrast, to demonstrate to your Lordships what the French, during the same period, have lost and sacrificed at the shrine of folly and infamy. This is no digression, my Lords, for every circumstance connected with the existence of our West India Settlements is also essentially connected with the existence of the Slave Trade. The French commerce, at the moment of the Revolution, stood thus:

	Tons
The French, excluding the foreign tonnage, employed	350,000
Seamen (French)	.. 50,000
About fourteen seamen to every 100 tons.	
Their West India commerce alone, 600 ships	
at 350 tons each	.. 29,000
Seamen, fourteen to 100 tons	.. 29,000
Imports from the West Indies 185 millions livres	
Exports to ditto	78 ditto

From these estimates I have clearly proved, that in the year 1788 the British property in the West Indies amounted to

£.70,000,000 sterling. Admitting that the price of Negroes, since the commencement of the war, has risen from £.50 to between £.80 and £.90 sterling per head, the improvement of property in the same period much more than counterbalances the advance; and hence I am perfectly well warranted in saying, that the whole capital of the Old British West India property amounts to at least £.80,000,000 sterling. If allowed to add the value of the New West India property, namely, the conquests from the French, Spaniards, and Dutch, amounting to at least £.20,000,000, I may safely assert, that the present British Capital in the West Indies, is equal, upon a fair calculation, to ONE HUNDRED MILLIONS STERLING! A sum, my Lords, which demands your most serious consideration, before you consent to the Abolition of that Trade without which it could not exist. When I say, that, on the proof of this interesting fact I repose the whole strength of my argument, I am confident that your Lordships will pause, and fully weigh the consequences of your vote this evening.—I am confident that, as the hereditary guardians of British subjects, you will stretch out your hands to protect, not to destroy—I am confident that, as hereditary councillors of the crown, you will give life and spirit, instead of dejection and death, to a most numerous and most loyal description of His Majesty's subjects.

I now, my Lords, beg leave to return my warmest thanks for the great indulgence which I have experienced this evening. The sentiments which I have delivered against the Bill are the pure dictates of my conscience; and I am highly flattered by the patient hearing which your Lordships have given me in the discharge of the duty which I owe to my King and Country.

After a long and interesting debate, the numbers were,

For the Commitment of the Bill	25
Proxies	36
	—
	61
	—
Non-Contents, Lords present	32
Proxies	36
	—
	68
	—
Majority against the Bill	7

Printed by C. Whittingham, Dean-street, Fetter-lane, London.

LETTERS

CONCERNING THE

ABOLITION

OF THE

SLAVE-TRADE

AND OTHER

WEST-INDIA

AFFAIRS.

═══════════

By MERCATOR.

═══════════

London:

PRINTED BY C. AND W. GALABIN, INGRAM-COURT,
FENCHURCH-STREET.

————

1807.

LETTERS, &c.
ABOLITION OF THE SLAVE-TRADE.

SIR,

It is understood, that, on opening of parliament, a bill is to be brought in, under the auspices of his majesty's ministers, for the immediate and total abolition of the slave-trade.

I am not about to discuss the expediency of this measure on hackneyed grounds. To vindicate the slave-trade is not a duty incumbent on the West-India planter or merchant, but on the British legislature, in whom it originated, by whom it was sanctioned and encouraged, and who even imposed on the court of Spain the famous Assiento contract, the object of which was to secure this country the exclusive supply of all the Spanish colonies with negroes. The West-India planters and, merchants have only been the humble instruments of accomplishing the declared purpose of the British parliament; and, encouraged by the high sanction of the legislature, which in every country impresses its principles on the minds of the people, they cannot be blamed for having participated in the execution of this once-favoured project, for extending the commerce and thereby adding to the wealth and strength of the British empire. If the principles of parliament are now so much more pure, that the proscription of this traffic is necessary as a sacrifice at the altar of humanity, let them not heap obloquy on the West-India planters, but fix the odium where it is justly due, and acknowledge, while they expiate, the crimes of their predecessors. Let them also remember, that one moral virtue is not to be trampled upon that another may be exalted; and that those who pretend to be the votaries of humanity must not be the violators of justice.

The West-India planters, while they call upon parliament to indemnify them against the pecuniary consequences of the abolition, warn them of other consequences against which no indemnity can be given; and strongly protest against this violent innovation, by which their property, depending on a trade established, and hitherto protected, by the laws of their country, is now to be sacrificed. They ask, too, whether it is consistent with that purity of principle by which the abolitionists profess to be actuated, to retain the profits of this execrable traffic, whose continuance they are about to abolish: while they reprobate the crime, will they pocket the fruits of it? If so, the point to which their morality extends can be precisely ascertained; that it goes on so far as it affects only the interests of others, but stops short the moment that it touches their own. For near a century and a half, the British nation has reaped profits almost incalculable from this very slave-trade. It produces, annually, near three millions to the revenue, in the duties paid on West-India produce, and takes off almost double that amount in British manufactures. As the source of the West India trade, it furnishes employment for 200,000 tons of British shipping and 16,000 British seamen; and thus is one of the great supports of that naval power to which she owes her independence and even existence as a nation. If parliament choose to abolish this trade, to be consistent, they must, in future, renounce these ill-gotten gains, derived from so impure a source; and, to be just, they must refund so much of those which they have already received, as will indemnify the planters and merchants, who, on the faith of parliamentary sanction, have invested their property in the British colonies.

Some advocates for the abolition have asserted, that this

measure will not be injurious to the planters; for, that, by proper care and humanity in the treatment of the slaves, their numbers may be kept up, and even increased, without importation from Africa. In arguing with men on subjects of which they have no local knowledge, (and I cannot consider those persons as conversant with the West Indies who have hazarded this assertion,) the best mode of reasoning is by analogy. It is admitted, that, in the manufacturing towns of England, the population decreases. Every estate in the West Indies is a manufactory; the process of boiling sugar and distilling rum is unfavourable to health, and necessarily carried on by night as well as by day, without intermission, during the whole of the crop-season. If the population decreases in the manufacturing towns of England, where a temperate climate unites with the laws of the land in promoting general regularity of conduct and domestic attachments, how much more must it decrease in the West-Indies, where the negroes yield to the ardent and uncontrolled influence of the passions, where a promiscuous intercourse of the sexes takes place, where, consequently, fewer children are born, and where the climate is unpropitious both to health and longevity? These considerations will probably establish in unprejudiced minds here what experience has long ago established in the West Indies, that a constant supply of negroes from Africa is requisite to continue the cultivation of the islands; and, as a necessary consequence, the just claim of the planters to an indemnification, if that supply be prohibited. To refuse it would be to contaminate a measure, founded on the pretence of humanity, by a manifest act of injustice.

Considering the slave-trade as an abstract question, it must be admitted, that it is irreconcileable to the principles of humanity and natural justice; against which, considerations of interests or policy ought not to be set in competition. Did not this trade actually exist, I am persuaded that not a man in the kingdom would argue in favour of its being established; but, having been so long established and acted upon, we are not now to consider the abolition of it abstractedly, but relatively, in all its bearings and consequences; or, in the excess of a blind though laudable zeal, we may occasion more mischief than we remedy, and injure the cause we mean to promote. To those who contend, that, disregarding all possible consequences, we ought, in the first instance, to set right what we feel to be wrong, I answer, that I know of no obligation which compels us to act upon such a principal. That the slave-trade is sanctioned by the laws of the land has already been shewn. That it is forbidden by any religious precept, either under the old or new dispensation, I have not been able to discover. For reasons inscrutable to our finite understandings, the carrying away the women and children of the conquered countries into captivity, after putting all the males to the sword and destroying their cities by fire, was the divine command given through the Jewish legislator.[1] Slavery, therefore, was expressly ordained by the law of Moses; none of the inspired prophets lifted up their voices against it; the abolition of it formed no part of the divine mission, either of our Saviour or his apostles; and one would have thought, that an institution of civil society, tolerated by such high authorities, might have escaped such very violent and unqualified anathemas as have been denounced against it, and all those connected with it, by our modern reformers.

The rights of man have been strongly urged against the slave-trade. Of these new-fangled doctrines we have lately heard too much; and the conduct of their supporters in a neighbouring country should operate as a warning, not as an example. Without drawing arguments from the state of society under arbitrary governments, in the happiest communities, great sacrifices of the liberty of the individual are made for the general good, and something very nearly allied to slavery exists even in this justly-boasted land of freedom. Is the impressing our seamen consistent with the rights of man or the liberty of the subject? Is it consistent with these principles, that a youth, inveigled into the army, should be irrevocably bound by his engagement, made at a time of life when the law absolves him from every other contract, except for food and raiment? These men were born to political rights and know their value. The slave was born a slave, without political rights, and is ignorant even of the meaning of the term. The poor, in England, are as effectually doomed to labour in the parishes where they are born as the slaves in the West Indies are on the estates to which they belong. If a poor man attempts to change his place of abode, unless he can give security that in case of sickness or want of employment he shall not become chargeable in his new residence, (which no poor man can do,) the afficers of the parish to which he emigrates have the legal right of sending him back to prevent his gaining a settlement, just as a run-away negroe is liable to be apprehended and sent back to his master. Any magistrate can oblige the poor man to work at the established rate of wages for the support of himself and his family; or, in case of refusal, commit him to hard labour in the house of correction. Labour, therefore, is not peculiar to a state of slavery, nor is the compulsion of it exceptionable, if imposed in a fair proportion to the physical strength of the parties: and, from what I have seen of the situation of the negroes in the West Indies, I can safely aver, that it is far more comfortable than that of the labouring classes of the community in Great Britain.

But, it is said, that the abuses of authority on the part of the masters, and the tyranny and cruelty exercised on the slaves, make it necessary to abolish the system altogether. Instances of this sort have been grossly exaggerated; and, admitting the charge to be, in some degree, well founded, have we not heard of abuses of authority, of cruelty, and tyranny, being exercised in every relation and condition of life? We have heard of them in the army, in the navy, and in the merchant-service; but is it to be argued thence, that our army, our navy, and our commerce, ought to be abolished? We have heard, too, of brutal ill-treatment of parish-apprentices: but are we, on this account, to put out no more children apprentices, and suffer them all to run idle about the streets, instead of being brought up in habits of useful industry? To argue from the abuse of an institution against the use of it is very unsound logic. Perfection is not the lot of humanity, and no human institution can be free from abuses. The laws are framed to punish what they cannot prevent and are intended to protect the negroes in the West Indies as well as they are to protect the poor in Great Britain.

But, notwithstanding these considerations, humanity still feels outraged; and arguments drawn from the state of society, in this or any other country, though they may palliate, cannot justify, the slave-trade. I mean to use them no farther than to stop that furious zeal, which, in its eagerness to gain its object, uses means without considering their end; and only to establish this proposition, that it is not merely the theoretical propriety, but the pratical consequences, of the abolition of this trade that ought to be considered. Let us then examine how they are likely to affect the interests of humanity, justice, and policy, the declared objects of this measure, and to the principles of all which, parliament, by a hasty resolution, has declared the slave-trade to be repugnant.

Let us first consider, how the cause of humanity will be benefited by our abolition of the slave-trade. Are ministers prepared to say that his majesty has made such arrangements, in concert with other powers, as will secure the universal abolition of the traffic? I know they are not. I know, farther, that America is launching rapidly into this trade, to carry on that branch of it which we renounced last sessions of parliament, the supply of the foreign colonies. If we imagine, that, when slaves can no longer be imported into the British colonies, the trade will, in some degree, be put a stop to, we deceive ourselves; for, if none are brought to the British islands, their produce will gradually decrease in consequence, and just so many more will be brought to the foreign colonies, whose produce will increase in the same proportion. This will be the whole difference; and just the same number of slaves will be annually exported from the coast of Africa as hitherto has been. The result, then, of the abolition of the slave-trade, by Great Britain alone, will be the aggrandizement of foreign merchants and foreign colonies at the expense of her own; and that the slave-trade, instead of being carried on in British ships, subject to the humane regulations adopted by parliament for the accommodation of slaves on their passage, will be carried on in American and other foreign ships, not subject to these restrictions; and thus the cause of humanity will be injured instead of being benefited.

How the cause of justice will be affected will appear from inquiring into the consequences of this measure to the British planters. Their negroes will no longer be joined by new recruits to share and lighten their labours. As their crops diminish, their resources will fail; and of course their means of affording the usual comforts to their slaves, among whom increased toil and diminished enjoyments will soon excite discontent. The negroes, too, will rationally conclude, that, if it be unlawful to make them slaves, it must be unlawful to keep them so; and will no longer brook that state to which they are now habituated. Insurrections and massacres will be the consequence; the horrors of St Domingo will be renewed in our islands and the race of whites be speedily exterminated. I seriously believe, that the abolitionists are not aware of the dreadful events to which their favourite measure leads, nor did the first leaders of the French revolution foresee the horrors that would mark its progress. They, who profess to distinguish abolition from emancipation and disclaim the one while they support the other, might as well say to the waves of the sea, thus far shalt thou go and no farther, as attempt to stop the torrent that will rush through the breach they are about to make in the present establishment of civil society in the West-India colonies; nor can they, with any claim to consistency, support the distinction; for, the reasoning that I have already put in the mouths of the negroes is obvious to the meanest capacity, and demonstrates that abolition justifies and even consecrates every attempt on their part at emancipation, however sanguinary the means by which the end may be pursued.

One topic yet remains; and that is, the policy of this measure in its effects on the interests of Great Britain. The important benefits, which she derives from her West-India colonies, have already been stated, and by them her loss may be estimated. These colonies, if they can possibly escape falling a prey to revolutionary horrors, will sink under the no less sure, though slower, operation of gradual decay, and the planters will emigrate from our own islands to foreign possessions, where their labours will be properly appreciated and rewarded. Surely it could not be with the view of guarding against this consequence that a clause was introduced into the bill, passed last year, for preventing the supply of foreign colonies with slaves, which prohibits the British planter from sending his negroes off the island on which he resides to any foreign colony; thus denying him the last melancholy privilege of emigrating from the country in which he is oppressed, and, under pretence of giving liberty to the slaves, forging chains for their masters. Could it have been expected, that a clause so intolerably grievous would have originated in an administration who profess themselves advocates for freedom? Is there no danger that our colonies may fall victims to the injudicious measures now in contemplation and that those of our enemy may rise upon their ruins? Then, indeed, would he attain the consummation of his wishes; ships, colonies, and commerce. In the loss of our colonies both the others are included; and, together, they are the support of that naval pre-eminence which is now the only barrier of Great Britain against the overgrown power and insatiable ambition of her implacable foe.

The institution of the slave-trade has involved us in a choice of difficulties; but, from what has been stated, one inference may clearly be drawn, that it cannot be abolished, with any good effect, till the judicious recommendation of parliament has been acted upon, and his majesty has made such arrangements, in concert with other powers, as will enable him to stop the traffic altogether. Without this general cooperation, the trade would only change hands, and, as has already been observed, the cause of humanity be injured rather than benefited. The West-India planters and merchants, who have invested their capital in the colonies, depending on the privilege of exercising this traffic, must also be indemnified for whatever losses they may sustain by the prohibition of it, or every pretension to justice must be abandoned: and policy dictates the utmost caution in guarding against the evils which such a revolution may occasion; for, our colonies, our commerce, our revenues, and our very existence as an independent nation, are involved in the consequences of this measure. Let us, then, pause, and deliberate before we decide: but, much I fear, from the temper manifested in the last sessions of parliament, that our legislators will be governed by their feelings rather than by their judgement; that the abolition will be carried by acclamation, not by evidence and argument; and that, as a false philosophy lately deluged France with blood and revolutionary horrors, so a false philanthropy is preparing similar evils for Great Britain.

MERCATOR.

Sir,

In my last letter, I considered the proposed abolition of the slave-trade, in a commercial and political point of view, as it affected the interests of Great Britain and of her West-India colonies. I shall now offer a few observations on the subject as a measure of political economy, considering it solely as it relates to the inhabitants of Africa.

These people, like other uncivilized nations, from their aversion to regular labour, attend more to pasturage than agriculture; and subsist, in a great degree, on the spontaneous fruits of the earth, and such animals as they can either domesticate or procure by the chase. Mr Mungo Parke, whose recent travels in the interior districts of Africa have afforded him better opportunities of information, respecting the habits and manners of the inhabitants, than any other European ever possessed, gives this general description of them, and says, "it was not possible for me to behold the wonderful fertility of the soil, the vast herds of cattle, &c. without lamenting, that a country, so abundantly gifted and favoured by nature, should remain in its present savage and neglected state.'

It is evident that mankind (like any other race of animals) cannot exist beyond the number for which food is provided by the hand of nature, unless they add to the natural productions of the earth by labour and cultivation: and that, if they increase in a greater degree than the labour so applied furnishes additional means of subsistence, the surplus of the population must either emigrate to some other country or starve. When the latter dreadful alternative takes place, it operates partly by the immediate effect of absolute famine, and partly by the diseases incident to the various stages of want, which, at the same time, injure the health and weaken the procreative faculties of those who survive. After the population is thus reduced, the supply of food becomes more plentiful. In proportion as the remainder are better fed, they increase in number till food becomes scarce again; and thus, the same cause producing the same effect, the wheel continually goes round. Sir John Sinclair, in his Inquiry into the Principles of Political Economy, illustrates this position by the following example: "Put two or three pair of rabbits into a field proper for them, the multiplication will be rapid; and, in a few years the warren will be stocked. You may take yearly from it a hundred pair, I shall suppose, and keep your warren in good order. Give over taking any for some years, you will find your original stock rather diminished than increased, for the reasons before-mentioned. —Africa yearly furnishes many thousands for the cultivation of America; in this she resembles the warren. I have little doubt, but that, if all her sons were returned to her, by far the greater part would die of hunger.' In confirmation of this opinion, which was given without any reference to the abolition of the slave-trade, and long before that measure was ever agitated, Mr Mungo Parke informs us, that in Africa, during periods of famine, slaves are sold to purchase provisions for the master and his family; that, under similar circumstances, the inhabitants sell their children, and that (I quote his exact words) there are many instances of free men voluntarily surrendering their liberty to save their lives. During a scarcity, which lasted three years in the countries bordering on the Gambia, great numbers of people became slaves in this manner. Dr Laidley assured me, that at that time many free men came and begged with great earnestness to be put upon his slave-chain to save themselves from perishing with hunger.'

The only effectual remedy for these miseries is, to make civilisation keep pace with population. Man, in a savage and independent state, scorns labour; considers it as a degradation, and imposes it on those over whom he can exercise authority. This is the case in Africa. Mr Parke states, that 3-4ths of the people are in a state of hopeless and hereditary slavery, and are employed in cultivating the land, in the care of cattle, and in servile offices of all kinds, much in the same manner as the slaves in the West Indies.'[2] In civilised countries, where slavery is abolished, the necessity of labour is impressed upon the minds of the whole, and actuates the conduct of the greater part of the community. Agriculture, too, is so much improved, that the earth is made to furnish subsistence for a much larger number of inhabitants; while luxury and refinement, by creating artificial wants, supply endless sources of occupation and keep up a constant circulation of property, which is diffused throughout all the members of the body politic, and provides every individual with the means of maintaining himself by the earnings of his own industry.

The superfluous population of the barbarous nations in the north of Europe formerly overflowed in periodical eruptions upon their more civilised neighbours, among whom they either gained a settlement by conquest, and adopted the manners of the people with whom they mixed, or were defeated and extirpated in the attempt. The Inhabitants of Africa have no such resource, either for emigration or improvement. Bounded by the seas and the desert, their wars are carried on with the surrounding tribes, whose manners are as ferocious and whose country is as uncultivated as their own. If their incursions are successful, no civilization ensues; they carry their enemies into captivity, drive off their cattle, destroy the provisions they cannot consume, and return home in triumph. The vanquished nation, thus rendered desperate, is driven by necessity to retaliate the injuries it has experienced, either upon the assailants or on some other less powerful people: and, in this manner, the Africans are and have been, from time immemorial, engaged in a constant series of petty warfare. Formerly the massacre of their prisoners contributed to keep their population within the bounds prescribed by their aversion to labour. This cruel practice has now in a great messure ceased; and the prisoners are sold instead of being put to the sword, except such as are reserved for slaves to the conquerors, or us from their age and infirmity are found unfit for sale, who are considered as useless, and who, Mr Parke declares, "he has no doubt are commonly put to death.' The slave-trade, therefore, is now the substitute for famine and the sword; and the population of Africa is kept down to its necessary level, by the export of the superfluous numbers to the West Indies.

The aversion to labour, so conspicuous a feature in the character of all uncivilized people, was probably the origin of slavery; as it induced those who possessed any superiority, either natural or acquired, to avail themselves of it, by compelling others to labour for them. When society was formed into states, chiefs and leaders exercised this authority over their prisoners; and the greater number of them they could obtain to employ in the labours of agriculture, the greater number of their own people they could employ in military service, and the wider range they could give to the pursuits of ambition or the dictates of revenge. Thus, slavery, as a right of war, became universally established, and continued to be in force till the laws of war were softened by civilisation. This right, however, is still exercised in many nations, and particularly in Africa; "where,' Mr Parke says, "prisoners of war are the slaves of the conquerors; and, when the weak or unsuccessful warrior begs for mercy beneath the uplifted spear of his opponent, he gives up at the same time his claim to liberty and purchases his life at the expense of his freedom."

From the preceding observations we may reasonably infer, that, by suddenly abolishing the slave-trade, and thus preventing the exportation of the superfluous inhabitants of Africa, we should occasion one of these two consequences: either that the excess of the population, beyond what the present productions of that country are sufficient to maintain, must starve, or, that the practice of putting prisoners to death, instead of selling them as slaves, would be revived in its full extent; neither of which events would certainly tend to promote the cause of humanity. The sentiments of Mr Parke on this subject are entitled to great weight; and, in considering them, we should recollect, that, at the period of his publication, the zeal of the advocates for the abolition, and the odium against those who opposed it, raged at their greatest height. Under these circumstances, coupled with the avowed sentiments and wishes of his patrons, a negative opinion was as much as he could be expected to hazard in favour of so unpopular a cause, and his reflections upon slavery are summed up in the following words: "Such are the general outlines of this system of slavery which prevails in Africa; and it is evident, from the nature and extent of it, that it is a system of no modern date. It probably had its origin in the remotest ages of antiquity, before the Mahomedans crossed the desert. How far it is maintained and supported by the slave-trade, which, for two hundred years, the nations of Europe have carried on with the natives of the coast, it is not within my province nor in my power to explain. If my sentiments should be required, concerning the effect which a discontinuance of this commerce would produce on the manners of the natives, I should have no hesitation in observing, that, in the present unenlightened state of their minds, my opinion is, that the effect would neither be so extensive nor beneficial as many wise and worthy persons fondly expect.' The testimony of this writer completely exculpates the Europeans from the charge of having established a system of slavery in Africa, by furnishing a market for its unhappy objects;[3] and although, in guarded and qualified terms, he discountenances the abolition of the slave-trade in the present

383

unenlightened state of the minds of the Africans, and treats the beneficial consequences expected from it, by many wise and worthy persons, as chimeras of the fond imagination.

The fair conclusion to be drawn from these premises, is, that the abolitionists begin at the wrong end of their undertaking. They should, in the first instance, prepare the minds of the people of Africa for the change which they wish to introduce in their present system. This can only be effected by promoting their civilisation and instruction, and thus gradually bringing about the necessary alteration in their habits and manners. When their ferocity is softened, when their minds are enlightened, when they can be induced to apply themselves to labour, and by their industry render their country capable of producing a much greater quantity of food, and of maintaining a much greater number of inhabitants than it can do in its present state, then the necessity of exporting their superfluous population will no longer exist, and it may be retained without those miserable consequences which such a measure would, in all probility, now occasion.

Let the abolitionists direct their immediate attention to these objects: let them pave the way by proper measures, for that increase of human happiness, to which no feeling mind can be indifferent, and to which all considerations of interest or policy ought to be subservient, and they will have the prayers of all good men for the success of their laudable endeavours. But the experience of history demonstrates, that the established customs of any country can only be altered by slow degrees; and that every attempt at sudden innovation, without due regard to the spirit and prejudices of the people, must prove mischievous as well as abortive.

MERCATOR.

Notes

1. Deuteronomy, chap. XX ver. 13 to 15. Numbers, Chap. 31.
2. If there can be any doubts which are entitled to the most credit, the accounts drawn from imagination by the abolitionists, of the happiness and independence enjoyed by the Africans in their own country, or that given from actual observation by Mr Mungo Parke, and above quoted, such doubts may he set at rest by this plain fact; that, out of the many thousands of negroes who have obtained their freedom in the West Indies, and have acquired sufficient property to indulge their inclinations in point of residence, scarcely a solitary instance can be adduced of any of them returning to the coast of Africa. What can be inferred hence, but that their own country has not those charms for them which some writers would lead us to imagine? Were it otherwise, they would feel the force of that principle which animates the European, who, while exposed to the heats and dangers of the torrid zone, looks forward to the sight of his native land as the recompense of all his toils.
3. The society who have lately published the substance of the debates in both houses of parliament, on the resolution for abolishing the slave-trade, assert, in what they are pleased to term their illustrations, that, "the European nations have not, as has been alleged, merely diverted the trade in slaves from its antient channel; but of themselves originated that trade, with all its enormities.' This may serve as a specimen of the truth and candour which pervade their publications on this subject.

THIRD LETTER

ON THE

ABOLITION

OF THE

SLAVE-TRADE

AND OTHER

WEST-INDIA

AFFAIRS.

By MERCATOR.

London:

PRINTED BY C. AND W. GALABIN, INGRAM-COURT,
FENCHURCH-STREET.

1807.

LETTER, &c.
ABOLITION OF THE SLAVE-TRADE.

SIR,

IN Consequence of my two letters on the abolition of the slave-trade, which appeared on the 13th and 20th of December last, a writer, under the signature of a Planter, has done me the honour of addressing me in a pamphlet.

A house that is divided against itself cannot stand; and the abolitionists cannot fail of success if planters become their advocates. Well might I exclaim, *et tu, Brute!* This schismatic from the established faith of the church in whose communion he was born and bred, candidly confesses, that "his only hope of salvation (from ruin) is placed in the adoption of this measure;' and tells us, that, "he has a greater dread from the land of the islands being worn out than that the population of negroes will not be sufficient for their cultivation, adding, that this evil is at present somewhat alarming to his mind.' This gentleman, having a population of negroes more than equal to the cultivation of his almost worn-out land, (like the fox who lost his tail and wished to persuade his brethern to cut off theirs,) very sagaciously and disinterestedly argues against other planters being permitted to make that improvement of their estates of which his own is no longer capable. He asks, "if a farther extent of cultivation is desirable for the West-India interest, at this or any other time, when the product is greater than the demand? and whether the true interest of the West-India planter is not confined to the supply of that market to which alone he is allowed to transmit his produce for sale.'

Overlooking all the great considerations of national interest, which are involved in his questions, and anxious to secure a good price for his produce, or, as he very intelligently terms it, "to guard against the market being in the hands of the buyer and not of the seller,' he is for limitting the cultivation of the colonies altogether, to the consumption of the mother-country.

Though this system may suit the narrow policy of the Planter, will his doctrine, that, "to extend the cultivation of the colonies is to open the box of Pandora still wider,' accord with the enlarged policy of the statesman? Is Great Britain no longer to retain her supremacy as queen of the isles? Is the genius of commerce to be banished from her shores? Or, to speak without a metaphor, are all the great manufacturing and maritime interests, which depend upon the extension of her colonies, to be abandoned? must she renounce all share in the supply of those powers who have no colonial possessions? If her surplus of colonial produce fails, whence is she to derive resources for the payment of all the commodities which she constantly imports; or how is she to provide for those incidental drains occasioned by subsidies to foreign powers in time of war, or the purchase of foreign corn in years of scarcity? It should be considered that the commerce relinquished by Great Britain is not only lost to her but gained by her rivals and enemies: that foreign colonies will flourish in the same proportion as the British colonies decline, and foreign navigation increase as British navigation diminishes. Buonaparte has wisely said, that ships, colonies, and commerce, are all he wants: for it is by them alone that we retain that naval supremacy which enables us to set his menaces at defiance; and our legislators must guard them with the most jealous vigilance, as they value the independence and safety of the empire.

It is not the excess of our colonial produce, but the

impediments opposed to its usual circulation that have caused the present urgent and extreme distress of the West-India interests. Ministers have the means of redress in their own hands, and I trust will speedily and effectually apply them, either by substituting sugar for corn in the distilleries and breweries, or by interdicting the supply of the enemy from his own colonies in neutral vessels, which will oblige his subjects to resort to the British market in spite of his prohibitory decree. This temporary pressure may be removed by more judicious expedients than that which the selfish policy of the planter recommends, the sacrifice of those permanent and important advantages resulting from our colonial and commercial pre-eminence.

Having thus shewn, by the avowal of this writer himself, that he supports the abolition of the slave-trade from motives of personal interest, and, in the discussion of this extraneous point, that, where his interest is concerned, his judgement is not the most profound nor his advice the most salutary, I shall now more immediately confine myself to the subject to which I am indebted for his correspondence.

In conceding that the slave-trade, considered as an abstract-question, is irreconcileable to the principles of humanity and natural justice, I am told, that I have admitted all that I attempt to deny: but the very next lines of the sentence, from which these words are quoted, refute this charge; and, unless I deceive myself, render the whole consistent: for, I added, "that, having been so long established and acted upon, we are not now to consider the abolition of it abstractedly, but relatively, in all its bearings and consequences; or, in the excess of a blind though laudable zeal, we may occasion more mischief than we remedy, and injure the cause we mean to promote.' The Planter does not reason fairly in taking only so much of a passage as suits his purpose, and I might retort upon him, what he imputes to me, a wish to assume the character of arguing with some degree of plausibility.

I leave it to the Planter to reconcile his assertion, "that there was no law in Rome against parricide;' with his observation, "that, when opinions are offered to the public to guide the mind, they should be the result of experience, and that experience should be such that nothing should be left at hazard upon the result.' In this instance he has, like many other persons, laid down rules for others which he has not observed himself. He will hardly venture to oppose his authority on the Roman law to that of Cicero, one of whose Orations, which no man who has read can possibly forget, was not only composed in defence of a person who stood arraigned for that crime, but even describes the horrible and disgraceful death by which it was punished.[1] I have a decided, though not a clear, recollection of it, too, in some other writer, by the term of "projectio in profluentem;' but, as my attention is more directed to mercantile than classical pursuits, my readers must excuse my not referring them to my author.

The Planter has been rather unfortunate in rummaging the Roman law to find a peg to hang an argument upon; nor, do I think he has been much more successful in his researches into divine law. He quotes the tenth commandment, as containing an implied abolition of slavery, though that precept obviously bears a very different import. Slavery had been ordained long before, and was continued for ages after, the delivery of the commandments to Moses, who may be presumed to have been a better commentator upon the decalogue than my new correspondent; and we may reasonably assume, that this practice would have been expressly abolished by the divine command, either under the old or the new dispensation, had it been repugnant to the divine will. Let me observe, too, that the slave-trade was established here at a period which was distinguished by the brightest constellation of statesmen, divines, and philosophers, that ever shone in the political horizon of Great Britain. Among the latter we find the illustrious names of Newton, Boyle, and Locke; men who took an active part in the politics of those days; and, in whose characters, philosophy was exalted into piety. With these reflections on our minds we must admit that this traffic is not condemned by the weight of authorities either divine or human.

The Planter asks me if I did mean to say what I certainly did not mean to say, and then reasons as if I had actually said it. I did not mean to say that the time of taking off the crop is not the most healthy of any period in the year; for, the mortality amongst both whites and blacks in the West Indies is principally in the wet season. During the dry months, the air is more salubrious, the provisions are more nutritive, and thus the effects of the laborious occupation of the negroes are more than counteracted. My assertion that the process of boiling sugars is unfavourable to health, is founded upon this plain principle; that, working day and night is so in the nature of things. In saying, that the distillation of rum was carried on without intermission, I expressed myself with a want of accuracy which he has very properly reprehended. I cannot consider the growing of sugar more like the cultivation of a farm than a manufacture; for, I never heard of the cultivation of a farm being carried on by night as well as by day, which, on a sugar-estate, is constantly the case in the crop-season. Being totally unacquainted with the interior process of breweries of distilleries, I can draw no comparison from them: the only persons I am in the habit of seeing, who are employed in the one or the other, are the men who go about with the drays. I consider them as carmen rather than brewers, and am inclined to suspect, that their athletic appearance, to which the planter alludes, is more owing to the beer they drink than to the beer they brew.

Of all the other causes of decreased population in the West Indies, which I enumerated, the Planter takes no notice; but asserts, that the number of slaves may he kept up on some estates in the old islands where the number of creoles is great; and thus, by quoting particular exceptions, admits the general rule for which I contend. With respect to the policy of ceasing to employ negroes in the West Indies, if their numbers cannot be kept up without importation, I have only to observe, that a great variety of occupations in this country are so notoriously unhealthy, that, (to use his own words,) "a succession must always be ready to supply what the hand of death takes off,' and yet the legislature has not thought fit to abolish them.

This strenuous advocate for the rights of man, who accuses me of deriding them, for having adduced instances to shew, that, in the happiest communities, great sacrifices of the liberty of the individual must necessarily be made for the general good, and that the compulsion of labour is not peculiar to a state of slavery; when he comes to discuss his title to his creole-slaves, entirely shifts his ground, and abandons the rights of man, abandons every moral principle, every consideration of humanity and natural justice, all which he had urged against the slave-trade, and attempts to support the right of slavery upon that legislative authority, by which he contends, that the continuance of the slave-trade ought not to be sanctioned; refers to laws, declaratory of the legality or illegality of the slavery established in the colonies, and asks how the present bill declares it to be unlawful. This bill certainly makes a most curious and extraordinary distinction; for, it declares, "that it shall be unlawful to use or deal with any person as a slave, in any place, not being within the dominions of his Majesty.' Thus we, who challenge to ourselves the proud title of freemen, and boast of our country as the land of freedom, legalise slavery in the British dominions and abolish it in all the world besides! Such are the absurdities to which men are driven who endeavour to bend the immutable principles of justice to interest or policy. On what grounds can those who contend for the abolition of the slave-trade justify slavery? While they vindicate the end will they condemn the means? and the slave-trade is but the means of which slavery is the end.

The Planter does not admit my position, that, if it be unlawful to make men slaves, it must be unlawful to keep them so; but says, it is quite clear that a man may forfeit his liberty, and equally clear that no man "can by force deprive another of his liberty.' It is admitted that a man may forfeit his liberty by crimes against the state, which make it necessary to banish or confine him; but, how have his creole-slaves forfeited their liberty? what crimes have they committed for which they can justly be doomed to bondage, they and their descendants yet unborn to the remotest generation?—None. By what just right, then, can he keep them in slavery, if the slave-trade be unlawful? While he asserts that no man can deprive another of his liberty by force, he contradicts the assertion by his own practice. He deprives his slaves of their liberty by force; for, he will not pretend to assert that they continue his slaves voluntarily. It is the Planter himself, and not Mercator, who "forgot the birthright of the negro, and considered only the acquired right of his master by purchase.' As a farther argument in support of slavery, the Planter asserts, "that a person born in bondage does not acquire freedom for his inheritance,' and "that, in the northern part of Europe, the peasants are appurtenant to, and pass with, the soil,' still abandoning every consideration of right and wrong where his own interest is concerned; and, if the doctrines by which the abolition is supported are admitted and recognised, justifying his own oppression by the oppression of others.

By the force of imagination, the Planter seems to have transported himself to his own estate, and to have dreamt that I was haranguing his gang of negroes in the West Indies, instead of addressing myself to my readers in England. The alarm which he betrays, shews his apprehension that the insurrection and massacres which I have predicted as the natural consequences of the abolition are too likely to ensue. He inquires "what object this part of my publication could have in view?' My answer is, if possible, to prevent them, by lifting up my warning voice against that blind enthusiastic zeal, which, in alliance with selfish policy, threatens our colonies with desolation. I rejoice that the Planter is alarmed. Reflection may, perhaps, induce him rather to risk "the supply of sugar, exceeding the consumption,' than put both life and fortune to the dreadful hazard that awaits the abolition, as the forerunner of attempts at emancipation. The external causes of discontent, which I stated as necessarily arising from that measure, are founded on the self-evident proposition, that many hands make light work, and cannot be reasoned away till the truth of that proposition be controverted. The creole-negroes are not deficient in understanding; and, unless the Planter can extinguish every spark of reason in their minds, will not internal causes of dissatisfaction operate? He asks, jocosely, "whether they can be worked upon to avenge the captivity of their grandfathers and grandmothers?" I fear the sense of their own wrongs will be quickened by the remembrance of those done to their ancestors, as well as by the prospect of those in store for their children, if once they are taught that the slave-trade has been abolished by the British legislature, as being contrary to the principles of justice and humanity. The Planter interrogates me respecting the different characters of the creole and the African negroe, and I must candidly tell him that my observations on this subject will not be very consolatory. Most of the plots and mischiefs that I ever knew of, in the West Indies, originated with the creoles. They possess more intelligence and intrigue, and therefore are more dangerous than the Africans. During the insurrection in Grenada, dreadful instances occurred of the most remorseless treachery and savage barbarity, which were chiefly exercised by those favoured slaves, in whose attachment and fidelity their unhappy masters placed the most implicit confidence, and thus became their victims.

The Planter wholly disagrees with me on the subject of the trade going into the hands of foreigners, and relies strongly on the "Americans having adopted the solemn pledge of the British parliament, and having anticipated them in the abolition, under penalties too severe to fear anything from that quarter." I have made some local observations in America, as well as in the West Indies, and am not quite so sanguine. I believe, indeed, that the bill for the abolition will be passed by the American government, but I also believe that the trade will still be carried on, as much, nay, more, than ever, because the temptation will be greater. It was abolished in the state of Rhode-Island, very soon after the independence; but has been continued there notwithstanding to a very great extent. If I was not afraid of writing a libel on the administration of justice in that country, I should say, that the case of Mr John Brown shews the impossibility of convicting any man of that offence by a Rhode-Island jury; according to the constitution of America no man can be tried but in the peculiar state where the offence is committed. The senate of Carolina have already rejected the bill, and this decision will, I suspect, render every attempt of the federal government to enforce it there completely nugatory. So far from his Majesty having made such arrangements in concert with other powers as will secure the universal abolition of the traffic, not one of all the nations of Europe has joined us in the measure, though the negotiation gave ministers a full opportunity of learning their sentiments. That those of Buonaparte are adverse to the abolition is indisputable; for he declares that he shall be governed by the interests of his colonies. Indeed, he has taken credit to himself for not having sold the inhabitants of Berlin as slaves, and given a hint that he may not always use victory with the same moderation. Admitting, then, for a moment, that the abolition would produce those happy effects on the inhabitants of Africa which its advocates anticipate, by passing the bill now before the house, without a general co-operation with the other powers, the slave-trade will not be abolished, it will only be thrown into other hands, and be carried on without any regard to those humane regulations which have been imposed upon it by the British parliament; foreign commerce and colonies will be aggrandized at the expense of those of Great Britain, and the cause of humanity will be injured instead of being benefited.

My object, in first discussing this subject, was to combat erroneous principles and to remove unjust prejudices. In replying to the letter of a Planter, I have been actuated by the same motive. Sentiments once delivered to the public are open to public animadversion. I complain, therefore, of none of his criticisms, but the uncharitable imputation, that "I had rather my forebodings should be verified, than my opinions be derided,' might have been spared: may heaven avert the one and the Planter is welcome to the full enjoyment of the other.

MERCATOR.

Notes

1. Insutns in culeum, per summum dedecus vitam mittere.— Oratio pro Sex. Roscio Amerino.

List of Illustrations

Figures 1,2, 4, 5, 6, 7 and 8 all Franklin Smith Collection. Reproduced by kind permission of Franklin Smith and photographed by David Gowers at the Ashmolean Museum, Oxford.

Figure 3 photograph by John Pinfold

Figures 9-21 all Bodleian Library of Commonwealth and African Studies. Individual shelfmarks below:

Figure 9   Shelfmark 100.221 r.38
Figure 10   Shelfmark 100.221 r.71 (8)
Figure 11 Shelfmark 100.221 s7
Figure 12 Shelfmark 100.221 r.196
Figure 13 Shelfmark 100.221 r.99 (28)
Figure 14 Shelfmark 100.221 r.175
Figure 15   Shelfmark 100.221 r.99 (4)
Figure 16   Shelfmark 100.221 r.71 (3)
Figure 17 + 18 Shelfmark 100.221 r.99 (2)
Figure 19   Shelfmark 500.22 r.101 (1)
Figure 20   Shelfmark 100.221 r.71 (6)
Figure 21   Shelfmark 100.221 r.71 (7)